D1603640

THE RANGE OF
INTERPRETATION

THE RANGE OF INTERPRETATION

Wolfgang Iser

The Wellek Library Lecture Series
at the University of California, Irvine

COLUMBIA UNIVERSITY PRESS

NEW YORK

Columbia University Press

Publishers Since 1893

New York   Chichester, West Sussex

Copyright © 2000 Columbia University Press

All rights reserved

Library of Congress Cataloging-in-
Publication Data
Iser, Wolfgang.
        The range of interpretation / Wolfgang Iser.
        p.   cm. — (The Wellek Library lecture
series at the University of California, Irvine)
        A revision and expansion of the Wellek
Library lectures given by the author in the
spring of 1994.
        Includes bibliographical references and
index.
        ISBN 0–231–11902–X (cloth)
        1. Literature—History and criticism—
Theory, etc. 2. Translating and interpreting.
3. Interpretation (Philosophy) 4. Canon
(Literature) I. Title. II. Series.
PN81.I79 I. Title. II. Series.
418'.02—dc21   99–41918

Casebound editions of Columbia University
Press books are printed on permanent and
durable acid-free paper.
Printed in the United States of America
c 10 9 8 7 6 5 4 3 2 1

EDITORIAL NOTE

The Wellek Library Lectures in Critical Theory are given annually at the University of California, Irvine, under the auspices of the Critical Theory Institute. The following lectures were given in May 1994.

The Critical Theory Institute
John Carlos Rowe, Director

CONTENTS

PREFACE

This book is an attempt to bring interpretation
under close scrutiny, not least as there is a wide-
spread opinion that such an activity is something
that comes naturally. What, however, does not come
naturally, are the forms interpretation takes; thus
their inspection will be the main objective of the
argument of this book. An anatomy of interpretation
is all the more pertinent as we currently witness a
burgeoning of its genres, so that interpretation is no
longer to be identified with hermeneutics, as it has
been in the past. Instead, hermeneutics is just a
prominent genre dealing basically with texts that are
opened up for understanding. But when it comes to
interpreting something that is neither textual nor
scripted, such as culture, entropy, or even the incommensurable, the procedures of interpretation
are bound to change. Highlighting these changes is
the basic intent of the following chapters.

Chapter 1, the introduction glances briefly at the
marketplace of interpretation in order to spotlight
the main trends and pinpoints what the different genres of interpretation have in common, namely, being
acts of translation that transpose something into
something else.

Chapter 2, The Authority of the Canon, focuses
on the rise of interpretation in the Rabbinic tradition, in which the commentary on the canon was
meant to translate the holy text into the life of the
community. Reading the Torah opens up a space
between the text and its exegesis, which makes the
authority of the text oscillate between the canon and

its reading. Such a shifting becomes all the more obvious in the tradition of the secular canon, in which the commentary claims an authority of its own by expounding how the canonical author is to be read. Dr. Johnson's exposition of Shakespeare will serve as a case in point.

Chapter 3, The Hermeneutic Circle, is devoted to the rise and development of modern hermeneutics, and it deals with what remained eclipsed in the commentary tradition, that is, the negotiation of the space opened up by the act of interpretation between what is to be interpreted and what the interpreted is transposed into. Coping with such a space requires a technique for bridging it, and to this challenge Friedrich Daniel Ernst Schleiermacher (1768–1834)—the most prominent modern hermeneuticist—responded by coming up with what has since been called the "hermeneutic circle." Schleiermacher, however, had a specific application of the circle in mind: it was his endeavor to understand an author better than he had understood himself. To achieve this, a circular movement has to be set in motion between the author's grammar and his psychology. If the focus for grammatical interpretation is on the language system as actualized by the author, the psychological interpretation spotlights the way in which the tools provided by grammar are used; this enables the interpreter to find out how the author thinks. Such a circle has to be interlinked with the two methods of divination and comparison. Beginning with an initial hunch, the divinatory method grasps the individuality of an author by confronting what is alien to the interpreter; the comparative method subsequently controls the hunch insofar as the author, representing a certain type, can be compared to others of the same type. Thus a network emerges that is intended to span the gap between an author's text and its understanding.

Circularity tends to become more complicated when the matter to be understood is not a text produced by an author for comprehension by its recipient. Such a question posed itself for Johann Gustav Droysen (1808–1884) who—as one of a the great historiographers of the century—tried to achieve an understanding of history, which for him was no longer a text written by an author but to be construed from a welter of fragments through which the past extends into the present. This makes the task of interpretation twofold: it has to constitute the subject matter, and it has to furnish understanding of what has been constituted. Such heightened complexity is coped with by a multiplication of circles. These run not only between the discernible remnants of the past but also between the construal of history and a humankind meant to perceive itself in the mirror of its deeds.

The hermeneutic circle is again conceived differently when the concern is no longer with something given but with something hidden that is to be translated into comprehension. This is the case with psychoanalysis. Droysen could deal with observable facts from the past in order to detect their eclipsed relationships, but the situation changes drastically when something hidden shows itself in disguise. What the patient reveals has to be interlinked with what this revealing is meant to conceal. In such a back-and-forth movement the hermeneutic circle operates in transactional loops, due to the fact that what is mutually transposed is never fully in view but masked by symbols. As there is no external reference for such a procedure, the looping can only be fine-tuned by continually scrutinizing what the transactional loops render tangible. Thus interpretation, owing to the trial-and-error pattern that structures transactional looping, becomes self-correcting. There is no longer a gap to be spanned between the subject matter of interpretation and the understanding into which it is transposed; rather, a chasm has opened up, thus transforming the hermeneutic circle into transactional loops.

This reconception is preconditioned by the mode in which the subject matter is offered to the interpretive act. It makes all the difference whether the subject matter is present, or has to be constituted, or has to be teased out of its hiddenness. In each of these instances, the gap between what is interpreted and the register into which it is translated is of a different dimension, which has repercussions for the method of negotiating it. The circle functions as a relay when the subject matter is given (Schleiermacher); it changes into a nesting of circles when the subject matter has to be constituted (Droysen); and it turns into transactional loops when the subject matter has to be brought out into the open. The wider the gap, the more complicated the circle tends to become.

Chapter 4, The Recursive Loop, highlights a decisive shift in the generic differentiation of interpretation. If it is true that interpretation—primarily a form of translatability—is dependent on what is translated, it is bound to be different when it concerns itself with how entropy is translated into control, how randomness is translated into what is central, how the largely intangible reciprocity of hominization and the rise of culture is translated into conceptual language, and how cultures or cultural levels are translated into terms that allow an interchange between what is foreign and what is familiar. This chapter inspects the interpretive procedure in both ethnographic discourse, which is devoted largely to the elucidation of the rise of culture, and systems theory, which is concerned with the self-organization of systems as their principal mode of operation. What the paradigms chosen have in common is that they are neither textual nor scripted; therefore the subject matter to be interpreted calls for a retooling of interpretive techniques.

The cybernetical loop forms the interpretive procedure of ethnographic discourse, which develops as an interchange between input and output, in the course of which a prediction, anticipation, or even projection is corrected insofar as it has failed to square with what it has targeted. Consequently there is—at least potentially—a dual correction: the feed forward returns as an altered feedback loop that in turn feeds into a revised input. This applies to the whole range of learning, from machines to human behavior, all of which are regulated according to Norbert Wiener's basic formula that recursive looping "adjusts future conduct to past performance." The ethnographic discourse of Clifford Geertz serves as an example for such a procedure. It demonstrates to what extent the information gap yawning between hominization and the rise of culture can only be coped with in terms of input/output recursion. Simultaneously, this very procedure also structures Geertz's explanatory strategy for cultural analysis, "thick description," which focuses on the gap between what is manifest and what is implied in the cultural signs ethnographers are given to observe. It operates as a recursive movement between the manifest and the implied, and because there is no given reference for this mutual transposition, such intertransposability realizes itself in a continual iteration between input and output. Thus iteration functions as a reference for recursive looping, which issues into an ever-expanding range of thick description.

Just as the hermeneutic circle was reconceived for the changing tasks it had to perform, something similar happens to the feedback loop of input/output when the subject matter differs from what the ethnographers were concerned with. Such a paradigm switch is to be observed in what has been called the Santiago school of systems theory, of which Francisco Varela is a major proponent. In conceiving how living systems, such as the nervous or immune system, or social systems operate, recursivity proves to be a powerful interpretive tool. A system is a self-regulating organization to be maintained through feedback loops. The recursive interactions between levels, components, and processes of the system result in a network of mutual interconnectedness, which keeps specifying their function by making them reciprocally select from and impinge on one another. This two-way traffic proceeds as a conversation through which an exchange of information is continually differentiated. Such an incessant internal recursion provides the closure of the system, not least because there is no external agency to do it. Thus the system's recursivity is its closure. Moreover the indefinite recursion is also instrumental in generating what is absolutely vital to the system: its self-maintenance. Thus the dual aspect of the feedback loop allows us to conceive the servomechanism through which an autonomous system sustains itself.

This makes the input/output conception of the feedback loop into a special case of recursion, as there are no fixed points in the autonomous system between which such an interchange might take place for the purpose of achieving control. Instead, the indefinite recursion that organizes the conversation between levels and components in order to generate the system's self-maintenance has to react to environmental perturbations, not least because systems have other systems as their surroundings. A perturbation, however, is not an input that an autonomous system might need for its self-maintenance; instead, it triggers a compensating operation within the system itself, and this is done by recursively reshuffling the latter's organization.

Now the register into which the otherwise impenetrable structures of systems are translated is moved into the very subject matter itself. The space opened up by any act of interpretation needs to be negotiated, however, and Varela splits his register into operational and symbolic components, in which the former highlights a system's recursive operation and the latter the epistemological comprehension of what the recursion appears to reveal to the observer.

Chapter 5, The Traveling Differential: Franz Rosenzweig, *The Star of Redemption*, delineates a genre of interpretation developed when incommensurabilities, such as God, have be translated into cognition. A translation of this kind cannot subsume God under frames of reference of whatever persuasion, because any such frame lies outside of what is to be ascertained and would conceptualize God according to existing beliefs or preconceived notions. Consequently, the incommensurable must be unfolded from inside itself in order to convey what it may be like. For such a task Rosenzweig had recourse to the differential, which is fundamentally a realizing operation and thus particularly apt when it comes to conceiving reality, continuity, or infinity. These too cannot be conceptualized from stances outside themselves, as that would imply conferring predicates on them with which they could not be identical. Since the differential—or the infinitesimal calculus, as Leibniz conceived it—operates as a principle of realization, it cannot be taken for an entity; instead, it splits what is to be perceived into a sequence of limited segments, thereby unfurling it as a transition between its discrete scissions. The operational mode of the differential is thus dual in character: Here as elsewhere the movement of the infinitesimal increment dissects God's immeasurability, as Rosenzweig termed it, into an ever-emerging series of finite scissions, thus presenting it as a transition between its divisions. In his own words, the "infinitesimal" borrows "all the characteristics of finite magnitude with the sole exception of finite magnitude itself." By initiating and driving a movement, the differential functions as a delimiting operation, allowing Rosenzweig to translate God's essence into a self-performing realization. The infinitesimal increment as a motion draws its impetus from the linking of what it has separated, thereby ceaselessly shading one scission into another. God's essence is thus given presence as infinite self-differentiation, which translates into a continual self-specification of the world and equally into the shifting configurations of the human self.

Chapter 6, Configurations of Interpretation: An Epilogue, draws a few conclusions from the discussion of the individual paradigms of interpretation. For the sake of analysis, the chapters up to this point purposely emphasize the distinctions among hermeneutics, cybernetics, and differential realization as types of interpretation. The difference in their operational modes are by no means rigid, however, and indeed the hermeneutic circle, the recursive loop, and the traveling differential shade into one another whenever interpretation occurs. What makes their interplay so important is the necessity to negotiate the liminal space opened up by any act of interpretation. The space is liminal because it demarcates the subject matter from the register and thus is not identical to either. The play among the modes turns out to be the interface through which the liminal space is negotiated and out of which something emerges. Therefore interpretation is not so much an explication but a performance: it makes something happen. This raises a final question: Why are we so continuously engaged in bringing something about by interpretation? A possible answer has to be sought in our anthropological makeup.

The appendix contains two essays that have a direct bearing on the issue developed in the preceding chapters, as each of them tries to elucidate the performative quality of interpretation. A shortened version of the Carlyle essay was an integral part of the Wellek Library Lectures. My intention was to show the workings of a recursively operating cross-cultural discourse as a staging of different cultures under mutually alien conditions. The essay on Pater focuses on modes of translatability within the discourse itself whose layers are continually enfolded into one another, thus making ever new adumbrations arise from what has been said.

A preliminary version of this book was delivered in spring 1994 as one of the Wellek Library Lectures at the University of California, Irvine. I am very grateful to the Critical Theory Institute for honoring me with their invitation to take part in this series. I should like to thank in particular professors Gabriele Schwab, J. Hillis Miller, and Alexander Gelley for their illuminating introductions to the lectures and also my many colleagues and students for their challenging comments in the subsequent discussions, which alerted me to the work still to be done.

The project of scrutinizing interpretation grew out of a workshop on institutions of interpretation that Sanford Budick and I organized under the auspices of the German-Israeli Foundation of Research and Development and The Center for Literary Studies at the Hebrew University in Jerusalem. The meetings held between 1988 and 1991 resulted in two publications: "Institutions of Interpretation," *New Literary History* 22, no. 1 (winter 1991); and *The Translatability of Cultures: Figurations of the Space Between* (Stanford: Stanford University Press, 1996). The scholastic interchanges that took place during this workshop proved to be very stimulating, and had lasting repercussions on my ideas.

An invitation to the Institute of European and American Studies at the Academia Sinica in Taipei, Republic of China, provided a splendid opportunity for me to try out the lectures before I actually gave them at Irvine. Presenting basically Western ideas to a non-Western audience forced me to consider the scope and efficacy of a cross-cultural discourse in the encounter between different cultures. I am extremely grateful for this experience, particularly to Dr. Shan Te-hsing, who not only organized the visit but also discussed with me extensively the problem of how intercultural relationships can be conceived.

Last but not least my sincere gratitude goes to my friend David H. Wilson for patiently polishing my English.

THE RANGE OF
INTERPRETATION

CHAPTER ONE
Introduction

The Marketplace of Interpretation

For a long time, interpretation was taken for an activity that did not seem to require analysis of its own procedures. There was a tacit assumption that it came naturally, not least because human beings live by constantly interpreting. We continually emit a welter of signs and signals in response to a bombardment of signs and signals that we receive from outside ourselves. In this sense we might even rephrase Descartes by saying, We interpret, therefore we are. While such a basic human disposition makes interpretation appear to come naturally, however, the forms it takes do not. And as these forms to a large extent structure the acts of interpretation, it is important to understand what happens during the process itself, because the structures reveal what the interpretation is meant to achieve.

Nowadays, there is a growing awareness of the effective potential of interpretation and of the way this basic human impulse has been employed for a variety of tasks. The very world we live in appears to be a product of interpretation, as had been suggested in books such as Nelson Goodman's *Ways of Worldmaking* or Günter Abel's *Interpretationswelten*.[1] I will

---

1. See Nelson Goodman, *Ways of Worldmaking* (Hassocks, U.K.: Harvester, 1978); Günter Abel, *Interpretationswelten: Gegenwartsphilosophie jenseits von Essentialismus und Relativismus*, stw 1210 (Frankfurt/Main: Suhrkamp, 1995).

therefore briefly glance at what is currently on offer in the marketplace of interpretation.

Spotlighting dominant trends is the starting point in what might be called an anatomy of interpretation. Anatomy—though a somewhat over-worked term—is a better guideline for this enterprise than is "interpreting interpretation," because it designates an endeavor to make procedures transparent, whereas "interpreting interpretation" implicitly entails a transcendental stance that, irrespective of its presuppositions, must inevitably lie outside interpretation. A study of what happens in interpretation can only proceed by unfolding interpretation.

A survey of the marketplace reveals three basic trends, one of which has already turned into a dead end. It may even be due to this dead end that inspection has become an issue at all. What are the trends or types that still hold sway?

First of all, there have been and still are types of interpretation that claim universal validity for their assumptions, thus pretending to provide an overall explanation of everything. A case in point is Marxism, which, in its heyday, claimed nothing less than a monopoly of interpretation. This type is now on the wane, in part because of the reification of its presuppositions. Such reifications occur in almost all forms of what has come to be known as ideology critique, Marxist or otherwise. The various brands of ideology critique elevate their presuppositions to the status of reality, just as do the ideologies they combat. Monopolies of interpretation thus present themselves as transcendental grandstand views, and although they see themselves as frameworks for the reality to be grasped, they actually seek to shape that reality according to their presuppositions. This is why we must refrain from interpreting interpretation, for to do so would be to fall into the same trap as Marxism and all the other ideology critiques.

Even William Elford Rogers, who with the title of his book *Interpreting Interpretation: Textual Hermeneutics as an Ascetic Discipline* claimed to provide a "theory of interpretation," finds himself in a similar predicament. Although he quite rightly and repeatedly maintains that "to understand an interpretive system from the inside . . . is the only way to understand it,"[2] he nevertheless tries to assess interpretation by developing a specific textual hermeneutics that verges on becoming a stance outside interpretation.

---

2. William Elford Rogers, *Interpreting Interpretation: Textual Hermeneutics as an Ascetic Discipline* (University Park: Pennsylvania State University Press, 1994), 93.

This is also borne out by his heavy dependence on Peirce's semiotics to underpin his approach (11–18).

Simultaneously, Rogers senses that interpreting interpretation moves him into a position outside what can only be understood from inside, and therefore he tries to resolve the dilemma by subjecting his semiotically fashioned stance to a drastic "asceticism": "But now I want to suggest that *textual hermeneutics can be looked at as an ascetic discipline*. Of course, one need not look at textual hermeneutics that way. But one way of describing what goes on in interpreting a text is to say that the interpreter tries, so far as possible, to become totally absorbed in the signs of the text, such that the interpreter purges from consciousness purely private feelings and awareness of the separate 'I' of the 'I think' " (135). This semiotically conceived stance requires self-effacement of the interpreter to mitigate what an outside stance would superimpose on what is to be assessed.

Rogers certainly does not claim a monopoly of interpretation, but total self-effacement is impossible when interpretation is interpreted; a stance still has to be adopted in order to explain what only can be grasped from inside itself. Thus we shall refrain from interpreting interpretation, and instead of asking "What is interpretation?" (13), we shall ask: Why is interpretation? If we can unfold an answer to this question, it will serve as a pointer to possible reasons for this unceasing human activity. But in order to do so, we must first lay bare the mechanics of interpretive procedures.

Another trend to be observed in the marketplace of interpretation is what Ricœur once termed "the conflict of interpretations."[3] This manifests itself as competition, with each type trying to assert itself at the expense of others in order to demonstrate its respective importance and the depth and breadth of its insights and range. What the conflict reveals, and what makes it interesting, is the inherent limitation of all presuppositions. The greater the awareness of such limitations, the more the conflicting discourses of interpretation begin to appropriate one another.

There is a kind of cannibalization going on among Marxism, psychoanalysis, structuralism, poststructuralism, and so on in their attempts to compensate for their various deficiencies. The offshoot is a magma of interpretive discourses, which Derrida once characterized as follows: "You can imagine to what kind of monsters these combinatory operations must

---

3. See Paul Ricœur, *The Conflict of Interpretations*, ed. Don Ihde (Evanston: Northwestern University Press, 1974).

give birth, considering the fact that theories incorporate opposing theorems, which have themselves incorporated other ones."[4] Such an amalgamation of interpretive discourses reveals that none is able to establish a monopoly of interpretation. As they vie with one another, their premises can only be taken as heuristic in character, and thus they have to be evaluated in proportion to the success they achieve. This holds true irrespective of whether they admit to the heuristic nature of their presuppositions or not. At any rate, the conflict of interpretations, the reciprocal appropriation of interpretive discourses, and the common need for support from outside themselves prevent each of these types from fulfilling its inherent claim to be all-encompassing.

The third trend prevalent on the marketplace of interpretation is represented by what has been called "oppositional discourses," ranging from minority to postcolonial. Oppositional insofar as they set out to subvert or dispute the standards of what they consider to be the hegemonic discourse, they are developed by social groups for the purpose of asserting their objectives, of gaining recognition for their agenda, and of striving for power. They face a problem, however, in that a great many of them use the very procedures developed by the hegemonic discourse; indeed, they have to do so in order to achieve the persuasiveness necessary to advance the group interest. Borrowing from the discourses they seek to subvert can turn out to be a structural handicap: in trying to gain validity for their objectives, they develop a frame of reference that, in the final analysis, is not far from being logocentric itself, because a certain rationality is required if an agenda is to be accepted. Logocentrism, however, is the hallmark of the hegemonic discourse, which, though dismantled by deconstruction and thus giving the green light to the rise of oppositional discourses, makes these latter discourses indirectly dependent on what they intend to discard.

Such dependence is double-edged. On the one hand, it certainly helps to promote the agenda, but, on the other, it may just compensate for a shortfall in persuasiveness. Even monopolies of interpretation need some corroboration from outside themselves, as evinced by the Marxist claim to provide a scientific interpretation of reality, wherein science

---

4. Jacques Derrida, "Some Statements and Truisms about Neologisms, Newisms, Postisms, Parasitisms, and Other Small Seismisms," in *The States of "Theory": History, Art, and Critical Discourse*, ed. David Carroll (Stanford: Stanford University Press, 1994), 67.

and politics are evoked to furnish necessary self-endorsement of their respective objectives.

What we may conclude from the current state of the marketplace of interpretation is the following: Starting out from presuppositions—irrespective of whether they are reified or taken heuristically—is certainly one approach, but it cannot be equated with what happens in interpretation. In view of the growing interpenetration of cultures and the newly emerging concerns of cultural studies, interpretation can no longer be exclusively conceived as a subsumption of what is to be grasped under a presupposition. Instead, we have to remind ourselves of what interpretation has always been: an act of translation.

We usually associate translation with converting one language into another, be it foreign, technical, vocational, or otherwise. Nowadays, however, not only languages have to be translated. In a rapidly shrinking world, many different cultures have come into close contact with one another, calling for a mutual understanding in terms not only of one's own culture but also of those encountered. The more alien the latter, the more inevitable is some form of translation, as the specific nature of the culture one is exposed to can be grasped only when projected onto what is familiar. In tackling such issues, interpretation can only become an operative tool if conceived as an act of translation. In Harold Bloom's words: " 'Interpretation' once meant 'translation,' and essentially still does."[5]

Interpretation as Translatability

Each interpretation transposes something into something else. We should therefore shift our focus away from underlying presuppositions to the space that is opened up when something is translated into a different register. "Translation, then," Willis Barnstone writes, "as all transcription and reading of texts, creates a difference,"[6] as evinced by the division between the subject matter to be interpreted and the register brought to bear. Its intent will be realized through the manner in which that difference is to

---

5. Harold Bloom, *A Map of Misreading* (New York: Oxford University Press, 1980), 85.
6. Willis Barnstone, *The Poetics of Translation: History, Theory, Practice* (New Haven: Yale University Press, 1993), 18.

be coped with. We shall call this difference a liminal space, because it demarcates both the subject matter and the register from one another, as it does not belong to either but is opened up by interpretation itself. Caused by interpretation, the liminal space is bound to contain a resistance to translation, a resistance, however, that energizes the drive to overcome it. Thus interpretation also turns into an attempt to narrow the very space it has produced.

The register into which the subject matter is to be transposed is dually coded. It consists of viewpoints and assumptions that provide the angle from which the subject matter is approached, but at the same time it delineates the parameters into which the subject matter is to be translated for the sake of grasping. This duality is doubled by another one. As the register is bound to tailor what is to be translated, it simultaneously is subjected to specifications if translation in its "root meaning of 'carrying across' " (15) is meant to result in a "creative transposition" (11).

This two-way traffic is due to the fact that the register does not represent a transcendental consciousness from which the subject matter is to be judged; if it did, translation would be redundant, as the subject matter—instead of being transposed—would just be determined for what it is. Therefore interpretation as translatability has its repercussions on the register by diversifying the framework into which the subject matter is transposed. For this reason the registers not only change but are also fine-tuned in each act of interpretation. Such reciprocity indicates that interpretation takes place within historical situations[7] that we cannot get out of. Whenever we translate something into something else, the register is nothing but the bootstraps by which we pull ourselves up toward comprehension.

If interpretation is primarily a form of translatability, it clearly depends on what is translated. Interpretation is therefore bound to be different:

1. when certain types of text, such as holy or literary ones, are transposed into other types, such as an exegesis of canonical texts or cognitive appraisals of literary texts;
2. when cultures or cultural levels are translated into terms that allow for an interchange between what is foreign and what is familiar, or when entropy is controlled, or when "reality" is to be conceived in terms of interacting systems;

---

7. See Cornelius Castoriadis, *Gesellschaft als imaginäre Institution: Entwurf einer politischen Philosophie*, trans. Horst Brühmann (Frankfurt/Main: Suhrkamp, 1984), 59f.

3. when incommensurabilities such as God, the world, and human-kind—which are neither textual nor scripted—are translated into language for the purpose of grasping and subsequently compre-hending them.

In each of these three types—which will form the framework for this discussion—the interpretive intent regarding the subject matter to be translated will be exposed to change. This implies that the liminal space will have to be handled differently, from which we may conclude that *the* interpretation does not exist. Instead, there are only genres of interpreta-tion, marked off from one another according to the manner in which translatability is executed. Such a process varies not only in relation to the subject matter but also in the way in which the liminal space is coped with in every interpretive act. Therefore interpretation is basically genre-bound, and the salient features of the respective genre are marked not least according to how the liminal space is negotiated.

This awareness of generic divisions is of recent vintage. As long as com-mentary on either holy or secular texts was deemed to be the only preoc-cupation of exegesis, it was identified with what has since been called interpretation. The idea that interpretation can only be conceived in terms of genres only arose after interpretation had become self-reflective. Self-reflection in terms of monitoring the interpretive activity reveals that the latter is dependent not only on the subject matter to be grasped but also on the different parameters of continually changing registers.

Furthermore, if interpretation has to cope with the liminal space result-ing from something being transposed into something else, then interpre-tation is primarily a performative act rather than an explanatory one, although more often than not performance is mistaken for explanation. Whenever this happens, the mistake is one of category: for an explanation to be valid, one must presuppose a frame of reference, whereas perfor-mance has to bring about its own criteria. The self-generation of criteria in interpretation allows us first and foremost to participate in whatever is highlighted rather than to validate the results achieved.

On such a basis we are able to make the following distinctions that will delineate our concerns.

1. As long as it is a text that is to be understood, or whose understand-ing is to be applied, or whose hidden constituents have to be brought to light, the hermeneutic circle in all its variations from Schleier-macher to Ricœur appears to be an adequate method of dealing with the liminal space.

2. If something nontextual, open-ended, or beyond the reach of one's own stance has to be made manageable, the hermeneutic circle may no longer be adequate. Translating open-endedness into graspability, or entropy into control, is different from translating a text into understanding, or from turning understanding into its application, or from deciphering what its disguises may either hide or reveal. Recursive looping therefore becomes a procedural necessity when it comes to charting open-endedness or controlling entropy; it operates as an input/output interchange or as systemic recursion that allows us to account for the self-maintenance of autonomous systems, particularly living systems such as those of the human organism.

3. A different problem poses itself when there are no longer any definable positions but only experiences of something whose existence appears incontrovertible but that exceeds knowability, such as God, the world, or humankind. Translating something immeasurable into language and even into terms of cognition—as undertaken by Franz Rosenzweig in his *Star of Redemption* (1921)—requires a different mode of translation from those mentioned so far. If the space between the immeasurable and cognition is to be coped with, the traveling differential appears to be an adequate mode for grasping infinity in finite terms.

These different modes point to the fact that each genre of interpretation focuses on a specific task regarding the translatability to be realized. In hermeneutics the circle is employed to interrelate the explicit with the implicit, the hidden with the revealed, and the latent with the manifest. It basically sets out to recover what an author has not been aware of when writing, or what lies beyond the historical material to be observed in the present, or what went awry in the human subject on the way to itself. Penetrating behind what is given in order to recuperate what is lost—that is, the author's subconscious, a historical past, or the buried telos of the fractured self—is what structures this type of interpretation.

While hermeneutics can be qualified by this excavatory tendency, cybernetics, operating in recursive loops, is a means of controlling entropy, elucidating the individual self-maintenance of autonomous systems, and configuring the structural coupling of systems. Its focus is on phenomena that emerge from coping with contingency, from the reciprocal "perturbation"[8] of systems, and from their being bracketed together. Recursivity operates either by an input/output relationship, when control is to be achieved, or by processing noise, randomness, and perturbation, when the self-organization of systems is to be conceived.

If cybernetics is concerned with grasping emergence, the differential method is designed to translate incommensurability into perception. Its operational mode is a traveling differential, because incommensurabilities can only be made tangible if unfolded from inside themselves. There is no external stance that would, for instance, allow us to grasp continuity, which posed itself as a problem for Leibniz, who developed the differential calculus. Consequently, the traveling differential operates as a mode of realization inside what it intends to unfold; it dissects incommensurabilities into a sequence of scissions, thus permitting access to what cannot be grasped from any external position.

These diversified tasks show clearly that interpretation is genre-bound, and they also reveal that interpretation has a history, which gains its salience through the way in which the problems that have cropped up have been coped with. Circularity became prominent when the authority of the text was on the wane; recursivity was developed when emergence had to be accounted for; and the differential—originally a mathematical operation—was reactivated when all the umbrella conceptualizations of immeasurabilities had broken down. Such a history does not proceed as a linear development toward a distant goal. Instead, it is nonlinear insofar as these modes of interpretation are responses to the ever-increasing open-endedness of the world, thus focusing on what appears to be pressing in the situation of the moment. This makes interpretation into a process of mapping the open-ended world, and such mapping is dependent on the here and now, which means new maps may be developed, or old ones reactivated, according to requirements. Although this activity unfolds as a history, it is in the end not so much the history itself that is of interest but rather what it might indicate. Hence interpretation, though primarily a technique, raises an anthropological question with regard to its necessity.

The paradigms used to unfold interpretation have all been chosen because they are instances in which interpretation is either expressly thematized or explicitly reflected on. The hermeneutic tradition is

---

8. See Francisco J. Varela, *Principles of Biological Autonomy* (New York: Elsevier North Holland, 1979), whose ideas are discussed in the second section of chapter 4.

represented by Friedrich Daniel Ernst Schleiermacher, Johann Gustav Droysen, and Paul Ricœur, who—all in their different ways—elucidate the workings of hermeneutic procedures. Those who advocate cybernetics as the infrastructure of interpretation—again all in their different ways—from Norbert Wiener through Clifford Geertz to Francisco Varela, practice their variegated interpretations by constantly reflecting on the efficacy of their underlying interpretive principles, which they sometimes analyze at length. The same applies to Franz Rosenzweig, who explicitly sets out the terms according to which he conceives of the traveling differential and the way in which he intends to make it operative. The very fact that paradigms of interpretation lead to thematization of, or reflection on, what is to be undertaken, indicates that there is no overarching reference for such activity; at best there are "routes of reference" that, when established, result in a reconditioning of both register and procedure.[9] The following discussion does not imply that the paradigms of interpretation to be examined represent the whole range of interpretive genres. What makes them conspicuous, however, is their attempt to develop changing mechanisms to cope with the liminal space that interpretation itself opens up.

Viewing interpretation from such an angle raises the question of its limits, as suggested by the title of one of Umberto Eco's books.[10] Whenever limits of interpretation come under scrutiny, two viewpoints seem to become prominent. First, the main focus tends to be on textual interpretation, and, second, limits do not apply so much to interpretation itself as to the frames and parameters that are brought to bear. This is apparent in Eco's wide-ranging analysis of interpretation, in which he explicitly states that the kind of limits he is going to examine are those intimately tied to a semiotic frame that he himself has developed, guided by Peirce's basic principles (12). He starts out by detailing three types of textual interpretation that provide the necessary orientation for the interpretive act: *intentio auctoris, intentio operis,* and *intentio lectoris* (22). Each of them, of course, has its limits, and therefore in reading a text one must take all of them into consideration.

Eco shows the implications of this in another context:

---

9. For what the notion "routes of reference" implies, see Nelson Goodman, *Of Mind and Other Matters* (Cambridge: Harvard University Press, 1984), 55–71.
10. See Umberto Eco, *I Limiti dell' Interpretazione* (Milan: Bompiani, 1990).

It is clear that I am trying to keep a dialectical link between *intentio operis* and *intentio lectoris*. The problem is that, if one perhaps knows what is meant by the "intention of the reader," it seems more difficult to define abstractly what is meant by the "intention of the text." . . . Thus, more than a parameter to use in order to validate the interpretation, the text is an object that the interpretation builds up in the course of the circular effort of validating itself on the basis of what it makes up as its result. I am not ashamed to admit that I am defining the old and still valid "hermeneutic circle."[11]

Now, the more "parameters" there are to be "dialectically" interlinked, the more liminal spaces are bound to emerge that have to be negotiated by circularity. If, however, only a single frame is privileged, interpretation, according to Eco, ceases, because the text is used for a certain purpose, which marks the limit of interpretation.[12] Consequently, the more rigid the frames, the more obvious the limits. Hence interpretation in itself is not limited; rather, it is the parameters chosen that impose restrictions. This does not mean, however, that frames or parameters can be dispensed with, because interpretation is an undertaking that has to produce its own frameworks in order to assess what it intends to elucidate.

This tendency is spotlighted in Eco's penetrating analysis of interpretation as well as in Patrick Colm Hogan's book *On Interpretation: Meaning and Inference in Law, Psychoanalysis, and Literature*, which starts out by criticizing Eco for attributing "meaning not to texts and dictionaries but to authors or to members of the linguistic community [because Eco] sees meaning as defined by a reader's intuition . . . thus shifting from authorial to individual readerly intent."[13] In the end, however, Hogan might be closer to Eco than he actually thinks he is, because what he calls "inference" is not very far from the "conjectures" Eco had spoken of. And "meaning" (let alone an entity such as "true meaning" [10])—being the "first concern of an

11. Umberto Eco, *Interpretation and Overinterpretation*, ed. Stefan Collini (Cambridge: Cambridge University Press, 1992), 64.
12. Richard Rorty, in Eco, *Interpretation and Overinterpretation*, 100, voices reservations about Eco's distinction "between interpretation and use," which might in itself be a frame according to which limits of interpretation are highlighted.
13. Patrick Colm Hogan, *On Interpretation: Meaning and Inference in Law, Psychoanalysis, and Literature* (Athens: University of Georgia Press, 1996), 2.

interpretive theory" (1)—is not a given but has to be arrived at by way of inferences. Focusing on meaning, however, is already a stipulation, for which again frames have to be conceived, so that "rational inferences" (93) can be made as to intent.

At this point an interesting turn occurs in Hogan's argument. There are "limits to stipulation," which are not to be taken for limits of interpretation, because the "intentional meaning . . . [of a] legislators's policy aim, speaker's unconscious beliefs, or author's aesthetical intent" (92) is an "ideolectal intent" (93), and therefore any conception of meaning presumed to be nonintentional does not exist. If meaning is only "ideolect or intent" (47), then all kinds of semantic essentialism, such as the assumption of social meaning or autonomous meaning as advocated by both analytic philosophy and structural linguistics, are invalid stipulations for assessing the semantic ideolect. This convincing criticism leveled at social, philosophical, and linguistic essentialism notwithstanding, Hogan makes one stipulation for interpreting the intent of the ideolect: it is the "Principle of Minimal Interpretation" (14), which is governed by "the ordering principle [of] simplicity" (15).

Whereas Eco combines different frames in order to stretch the limits of interpretation, Hogan excludes overarching frames in order to prevent encroachment on interpretation. Eco's basic stipulation is that interpretation proceeds as semiosis of the text, whereas Hogan's "stipulative view of meaning" (32) proceeds by inferences that are guided by the principle of simplicity.[14] The more restricted the initial objective of interpretation turns out to be, the more limited are the frames stipulated for interpreting basic intent. The more frames are combined, the more unmistakably their limits are meant to be overcome. If the assembly of frames is connected in a circular movement, liminal spaces begin to loom large. Therefore interpretation as translatability, proposed as a frame in the following chapters, proves to be a minimalistic stipulation, in consequence of which the liminal space and ways of negotiating it reveal themselves as a basic concern of interpretation.

---

14. When Hogan details the interpretive practice in law, psychoanalysis, and literature, however, he stipulates a great many frames as the basis for "rational inference."

CHAPTER TWO
The Authority of the Canon

Canonization and Midrash

Interpretation as we have come to understand it in the West arose out of the exegesis of the Torah in the Judaic tradition. Its inception is intimately tied to the canonization of holy texts, which itself reveals constitutive features of interpretation insofar as the canon is not established for its own sake. Broadly speaking, canonization is a process of choosing the texts that will become the object of interpretation, which simultaneously elevates them into a position of censorship over other texts, whose study and interpretation may even be forbidden, because the cancellation of their claims to validity helps to stabilize the authority of the texts that are chosen. Just as the canon does not exist for its own sake, the ascription of authority requires a negative foil to underpin its authenticity.

Endowing a text with authority may entail two things: (a) endowing itself can be a unique and unrepeatable act; (b) the authority attributed may be supplemented, augmented, broadened, specified, and so on. Each of these possibilities pertains to the Old Testament as conceived in Judaism. Consequently there is both a sealed and an open canon. The sealed canon is considered unique, as its canonization has been established; the status of the textual elements is exclusive, and no new text can be added to it. The Pentateuch is a case in point. The open canon, however, does allow for other texts to be added and hence canonized. The Book of Laws is an example, as it permits the addition of new laws whose legal status is as binding as those already included.

The consequences of the sealed and open canon are immediately obvious in the Judaic tradition. Moses was the greatest prophet and lawgiver of all times who legislated through prophecy. No other prophets enact their prophecies as law; instead, they advance reform or extrapolate laws from the Law of Moses, and these are already forms of interpretation. This distinction makes the consequences of the sealed canon apparent: (a) if it alone is authoritative, any subsequent prophecy is bound to lack authority; (b) henceforth the text provides solutions to all possible questions.[1] Such authority, however, implies that the text is bound to gain new dimensions that did not exist when it was sealed. Because the sealed canon was meant to offer guidance, the question of how its elements were to be understood became all the more pressing, a necessity that gave birth to interpretation as executed by the sages and the rabbis.[2] The latter, however, were not prophets and were consequently two stages removed from the Law of Moses; nevertheless, they assumed an important position through their exegesis of the Torah. This brings to light the double-edged relationship between the canon and interpretation as described by Moshe Halbertal:

> The sealing of the text engenders both the bestowal and the removal of authority. . . . The moment the text was sealed, authority was removed from the writers of the text and transferred to its interpreters; denied to the prophets and awarded to the Sages. "Henceforth you must incline your ear to the works of the learned." The sealing of the Scriptures does indeed indicate recognition of the exclusive authority of these texts, but at the same time authority is redistributed. . . . The new leadership model of the Torah scholar arises, the religious ideal of the Torah study becomes central, and new institutions such as the *beit midrash* acquire a prestigious position in the community.[3]

---

1. See Moshe Halbertal, *People of the Book: Canon, Meaning, and Authority* (Cambridge: Harvard University Press, 1997), 18. I had occasion to profit greatly from Halbertal's research at one of the workshops held in Jerusalem in 1988, entitled "Institutions of Interpretation," to which he made an important contribution with his essay "Canonization and the Politics of Interpretation," out of which he developed his book.
2. See Joseph Heinemann, "The Nature of the Aggadah," in *Midrash and Literature*, ed. Geoffrey Hartman and Sanford Budick (New Haven: Yale University Press, 1986), 46.
3. Halbertal, *People of the Book*, 19f.

This is so because the sealed canon does not invest itself with authority; authority is bestowed on it, for whatever reason, from outside. Thus the ineradicable duality of interpretation comes to the fore: it is an act that is both domineering and subservient in relation to what it sets out to elucidate. Such a duality must have been sensed as a problem very early on, because "Pharisaic Judaism," as Michael Fishbane writes,

> tried to minimize the gap between the divine Torah and ongoing human interpretation by projecting the origins of authoritative exegesis to Sinai itself. But even this mythification of a chain of legitimate interpreters did not so much obscure the distinction between Revelation and Interpretation as underscore it. From this perspective, the interpretive traditions of ancient Judaism constitute a separate, non-biblical genre: a post-biblical corpus of texts which stand alongside the Sinaitic Revelation as *revelation* of new meanings *through exegesis*. Moreover, this dignification of interpretation in Pharisaic literature highlights another feature of early Judaism (and is a root cause of early Jewish polemics): the realization that there was no pure teaching of Revelation apart from its regeneration or clarification through an authoritative type of exegesis.[4]

The House of Midrash that has arisen out of this type of interpretation is an exegetical procedure that basically pursues three main objectives:

1. Bringing out the seminal character of the inspired word.
2. Linking it up with the life of the people of Israel.
3. And dealing with other groups of texts that beat at the door of the canon.

What distinguishes midrashic interpretation from earlier stages of exegesis, in which the distinction between the sealed canon and its interpretive exposition was still blurred,[5] is its awareness of the difference between the Torah and the world outside the canon, a difference, however, that is simultaneously upheld and eliminated owing to the fact that the canon is

---

4. Michael Fishbane, "Inner Biblical Exegesis: Types and Strategies of Interpretation in Ancient Israel," in *Midrash and Literature*, ed. Geoffrey Hartman and Sanford Budick (New Haven: Yale University Press, 1986), 19f.
5. See Halbertal, *People of the Book*, 15.

to be translated into the life of the community. "The sages' commitment to discover all the ramified teaching in the Scripture," as Joseph Heinemann has phrased it, "finds expression in their dictum: 'Interpret and receive reward!' They were of the opinion that the Bible intended to impart moral and religious instruction, to teach us how to live."[6] But as the chasm between the word of God and the world can never be definitively bridged, the residual untranslatability leads to a limitless proliferation of midrashic interpretations. Interpretation highlights the fact that canon and community do not coincide, and although it created this split in the first place, it also strives to overcome it. Betty Rojtman stresses this point by saying: "In particular, one cannot eliminate, in any theory of exegesis, a variable parameter of exegesis, which reintegrates into the message a problematics of the subject and of reception: Midrash in fact acknowledges, as a technique of interpretation, the projection of the biblical model onto various planes of existential actualization."[7]

The possible implications of such a midrashic interpretation can be observed most strikingly when a text that was originally not part of the canon is later canonized.[8] The Book of Ecclesiastes is a case in point. In Ecclesiastes, history is portrayed as a series of events completely devoid of meaning. The sons repeat the wicked deeds of their fathers, and such repetition proves that there is nothing new under the sun. "I have seen all the works that are done under the sun; and, behold, all is vanity and vexation of spirit" (Eccles. 1:14). "The thing that hath been, it is that which shall be; and that which is done, is that which shall be done; and there is no new thing under the sun" (Eccles. 1:9). "All things have I seen in the days of my vanity: there is a just man that perisheth in his righteousness, and there is a wicked man that prolongeth his life in his wickedness. Be not righteous over much, neither make yourself over wise:; why shouldest thou destroy thyself?" (Eccles. 7:15–16). Ecclesiastes flouts almost everything that has been set out in the Torah; it contradicts the beliefs represented in the Bible, and yet it is part of the Scripture.

----

6. Heinemann, "The Nature of the Aggadah," 48.

7. Betty Rojtman, *Black Fire on White Fire: An Essay on Jewish Hermeneutics, from Midrash to Kabbalah*, trans. Steven Rendall (Berkeley: California University Press, 1998), 106; see also 116 ("Midrash, as we have seen, corresponds to a degree of actualization that draws the multiplicity of its projections from the existential").

8. Halbertal, *People of the Book*, 24–26, gives an elaborate account of this procedure.

How does interpretation deal with such a situation? There is a famous midrash by R. Samuel ben Nahmani, which changed the meaning of Ecclesiastes so completely that the text assumed a different status altogether. The midrash in question addresses two central themes: (a) the futility of all human expectations; and (b) the hedonistic suggestions offered by Ecclesiastes in view of such futility. For what the preacher explicitly recommends is indulgence in the pleasures of daily life, such as eating and drinking, in order to counteract the otherwise prevailing mood of hopelessness. "There is nothing better for a man than that he should eat and drink" (Eccles. 2:24). "Then I commended mirth, because a man hath no better thing under the sun, than to eat, and to drink, and be merry" (Eccles. 8:15).

The hedonistic message is reinterpreted by the midrash as a metaphor to mean that whenever Ecclesiastes "tells you to eat and drink, know that what he means is 'go and do good deeds and study the Torah.'" Thus the recommendation of hedonism as expressed by the text "becomes a threat: know that God will be the judge of your indulgence."[9] From the moment Ecclesiastes became part of the canon, it had to be read in such a way that it would be consistent with the rest of the Scripture. Such an exegesis shows that the meaning of the text is not authoritative; instead, it is the reading given to the text that endows the Book of Ecclesiastes with authority.

Such contortions point up the duality inherent in the canon. What is actually said by the text is discarded in favor of what the text is supposed to mean, and such a procedure implies that canonization of a text is, in the final analysis, the specific reading given to it. Shifting authority to the reading is not only an appropriation of the canon but is conditioned by the intention to make readers read according to what the text has been decreed to mean. Therefore "canonization of a text may at times serve to take the authority away from its original meaning, allowing the commentator to choose the meaning that will be deemed authoritative. In reality, he wields authority over the text" (27).

There are, however, two basic reasons for what might seem to be an "arbitrary distortion" of the text as evidenced in midrashic exegesis. The guiding principle operative in the reading of the canon is what Halbertal has termed the "principle of charity," a term he has taken from Quine,[10]

---

9. Halbertal, *People of the Book*, 25.
10. See ibid.; see also Willard Van Orman Quine, *Word and Object* (Cambridge, Mass.: MIT Press, 1960), 57–61.

although there is already an early reference to such a principle in St. Augustine, who maintained that whoever "thinks that he understands the divine Scriptures or any part of them so that it does not build the double love of God and of our neighbors does not understand it at all. Whoever finds a lesson there useful to the building of charity, even though he has not said what the author may be shown to have intended in that place, has not been deceived, nor is he lying in any way."[11] The principle of charity, as understood in the Judaic tradition, seeks to ensure the meaningfulness of the canonical text in instances where the literal meaning creates an impression of meaninglessness in relation to other texts of the canon; simultaneously, it aims to bring out the plethora of meanings enfolded in the text. Charity therefore entails giving a positive slant to whatever the text says, in order to bring it to full fruition, so that it can be perceived in the light of its inherent perfection. Because the Torah issued to a large extent from the word of God, whatever is added to the canon must be understood in the best possible manner: the word of God is free from inconsistencies and contradictions, so any inconsistent canonical elements have to be eliminated by the best possible reading. It is therefore the task of exegesis to highlight the correspondence between each word in the Bible and the perfection and plenitude that it connotes. An offshoot of this removal of apparent contradictions is the multitude of similes, stories, and metaphors with which the rabbinical commentaries abound and through which we may gain a first glimpse of the inherent problem of interpretation.

The other prominent reason for the shift of authority to the reading of the canon is the fact that the latter has to be translated into the life of the community that it is designed to structure.[12] Again, this assumption of

---

11. Saint Augustine, *On Christian Doctrine*, trans. D. W. Robertson, Jr. (Indianapolis: Bobbs-Merrill, Liberal Arts Press, 1958), 30. There is also a lengthy discussion in the Judaic tradition as to whether the principle of charity is to be employed by the exegete or whether it is determined by Scripture itself.

12. Rojtman, *Black Fire on White Fire*, 4f., writes: "The role of interpretation is to combine units from differing systems, to link the textual with the ritual, written characters with existential significations. . . . The uncertainty principle—situated between precise boundaries—will allow us to lay the methodological foundations of commentary. Jewish exegesis has constructed for itself an entire hermeneutic apparatus that regulates these relations between textual premises and existential conclusions, between original formulations and semantic translations."

authority appears justified, as the exegesis of the canon has to unfold the inspired word, which would otherwise lie dormant in the Torah. But once more the problem of the sealed canon becomes apparent: it has to be understood, and so the provision of understanding is bound to assume authority. Such authority, however, is already two removes away from the sealed canon; after the prophets, it is now the exegetes who claim validity for their reading, and this brings to the fore another aspect of the duality of interpretation.

If the reading is meant to exhibit the authority of the text, it is simultaneously bound to borrow that authority in order to translate the canon into the life of the community. In other words, the reading highlights the authority of the canon by bringing out its all-encompassing dimension, so that it can be turned into a measuring rod for all other texts; simultaneously, it transposes the canon into guidelines for the life of the community. But although the canonical text cannot be deprived of its authority, nevertheless the latter has to be siphoned off in order to invest the reading itself with authority. Consequently, authority rests exclusively neither in the canon nor in the reading; instead, it oscillates between the two, and this oscillation is an indication of the ineradicable space between the canon and its interpretation. The space is opened up by the necessity to understand the Torah and to translate it into guidance for the life of the community. The central problem of interpretation thus comes to light, namely, that any act of interpretation creates a liminal space between the subject matter to be interpreted and its translation into a different register. This "shuttle space between the interpreter and the text"[13] reveals very early on in history the nature of interpretation as an iteration of translatability. And this is due to the fact that texts in and of themselves do not legislate the conditions of their own reading,[14] although each text can only come to life through being read.

---

13. Geoffrey Hartman and Sanford Budick, introduction to *Midrash and Literature*, ed. Geoffrey Hartman and Sanford Budick (New Haven: Yale University Press, 1986), xi.

14. Halbertal, *People of the Book*, 44, comments on this situation as follows: "Since canonization determines the function of texts and affects the expectations of the community of readers, it has great impact not only on the status of texts but on their meaning. There is an increasing asymmetrical relation between canonization and hermeneutical openness. The more canonized the text, the broader interpretive possibilities it offers."

As the Torah and the life of the people of Israel are not totally synchronized, the authoritative reading of the canon has to bridge this gap, which has given rise to the elaborateness of midrashic interpretation. The procedures developed for this enterprise "do not mean so much to clarify difficult passages in the biblical text as to take a stand on the burning questions of the day, to guide the people and to strengthen their faith."[15] Therefore the "burning questions" decide what kind of register the canon has to be transposed into, and there seems to be no limit to the variety of registers. Moreover, the canonical text is punctured by indeterminacies, the clarification of which allows approaches from different angles, depending on what the passage in question is supposed to mean for the life of the community. Hence the different registers into which the holy text is translated may well "threaten to erode its 'original' and straightforward core,"[16] and such an obvious "threat" points to the variableness of registers into which the holy text can be transposed.[17]

The register, however, is not totally predetermined by the text, not least as one has to learn *from* the text and not learn the text (15). Therefore it rests almost entirely with the discretion of the interpreter what kind of register he or she decides to choose. Thus a further distribution of authority occurs: not only does the reading given to the canon claim authority for itself, but the authority is also transferred to the register on the ground that the canon has to set guidelines for communal life.

Because the register is highly selective with regard to the function the Scripture is meant to exercise, the authority arrogated to it became a matter of dispute, as is vividly shown by the controversies in midrashic interpretation. Even when the register is not in dispute, its multiformity is essential because the canon has to be made available for all domains of life, the structuring of which must allow for all types of human disposition. Thus the register is to a large extent conditioned by what the study of the Torah is designed to achieve, and the breadth of this function elevates learning to a religious obligation. Learning means two things at once: an ongoing reflection on the Torah, and an effort to derive the structure of

---

15. Heinemann, "The Nature of the Aggadah," 49.
16. Halbertal, *People of the Book*, 40.
17. In his chapter "Three Views on Controversy and Tradition," Halbertal, *People of the Book*, p.71f., writes: "The idea of the open-endedness of text and the constitutive role of the interpreter are the boldest options produced, both theologically and hermeneutically, by an internal rabbinic reflection on the canonization of controversy."

society from continual immersion in the holy text. The register therefore bears a dual inscription: it has a religious and a worldly dimension. The latter concerns itself with questions like the following: What do human beings actually do when they think, how do they think, and what guides their thinking? How do they view the world, and what are the subjects of their meditations? This means that human dispositions have to be explored as part of the study. The reason for such an exploration is again twofold: to make the Torah more adequately translatable into human lives, and to make human lives translatable into terms set by the Torah. As the register provides the framework within which the holy text may be anchored in human life, it is marked by a split, because it has to look in two opposing directions at once: the holy text and the community. This split, however, is glossed over by the decision through which the register is established in the first instance and through which it determines the function that the chosen text is to perform in the life of the community. This structure applies to all subsequent forms of register in the history of interpretation, as the terms into which something is to be translated have a strongly pragmatic orientation. Beside these pragmatic considerations the dualities and divergencies contained in all the registers of interpretation pale into insignificance.

Because the register posits the terms into which the given text has to be translated, it simultaneously opens up the liminal space between the text and the terms concerned. This liminal space cannot be glossed over, not least as it is created by the very act of interpretation itself, which cannot simply ignore, let alone undo, what it has caused. Thus the liminal space is always present in any interpretive activity, and in the final analysis it enables and indeed forces authority to oscillate between canon and exegesis, while being equally responsible both for its distribution and its division. Authority is divided among the canon, the reading given to the canon, and the register that sets the terms by which the canon is transposed into human life. Do we have several authorities, is there continual borrowing, or is authority forever shifting without having a definitive location at all? There is no need to answer these questions, for the shifting of authority is caused by the liminal space, whose basic indeterminacy makes authority float among canon, reading, and register. Again we encounter, at the very inception of rabbinic exegesis, a basic problem of interpretation: the necessity to negotiate the liminal space.

The House of Midrash might be called the first major attempt to grapple with the liminal space. It is, as Daniel Boyarin once remarked "a method of strong reading of the gaps of the text, filling them, as it were, by inserting the intertext into them."[18] Such an intertext is all the more necessary as the indeterminacies of the canonical text itself have to be dealt with in a manner that will prevent possible readings from using the text for subversive or heretical purposes. Basically, however, the gap-filling intertext is to blanket the liminal space.

The most prominent paradigm in the Judaic tradition of such an intertext to be inserted between the canon and its reading is the mashal. Generically speaking, the mashal is a parabolic narrative, similar to the fable or parable that suggests parallels "between an imagined fictional event and an immediate, 'real' situation"; "the parallel and its implications, or levels of implication . . . actively elicit . . . from its audience the solution of its meaning, or what we could call its interpretation."[19] Thus the mashal provides multiple interconnections, basically designed to fill the liminal space, as "it enables the rabbis to associate texts from different parts of the canon by assigning relations to these texts, by allowing them to be placed in a plot together."[20] In this respect, the Bible is turned into a self-glossing text, as linked passages from different books elucidate one another in an effort to disclose the inherent plenitude of the word. It is only through such an interactive reading of words, phrases, verses, or pieces of narrative that the gap between the overt and the covert nature of the word can be bridged. The mashal also frames and contextualizes the biblical verses to be interpreted. This is an attempt to reach out to the audience for whom the interpretation is intended, and therefore particular circumstances of basic human situations have to be part of the gap-filling narrative. Thus the mashal is primarily concerned "with maintaining the Torah's presence in the existence of the Jew, with bridging the gap between its words and their reader, with overcoming the alienation, the distance of the Torah, and with restoring it to the Jew as an intimate, familiar presence. The midrashic interpreter in this sense is literally a translator: one who carries the text across a divide, who negotiates the space between the text and its comprehension."[21] To achieve such an objective by means of a narrative, however, the author has to heed the pitfalls inherent in any

---

18. Daniel Boyarin, *Intertextuality and the Reading of Midrash* (Bloomington: Indiana University Press, 1994), 56.
19. David Stern, *Parables in Midrash: Narrative and Exegesis in Rabbinic Literature* (Cambridge: Harvard University Press, 1991), 5.
20. Boyarin, *Intertextuality*, 84.
21. Stern, *Parables in Midrash*, 44f.

narrative that, as it can never be told in its entirety, is punctured by indeterminacies that have to be coped with.

If the mashal as an intertext charged with multiple functions is to fulfill its purpose, certain constraints have to be imposed in order to turn the narrative into a closed text. Without such closure, the liminal space, instead of being filled, will tend to inscribe itself into the very device meant to blanket it. The constraints of the mashal are both thematic and structural. As a form of teaching and preaching, its themes are based on opposites intimately related to human conduct, such as obedience and disobedience, praise and blame, eulogy and consolation, complaints and reconciliation, regret and warning, reward and punishment, and the like (102–151). As a resolution of opposites, the mashal reflects both the liminal space between canon and register and the attempted elimination of this difference. The very fact that the mashal embeds the canonical text in situations taken from the life of the people of Israel points unmistakably to the context into which the Torah has to be translated, while the variable topics of the mashal reveal the respective register posited in the act of interpretation.

These two features in themselves, however, are not enough to guarantee that the intention operative in interpretation will be fulfilled. Therefore the mashal has to be structured along lines that will ensure this fulfillment. The rhetorical pattern of the mashal is threefold: the narrative is followed up by the nimshal, which spells out the application of what the story has shown, and the mashal ends with a "prooftext," which is always a passage from the Bible meant to endorse the inference made explicit by the nimshal. There is no doubt as to the priorities of the elements in this tripartite pattern. The narrative part is the least important, as it only provides the context into which the nimshal inserts the adequate application of what the Torah says, an application, however, that needs to be corroborated by the prooftext taken from a different passage of the Bible, as the application cannot be self-confirming. This three-part relationship is a rather ingenious form of interpretation because the interlinkage between narrative, application, and prooftext makes it seem as if the formulaic textuality of the mashal has spoken for itself, thus appearing to be a self-explanatory translation of the Torah into human life; this is all the more remarkable given that the mashal as a rule starts out with the name of the rabbi who has told the story. Although the rabbi provides the exegesis, the formulaic interrelationship among the parts of the mashal makes it appear to bear an authority of its own.

This seems to be pertinent for two closely interconnected reasons.

First, the prime concern of the mashal is to engage its potential audience. David Stern writes that the mashal "deliberately gives the impression of naming its meaning *insufficiently*. It uses ambiguity intentionally. Yet the mashal achieves this appearance—the appearance of ambiguity—not by being authentically ambiguous but by shrewdly incorporating openings for the questioning of meaning; in this way it artfully manipulates its audience to fill those openings so as to arrive at the mashal's correct conclusion" (15). This objective is achieved through the discontinuities of the text, "technically called a gap. A gap is a deliberately withheld piece of information in a narrative—(1) a missing link in a series of events; (2) an absent cause or motive; (3) a failure to offer satisfactory explanations for an occurrence in a story; (4) a contradiction in the text that challenges the audience's understanding of the narrative; (5) an unexplained departure from norms" (74f.).

Second, these gaps are doubled up by the empty spaces that separate the narrative, the nimshal, and the prooftext, as these textual patterns have different functions in relation to what has preceded them and what they are designed to interpret. The empty spaces, however, are structured insofar as the nimshal determines the application, and the prooftext is the authoritative corroboration of the latter. Thus the spaces serve as openings for the audience, which has to grasp the ulterior meaning that the mashal bears.

What looks like a predetermined strategy of rabbinical interpretation is not as intentional as it appears. In rabbinical literature there is little self-conscious awareness of the exegetical procedures that are employed. The rabbis considered the mashal "determined," as Stern has shown, "by its utility as an exegetical device, as means to the comprehension of the Torah [and] not as a reflection in any way of their own ideology" (67). Moreover, every text, whatever its patterning, is punctured by gaps that in turn become effective as structures that invite a response. And finally, if the mashal is the exegetical intertext that has to overcome the liminal space between the Torah and its translation into the presence of the community, it cannot help bearing the inscription of that space, which it can never totally eliminate. The leaps between narrative and nimshal and nimshal and prooftext are traces of the liminal space, which reveals its salience by marking off the story from its application and the application from its endorsement. The mashal's character as intertext is further highlighted by a unique feature. Although it has a resemblance to the parable, it assumes its singularity by the fact that it does not make any sense at all outside its specifically rabbinic interpretation, for it is designed to communicate "the 'correct' understanding of the Bible . . . through a mode of discourse that expresses both exegetical practice and ideological program" (184).

As a vehicle for transposing biblical truth into human life, the mashal does not actually carry authority, partly because the story told is a fiction. As a fiction, however, it has the advantage of fusing an "exegetical practice" with an "ideological program," thus helping to bridge the divide between the authoritative commentary and the impact it has to make on the life of the people. In this respect, the mashal is a basic genre of midrashic exegesis. It opens up an area that James Kugel once described as follows:

> And if we are to designate the halakhic reading of the Scripture as a bridge between the Bible and the present-day Jew, out of fairness one must add that the bridge has another (if anything, greater) lane going in the opposite direction. For in Midrash the Bible becomes . . . a world unto itself. Midrashic exegesis is the way into that world; it does not seek to view present-day reality through biblical spectacles, neither to find referents of biblical prophecy in present-day happenings, nor to find referents to the daily life of the soul in biblical allegory. Instead it simply overwhelms the present; the Bible's time is important, while the present is not; and so it invites the reader to cross over into the enterable world of the Scripture.[22]

Crossing over is what the mashal facilitates, but one must add that the traffic is two-way, because the bridge permits the reader to enter the world of the Scripture and simultaneously patterns the reader's behavior in the here and now.

The mashal as a gap-filling intertext of the liminal space is always guided by a specific concern according to which the translation of the canon has to be effected, and its scope is limitless, just as the exegesis of the Scripture itself expands into ever-new readings. As Gerald Bruns remarks, "Midrashic interpretations stop but do not end"[23] in consequence of which each interpretation engenders further interpretations. This applies

---

22. James L. Kugel, "Two Introductions to Midrash," in *Midrash and Literature*, ed. Geoffrey Hartman and Sanford Budick (New Haven: Yale University Press, 1986), 90.
23. Gerald Bruns, *Hermeneutics Ancient and Modern* (New Haven: Yale University Press, 1992), 111.

first and foremost to the exegesis of the Scripture, whose gaps, indeterminacies, ambiguities, and inconsistencies gave rise to "a native rabbinic
saying for this quality of the text: 'this verse cries out, interpret me!' "[24] A
vast web of textuality is generated by such a demand. The Scripture is
unfolded into its diversified meanings, and its translation into the human
condition issues into a welter of meshalim. A continual proliferation of
narratives extends what has already been narrated, as each newly arisen
situation will determine how the holy text is to be taken. Thus midrash, as
Bruns has shown, "presupposes that interpretation cannot mean simply
giving uniform representations of a text that is sealed off from the hetero-
geneity of human situations. Midrash understands that if a text is to have
any force, it must remain open to more than the context of its composition."[25]

This is one of the reasons why there are no definitive rules of interpretation in midrash; "Abstract rules for rhetoric or prophetic discourse are
not given. . . . Tradition is the warp and woof of creative talent, the textual content whose lexical and theological knots are exegetically unraveled,
separated, or recombined. In this sense tradition is also a retextured context."[26] Narratives spawn further narratives, whose continual expansion
gives rise to an ever-evolving textual tradition that in turn functions as
guidance in midrashic interpretation for illumination of biblical verses
and for the translation of the Scripture into individual situations. This
apparently self-reproducing textuality bears witness to an unceasing
attempt to overcome the liminal space that is caused by interpretation
itself but is necessary to mark off the inspired word from the register into
which the Scripture is transposed.

Although tradition as a continual reshuffling of textuality preserves the
accumulated wisdom of generations, it is, in the final analysis, constituted
by this seemingly endless proliferation of narratives. It points to the deep
need for continuity rather than to continuity itself, the need to anchor
practices and beliefs in something larger than the existing order. And such
a need has repercussions on how we conceive of interpretation, which is
not just a tool for transposing the divine word into guidelines for behavior
but, in bridging the chasm between Scripture and world, is always on the
verge of assuming a status of its own. Midrash, as David Stern contends,

24. Boyarin, *Intertextuality*, 41.
25. Bruns, *Hermeneutics*, 106.
26. Fishbane, "Inner Biblical Exegesis," 34f.

"is not simply exegesis, nor an exegetical stance, but the discourse *of* exegesis. As midrash is preserved in Rabbinic literature, it does not only interpret Scripture, but already organizes and exploits exegesis—smaller, independent, often local interpretive traditions—for larger ideological purposes that have increasingly sophisticated and polyvalent meanings of their own. Midrash thus *deploys* scriptural exegesis for its own end."[27]

Whenever reading gets the upper hand over what is being read, there is a potential erosion of the canonical text. Again it is interpretation that claims authority for both its reading of biblical verses and its behavioral guidelines. Such authority, however, cannot be spun out of interpretation itself but has to be borrowed from the canonical text in order to authenticate the decrees intended by the reading. Just as the readings of the sealed canon are a "bestowal" and "removal" of authority, midrashic interpretation makes the textual authority slide into what it takes the text to mean. The canon is saved from erosion, however, either by the latent conflict of readings or by the multifarious readings produced in the House of Midrash.

In this respect, interpretation reveals the inherent problem of authority. In providing access to the authoritative text, interpretation both divides and borrows from this authority, although borrowing alone is not enough to validate the claims of interpretation, because validity and authority are not totally identical. The authority of the text serves to underpin the validity claimed by interpretation. Validity thus appears dual in nature: it subsists on the authority of the text and simultaneously appears to enrich what it lives on. "The sealed text not only acquires the status of exclusivity but new information can be gained mainly through interpreting the text."[28] In relation to single passages of the Bible, midrashic readings illuminate the hidden meanings of the inspired word, and in relation to the people of Israel, interpretation translates the canonical text into guidelines for human conduct. Although all these efforts depend on the authority of the Scripture, interpretation makes something emerge that, strictly speaking, is not contained in the canon proper. In the words of Rabbi Akiva: "All is foreseen, but freedom of choice is given." Betty Roitman states that "all is determined, and yet all is open,"[29] and what is open is worked out through interpretation.

---

27. Stern, *Parables in Midrash*, 179.
28. Halbertal, *People of the Book*, 19.
29. Betty Roitman, "Sacred Language and Open Text," in *Midrash and Literature*, ed. Geoffrey Hartman and Sanford Budick (New Haven: Yale University Press, 1986), 160.

This brings us back to the concept of the liminal space. At this early stage in the history of interpretation its effect is twofold: The liminal space makes the authority of the text oscillate between the scriptural canon and its forms of translation, thereby indicating that it cannot be eliminated by the very act that has caused it. Furthermore, as an empty space that separates two different systems (text and exegesis) from one another, it calls out for negotiation, thereby revealing itself as a matrix for the emergence of a text-imbued life and a Scripture lived.

The Literary Canon: Dr. Johnson on Shakespeare

The shift of authority becomes all the more apparent in readings of the literary canon. "The concept of the canon names the traditional curriculum of literary texts by analogy to . . . the scriptural canon. The scriptural analogy is continuously present, if usually tacit, whenever canonical revision is expressed as 'opening the canon.' "[30] "The very fact that the body of literary works can be analogized to the scriptural 'canon' betrays the fact that vernacular writing must borrow the slowly fading aura of Scripture as a means of enhancing and solidifying its new prestige" (76).[31] In contradistinction to the discrimination between a closed and an open canon in Scripture, however, the literary canon is basically open, because new authors can be added to the stock of classical writers. Such a process, however, does not unfold itself as a mere addition of authors; instead, an open canon is subject to an ever-renewed "completion." As T. S. Eliot once remarked: "The existing monuments form an ideal order among themselves, which is modified by the introduction of the new (the really new) work of art among them. The existing order is complete before the new work arrives; for order to persist after the supervention of novelty, the *whole* existing order must be, if ever so slightly, altered."[32] Nevertheless,

30. John Guillory, *Cultural Capital: The Problem of Literary Canon Formation* (Chicago: Chicago University Press, 1993), 6.
31. Historically speaking, canon formation in the West originated from the grammarians of Alexandria, who gave the name "canon" to a collection of Greek texts that were considered as models "because of the purity of their language." See Mihàly Szegedy-Maszàk, "The Rise and Fall of Literary and Artistic Canons," in *Neohelikon* 17 (1990): 129.
32. T. S. Eliot, *Selected Essays* (London: Faber and Faber, 1951), 15.

the conviction prevails that a commentary made on the work of such authors is a definitive statement, although in actual fact it is partial insofar as it is a translation of a canonized text into a historically conditioned situation. "The aim of every commentator," Karlheinz Stierle writes, "is to open up ways to a more profound understanding of such a text which, being worthy of comment, is an exemplary concentration of meaning. However, the intense reading conditioned by commentary is not a wholly determined reading. The conception of ideal reading that each commentary has in view is functional to the institution where reading and commenting have their place."[33]

Dr. Johnson's commentary on Shakespeare may serve as an example of what is implied by the interpretation of a canonical author, not least as Johnson may well have been the last in the line of commentators committed to the traditional concept of the canon as the "monuments [of] an ideal order." This position highlights the inherent problems of canon formation, thus providing a foil for both the rise of hermeneutics and the function of criticism.

What holds true for the canon of holy texts applies equally to the literary canon: that is, it also has to be made available.[34] It is Dr. Johnson's aim therefore to provide the conditions necessary "to a perfect knowledge of the abilities of Shakespeare."[35] The conditions already point to a potential register into which these "abilities" have to be transposed. Thus Dr. Johnson starts out by saying: "Among the powers that must conduce to constitute a poet, the first and most valuable is invention" (47). The latter, however, is no longer identified with the combinatory rule of Aristotelian rhetoric, nor is it meant to anticipate the romantic power of genius:[36]

---

33. Karlheinz Stierle, "Studium: Perspectives on Institutionalized Modes of Reading," *New Literary History* 22 (1991): 118.

34. See also Szegedy-Maszàk, "The Rise and Fall," 151.

35. *Johnson on Shakespeare*, vol. 7 of The Yale Edition of the Works of Samuel Johnson, ed. Arthur Sherbo (New Haven: Yale University Press, 1968), 47. The sources of all other quotations from this volume are given in in-text references to the appropriate pages.

36. It is, however, interesting to note—as Walter Jackson Bate, *The Achievement of Samuel Johnson* (New York: Oxford University Press, 1961), 211, has pointed out—that Stendhal "had virtually translated part of the discussion of the neo-classic rules of drama from the *Preface to Shakespeare* and published it as a 'romantic' manifesto. The fact would have surprised Johnson."

[Of] all the degrees of invention, the highest seems to be that which is
able to produce a series of events . . . to introduce a set of characters so
diversified in their several passions and interests, that from the clashing
of this variety may result many necessary incidents; to make these incidents surprising, and yet natural, so as to delight the imagination without shocking the judgment of a reader; and finally, to wind up the
whole in a pleasing catastrophe produced by those very means which
seem most likely to oppose and prevent it, is the utmost effort of the
human mind.   (47f.)

Invention, it seems, is something impenetrable that can only be assessed
by way of its manifestations and therefore by the impact it is able to exercise. An event is an occurrence without referentiality and therefore surprising; passions and interest are entangled in conflict and hence issue
into an oxymoronic situation. This makes invention dual in nature: it is
both unpredictable and natural, exciting the imagination but paying trib-
ute to judgment. What keeps these countervailing tendencies from clashing is the experience transmitted to the recipient that Shakespeare's
"*heroes are men,* that the love and hatred, the hopes and fears of his chief
personages are such as are common to other human beings" (49). Here
we may discern an outline of the register into which Shakespeare is transposed. The reader's perspective provides the focus for ascertaining the
qualities and perfection of the canonical author, and such a focus implies
that Shakespeare's characters should be perceived as a mirror of common
humanity. The authority, in turn, is meant to offer guidelines for the self-
perception of contemporary readers, whose views have to be heeded for
the guidance to take effect. Such a dual orientation results in the growing
complexity of the commentary, which has both to highlight the authority
and to cast it in comprehensible contemporary terms. Highlighting
authority means giving reasons for canonization, whereas fashioning
authority in terms of a contemporary readership means making it conform to common belief.

The register thus has a dual orientation: while authority is conceived
in reader-oriented terms, these cannot establish authority but only help to
comprehend it. Obviously, comprehension begins to mold what is understood by authority. As Shakespeare's characters "are the genuine progeny
of common humanity" (62), they reflect the perennial qualities of human
nature, thus allowing Dr. Johnson to authenticate Shakespeare's achievement in terms of an eighteenth-century belief. The conviction that there
is a common ground of human nature held sway right up to the threshold

of romanticism.[37] The core of a common humanity bodied forth in Shakespeare, however, was not meant only to corroborate an eighteenth-century idea but also had to serve a particular purpose. What this supposedly perennial and unchangeable human nature might be like remained an open question; at best it was a blank that required filling. For this reason, Shakespeare's change of situations became an important issue for Dr. Johnson insofar as it refracted common humanity in the mirror of kaleidoscopically shifting facets that in turn could be connected up with another burning issue of the time: self-confrontation for the purpose of achieving human perfection. Dr. Johnson left no doubt that this was one of the main objectives of his commentary by explicitly stating that instruction is to be derived from such a mirroring of human nature: "The end of writing is to instruct; the end of poetry is to instruct by pleasing" (67). In order to channel Shakespeare to such an end, Dr. Johnson frankly confesses: "I have endeavoured to be neither superfluously copious, nor scrupulously reserved, and hope that I have made my authour's meaning accessible to many who before were frighted from perusing him, and contributed something to the publick, by diffusing innocent and rational pleasure" (103). This means no less than that the author's meaning is already there, so that the commentator need only devise the form of perception in order to transfer the meaning agreeably into the imagination of a contemporary readership.

The register, however, into which Shakespeare is translated is not as homogeneous as Dr. Johnson might have conceived it. First of all, interpretation of a canonical author means making him available. In this respect, readings of holy and secular texts are similar in their intention. Achievement of the objective requires access to the canon, for which the cultural code of the contemporary reader provides the parameter. Thus there emerges a liminal space between Shakespeare and the register, which poses a problem insofar as either authority is borrowed in order to authenticate the reading or the space is eliminated by fusing exegetical reading and canonical text together. Dr. Johnson does both, so that his register is marked by the duality I have already discussed. Furthermore, this duality is paralleled by a countervailing tendency within the reader-oriented register itself, as the reader has not only to face himself or herself in the mirror of Shakespearean characters but also to be instructed by

---

37. See, for instance, Sir Walter Scott, *Ivanhoe*, ed. Andrew Lang (London: Macmillan, 1901), footnote to xlvii.

what Dr. Johnson considers the meaning of Shakespeare, which he sets out to make as palatable as possible. The register now becomes increasingly complex owing to the diversified aspects that have to be taken into consideration. These aspects, however, relate not so much to the canonical text as to the framework into which it is meant to be transposed.[38]

This becomes all the more obvious in Dr. Johnson's references to earlier commentators on Shakespeare. Although it was his aim to bring about "revolutions of learning" (99), he did not want to achieve this objective by criticizing previous commentators, as "not one has left Shakespeare without improvement, nor is there one to whom I have not been indebted for assistance and information" (101). In spite of such avowals, Dr. Johnson cannot help criticizing some of his predecessors, whose predominant "errour" consisted in just "surveying the surface" without "penetrating the bottom" (98). If some of the commentators, in spite of their common effort, have failed to leave the canonical work better understood—as Dr. Johnson has explicitly claimed for himself (58)—what does he actually mean by "improvement"? Apart from textual emendations, it can only refer to making the text available to the contemporary situation. And as situations change, the perception of previous commentators may become irrelevant or may have to be 'rectified' in order to make the canonical author fit new needs.

Such a shift is all the more surprising as the tradition of the commentary is deeply imbued with the belief that eventually an exhaustive understanding of the canonical author will be reached. The very fact that the road toward total comprehension does not develop in a straight line bears witness to the dual orientation prevailing in the commentary: that is, the authority rests with the canonical author, yet that author is continually shifted into a different perspective, and therefore what earlier commentators may have brought to light has to be reshuffled. The reshuffling marks the rise of criticism within the tradition of commentary itself,[39] and this development is largely due to the growing complexity of the register into which the canonical author is translated. The register is not exclusively determined by understanding the canonical author but depends even more on the prevailing exigencies that condition his availability. The latter will

---

38. Szegedy-Maszàk, "The Rise and Fall," 143, quite rightly states: "Canons are closely tied to communities."
39. For Johnson's relationship to tradition, see Bate, *The Achievement of Samuel Johnson*, 217.

inevitably entail reassessment of both the canonical author and the standards that govern the register.

This duality becomes apparent through the connection Dr. Johnson establishes between the universals of Aristotelian poetics and Shakespeare's work. A brief look at some of these links will once more bring to the fore a fundamental problem inherent in the canon generally: the inevitable slippage of authority from the canon to the reading. In conveying Shakespeare's greatness to a contemporary readership, Dr. Johnson invokes the stock-in-trade of the then still current Aristotelian poetics that it is the poet's task to imitate nature. As Shakespeare had excelled all other poets in this respect, such exemplarity invested his work with authority.

As to nature and imitation, however, Dr. Johnson appears to have had his own ideas. Shakespeare as "the poet of nature . . . holds up to his readers a faithful mirrour of manners and of life" (62); thus nature is first and foremost human nature. Dr. Johnson continues to elaborate on this by saying: "Mankind was not then to be studied in the closet; he that would know the world, was under the necessity of gleaning his own remarks, by mingling as he could in its business and amusements" (88). As "his drama is the mirrour of life" (65), "exhibiting the real state of sublunary nature, which partakes of good and evil, joy and sorrow, mingled with endless variety of proportion and innumerable modes of combination" (66), Shakespeare makes manners fan out into a hitherto unforeseeable diversity, unfolded in an ever-changing sequence of vivid images. Such a catalog, which Dr. Johnson keeps detailing, is a blend of ideas developed throughout the eighteenth century, although he gives them his own individual slant. Because he maintains that all these ramifications of nature are featured in Shakespeare's work in unsurpassable perfection, Shakespeare's authority implicitly serves to authenticate the standards of excellence laid down by an eighteenth-century commentator.[40]

There is a price to be paid for such a claim, however. Equating nature with "the real state of sublunary nature"—elucidated by the vividly perceptible variety of manners—is in direct conflict with a statement made immediately before in the "Preface," where Dr. Johnson invokes the old Aristotelian notion by saying: "Nothing can please many, and please long,

---

40. Though it must be said, as Bate maintains, that "Johnson uses the critical vocabulary of European criticism before the romantic movement: he uses words like 'reason,' 'nature,' 'propriety,' and 'wit,' though he gives them a far larger meaning than others did at the time" (*The Achievement of Samuel Johnson*, 191).

but just representations of general nature" (61). Murray Krieger has drawn attention to this apparent dichotomy:

> We can note in the statement that curious juxtaposition of the rational-
> ist's assumptions of a general nature with the empiricist's concern with
> audience reaction (the notion of pleasing many and pleasing long).
> Thus, although there is no questioning of the dogmatic belief in the
> objective existence of discoverable universals, there is also the insis-
> tence that the sanction for these universals comes, not from a priori
> deductions from the nature of things, but from the combined judg-
> ments of individual experiences.[41]

Dr. Johnson appears to borrow the universal character of "general nature" in order to back up the assumed exemplarity of "sublunary nature." Even if he may not have been aware of this dichotomy, the very fact that it occurred bears witness to strategic procedures operative in the commentary. The tra-ditional concept of nature has to lend validity to the diversification of human nature as the actual object of imitation, and this diversity in turn is tacitly equated with basic standards of Aristotelian poetics. The reason for such a maneuver is obvious, because the canonical author is not appealed to for his own sake, in order to utilize "the greatest graces of a play," that is, "to copy nature and instruct life" (80). For such an overriding concern, "gener-al nature" as a universal has to be appropriated so that the multiformity of human nature can be forged into an instrument for instruction. Therefore human dispositions have to be observed if the intended lesson is to be effec-tive. In his "Preface" Dr. Johnson juggles the attributes of nature, and this interplay of the "general" and the "sublunary" draws attention to the limi-nal space between the canonical author and his translation into instruction for an eighteenth-century reader. This space cannot be definitively glossed over, and as a result Dr. Johnson is forced to bisect nature.

Use of the Aristotelian concept of nature to authenticate ideas advanced by the commentator is not, however, a one-way process. The very fact that Dr. Johnson considers Shakespeare a perfect embodiment of what he took nature to be implicitly helps to underpin the authority Shakespeare commands. Such underpinning is all the more necessary because the authority of a canonical author does not hail from the word

---

41. Murray Krieger, *Poetic Presence and Illusion: Essays in Critical History and Theory* (Baltimore: Johns Hopkins University Press, 1979), 56.

of God, as is the case with holy texts. Therefore a secular authority has to be made plausible in terms shared by the readership meant to acknowledge this authority. The two-way traffic makes the commentary double-edged, as becomes evident when Dr. Johnson details the way in which Shakespeare imitated nature.

On the one hand, he praises "the great excellence of Shakespeare, that he drew his scenes from nature, and from life" (53), and yet, on the other, by copying everything from nature Shakespeare came so close to life that he created "obscurities" (52ff.). It is now for the commentator to "explain what is obscure" (51), and, as he does so, authority is bound to shift once more, because the commentator now speaks authoritatively about clearing up the obscurities through "conjectural criticism" (51). Dr. Johnson explicitly states that he does not "intend to preclude himself" when it comes to comparing Shakespeare's "sentiments or expression with that of ancient and modern authours" (58). In the course of such an endeavor, Dr. Johnson finds a great many "faults" in Shakespeare that implicitly appear to diminish the authority of the canonical author, who is criticized for what he either did or failed to do when imitating nature. Thus another dichotomy opens up, as Krieger has shown, in that Dr. Johnson "could scold Shakespeare for moral indifference after praising his truthful adherence to our morally indifferent world," and in doing so he "is only enunciating again . . . that age-old dilemma which vainly seeks to make the mimetic compatible with the didactic" (77).

Whenever the didactic intent gets the upper hand in Dr. Johnson's commentary, the liminal space can only be overcome by projecting standards onto the work of the canonical author, thus turning the function of the commentary upside down. Instead of deriving standards from the canonical work, Dr. Johnson lists the faults he has spotted in Shakespeare's otherwise praiseworthy imitation of nature. The great many faults are "sufficient to obscure and overwhelm any other merit" (71). Shakespeare, Dr. Johnson maintains, "sacrifices virtue to convenience . . . makes no just distribution of good or evil . . . carries his persons indifferently through right and wrong, and at the close dismisses them without further care, and leaves their examples to operate by chance" (71). His plots omit opportunities to instruct or delight the reader; the jests in the comedies are more often than not gross, and their pleasantry licentious; "whenever he solicits his invention," in the tragedies, " the offspring of his throes is tumour, meanness, tediousness, and obscurity" (73). Shakespeare, however, is not only criticized on moral grounds but also for sloppiness in craftsmanship. "He had no regard to distinctions of time and place . . . was . . . a violater of chronology . . . confounded the pastoral with the feudal times" (72). On and off he became "entangled with an unwieldy sentiment, which he cannot well express, and will not reject" (73). Whenever a quibble springs up before him, "he leaves his work unfinished. A quibble is the golden apple for which he will always turn aside from his career, or stoop from his elevation" (74). Dr. Johnson continually lists Shakespeare's defects in this vein.

This procedure has two important implications: First, Dr. Johnson dispenses with the principle of charity basic to the exegesis of holy texts, whereby everything written has to be presented in the best possible light.[42] Although Dr. Johnson dwells at great length on Shakespeare's "excellencies," he does not expound his apparent faults as hidden, not yet fully recognized virtues. Obviously, Dr. Johnson's own standards regarding moral instruction, decorum, and craftsmanship provide the parameters for exposing Shakespeare's shortcomings. Therefore he has to phase in what he considers Shakespeare's defects in order to ensure the success of the moral instruction he has in mind. This makes instruction the overriding issue, which Shakespeare, in spite of the guidelines he appeared to offer for such an endeavor, did not fully comply with. Substituting the criticism of faults for the principle of charity need not diminish Shakespeare's authority; it aims rather at a completion of the model required for Dr. Johnson's didactic purpose. Nevertheless, the interchange between charity and criticism makes the commentary duplicitous insofar as interpretation is no longer exclusively devoted to an understanding of the canonical author, because the latter is made subservient to contemporary exigencies that may not have been in his orbit. Dr. Johnson appears to be aware of such duplicity: although he wants "to leave his authour better understood" (58), he simultaneously confesses "it would be ludicrous to boast of impartiality" (80).

This brings the second implication to the fore. The standards inherent in the criticism voiced and that Shakespeare failed to comply with, have to be inferred from the faults registered and thus remain virtual in character. Any form of criticism is motivated by hidden standards that do not have to be verbalized when judgment is passed. Projecting virtual standards onto Shakespeare makes the canonical author implicitly serve to authenticate Dr. Johnson's nonverbalized standards, and although ultimately the canonical author is not necessarily divested of his authority,

---

42. For further elaborations on the principle of charity, see Moshe Halbertal and Avishai Margalit, *Idolatry*, trans. Naomi Goldblum (Cambridge: Harvard University Press, 1992), 88.

he is reconceived in such a manner that he appears to endorse Dr. Johnson's implicit criteria of excellence. The commentary has to prop up the authority of the canonical author in order to utilize that authority for its own purposes. Again it is the register that decides the use to which the canonical author is put; hence the work is made to conform to it.

Once again we see an inherent duality in the commentary, which seems to look in two different directions at the same time. Stierle writes:

> Whether the commentary wants to lead back to the original text and its meaning or to give the past text its present significance, each time the commentary is a bridge between the reader and the text he is approaching. The commentator, too, is an interpreter living in two worlds, that of the text and that of the reader, and organizing the exchange between them. Whatever the concrete intention of the commentary may be, it presupposes a difference between the text and its readability that it wants to abolish.[43]

It is exactly this difference that can never be abolished, however, and so authority is made to pivot around the space that separates the text from its reading. What happens in such a pivotal moment is not only the transfer of the canonical author's authority to what Dr. Johnson claims to be a more adequate understanding of Shakespeare. It also entails preserving the authority by means of a more plausible and hence persuasive exegesis of the canonical author. Such a duality has far-reaching implications for the business of interpretation as it evolves toward the end of the eighteenth century.

The secular authority wielded by canonical authors derives not from a transcendent agency but from a collective assent prone to change, not least as the secular canon is principally open and thus subject to rearrangement and revaluation. Consequently, the authority of a canonical author is not guaranteed forever but has continually to be made plausible by highlighting his achievements. Time and again authority has to be underpinned by exhibiting the exemplarity of the model to be emulated, which in turn is not monolithic but multifaceted and hence assumes different shapes in the course of history. Thus a mutual translatability occurs: The commentary borrows the authority in order to substantiate its claims as to how a canonical author should be translated into the terms of a prevailing situation. By highlighting the applicability of a canonical author, the

---

43. Stierle, "Studium," 119.

commentary furnishes evidence for the authority that rests with that author. Therefore the commentary as a genre of interpretation does two things at the same time: in using the authority, it underpins the validity of its own postulates; in providing a better understanding, it both stabilizes and augments the authority of the canonical author. Dr. Johnson wanted to establish more adequate access to Shakespeare's works in terms of both an uncorrupted text and what he took to be the meaning of the text. For this reason, his criticisms of Shakespeare are an attempt to achieve conformity between the canonical author and the register into which the latter had to be translated, and this results in a switch of authority.

Such a switch points to the fact that the space between the canon and the commentary cannot be as easily glossed over as it used to be when the commentary acknowledged that the canon alone commanded authority. Whenever the nascent criticism gets the upper hand, which may not have been Dr. Johnson's intention, the authority of the canon is in jeopardy, because what is now considered to be valid is decreed by criticism.[44] What Dr. Johnson had to say in this respect was governed by his conviction that the ideas he was criticizing were identical to the text he was representing. In other words, the liminal space did not move into focus, and thus the question of misreading did not dawn on him either as commentator or commentator turned critic. Criticism, as practiced in the "Preface," is not exactly a colonization of the liminal space, but the necessity of having to repair the exemplarity of the canonical author, as indicated by exposing Shakespeare's so-called faults, points to a difference. In spite of such a repair, Dr. Johnson—for whom criticism was still subservient to commentary—did not seem to consider the gap between canon and reading as a problem that had to be addressed.

When criticism eventually emancipated itself from commentary at the beginning of the nineteenth century, it aimed no longer to translate the canonical author into contemporary understanding but, as Matthew Arnold phrased it, "to see the object as in itself it really is."[45] Therefore

44. This has been convincingly demonstrated by Guillory, for whom the canon is nothing but an "imaginary list" of texts that "is always in conflict with the finite materiality of the syllabus"(Cultural Capital, 32) and that nowadays is conceived as "cultural capital" coveted by diversified group interest. Such an understanding of the canon is rather different from that entertained by the tradition of the commentary.

45. Matthew Arnold, Lectures and Essays in Criticism, vol. 3 of The Complete Prose Works, ed. H. R. Super (Ann Arbor: Michigan University Press, 1962), 258.

the "critical effort" set out first and foremost to cleanse the "object" from the disfigurements imposed on it by all the appropriations to which it had been subjected.

But it was the contemporaneous rise of hermeneutics that explicitly thematized the gap between the text and its understanding in an attempt to couple what remained ineluctably separate. The liminal space, caused by interpretation itself, had not been an important issue in the tradition of the commentary, although it posed a problem insofar as its widely unrecognized presence made authority slip between canon and reading. Such a floating authority indicates that this space cannot be eradicated, and whenever it is glossed over, this has repercussions: authority is no longer exclusively grounded in the canon; instead it hovers between text and commentary, thus being exposed to erosion.

There is, however, a reason why this precarious situation did not move into focus: the commentary did not deliberately arrogate the authority of the canon to itself, but in making the canon available it participated in its authority. The commentary was pervaded by the belief that participation entailed authentication of what the expositor of the canon had made available, and availability is a question of distribution, for which participation is a prerequisite. This distribution, however, eventually resulted in the dissipation of the very authority that the commentary was meant to make accessible.

The extent to which participation is the hallmark of any relationship to the canon is borne out by the current debate concerning canon and canon formation. As the commentary has long since eroded the notion of authority, the canon meanwhile has changed its basic attribute altogether: instead of being an authoritative assembly of literary texts, it is now considered to be cultural capital. Therefore "the problem of what is called canon formation is best understood as a problem in the constitution and distribution of cultural capital, or more specifically, a problem of access to the means of literary production and consumption." For this reason, "literary works must be seen rather as the vector of ideological notions which do not inhere in the works themselves but in the context of their institutional presentation, or more simply, in the way in which they are taught."[46] In spite of the revolution that the concept of the canon has undergone and notwithstanding the latter's diminished importance, participation—though no longer in authority but in the now-available

46. Guillory, *Cultural Capital*, ix.

cultural capital—is still the overriding activity that links the current view of the canon to the old tradition of commentary. Participation is always on the verge of appropriating what it intends to make available, be it authority or cultural capital. The latter is esteemed not because it commands authority but because it is something to be coveted; this is the basic difference. Again, in the final analysis, such participation leads to an erosion of what the canon either commands or has to offer.

CHAPTER THREE
The Hermeneutic Circle

Friedrich Daniel Ernst Schleiermacher:
Self-Reflective Circularity

The major event in the developing history of interpretation was not so much the Arnoldian type of criticism, which arose out of the demise of the commentary as a genre of interpretation, but rather the emergence of hermeneutics, as advocated by Friedrich Daniel Ernst Schleiermacher (1768–1834).

He started out from what he called "the quite limited purpose of interpreting the Holy Scriptures,"[1] but with the awareness that such an undertaking required a "rigorous practice . . . based on the assumption that misunderstanding occurs as a matter of course, and so understanding must be willed and sought at every point" (110). Instead of invoking an authority, Schleiermacher focuses on the gap between the text and its recipient, which makes the text into a "foreign or strange speech" (175), the grasping of which is continually threatened by misunderstanding.[2] Therefore he considered interpretation as the rigorous practice of discovering and elucidating the ramified conditionality of how understanding comes about. Thus hermeneutics marks the stage at

---

1. Friedrich Schleiermacher, *Hermeneutics: The Handwritten Manuscripts*, trans. James Duke and Jack Forstman, ed. Heinz Kimmerle (Missoula: Scholars, 1977), 67. The sources of all other quotations from this volume are given in in-text references to the appropriate pages.

which interpretation becomes self-reflective; this results in a continual self-monitoring of its operations and eventually a thematizing of what goes on during the activity of interpretation itself. Such a self-monitoring is all the more necessary as hermeneutics cannot appeal to indisputable standards, let alone to authority, which it might arrogate to itself. Instead, it can only be practiced—according to Schleiermacher—as an art,[3] whereas an analysis of *how* understanding is to be achieved is considered to be a replacement for authority.

When hermeneutics entered the stage, both commentary and criticism shrank to subgenres of interpretation. Such a change is important insofar as neither commentary nor the Arnoldian type of criticism had ever been considered as a genre of interpretation by those who practiced them. On the contrary, the practitioners identified what they did with interpretation, whereas Schleiermacher makes interpretation into an independent subject matter that has to be inspected and subjected to critical assessment. If the commentary obtained its legitimation from the authority of the canonical text that it was expounding, and if criticism appealed for its validity to a postulated idea of culture, hermeneutics strives to gain its legitimacy by both analyzing and 'sanitizing' the procedures of interpretation in order to ensure understanding. Therefore Schleiermacher has little if anything positive to say about commentaries, because they submit "to an authority, and in order to arrive at an independent understanding one must subject these authorities to one's own judgment" (217). Consequently, an analysis of understanding is no longer linked to any kind of authority. On the contrary, it has to be freed from all traditional and time-honored conceptualizations in order to ensure the transparency of what happens in understanding. Even the holy texts have to be subjected to hermeneutical procedures, as the objective is to translate them into terms not of communal life but of how they can be understood in relation to their original intention.

---

2. Hans-Georg Gadamer, *Truth and Method*, 2d ed., trans. rev. by Joel Weinsheimer and Donald G. Marshall (New York: Crossroad, 1989), 184f., has elaborated on what "misunderstanding" meant for the rise of hermeneutics and for Schleiermacher in particular.

3. Friedrich Schleiermacher, *Hermeneutik und Kritik*, ed. Manfred Frank (Frankfurt/Main: Suhrkamp, 1990), 91, gives a detailed account of what the "art of interpretation" is like and also of why interpretation is an art—because it is not an application of given rules.

The achievement of such an objective requires a ground-clearing operation, as undertaken by Schleiermacher's criticism of what he calls forms of "special hermeneutics," which are conditioned by the subject matter to be interpreted. This holds true not only for commentaries but also for all types of theological, legal, philological, and other subject-oriented interpretation. General hermeneutics, however, which Schleiermacher seeks to develop, "deals only with the art of understanding, not with the presentation of what has been understood. The presentation of what has been understood would be only one special part of the art of speaking and writing" (96). "Special hermeneutics is only an aggregate of observations" (95) and hence not so much concerned with understanding as with application, which is borne out by the use to which its findings are put. In such cases, the procedures of interpretation are geared to what the application intends to achieve. Although understanding may also play a part in special hermeneutics, it is not the focus of interpretation, and this is the prime reason why Schleiermacher takes exception to all kinds of special hermeneutics. What these are bound to lose sight of while dealing with specifics is the fact that understanding is a precondition for all these operations; by itself, a subject matter can never provide an adequate basis for investigating what understanding entails and how it comes about.[4] The latter is universal in nature, and none of the multiple applications executed by special hermeneutics would function if they did not rest on the achievement of understanding. Furthermore, all forms of special hermeneutics start out from certain presuppositions, which have to be analyzed in the light of their purpose.

What makes the investigation of understanding into a revolutionary event at the threshold of the nineteenth century is Schleiermacher's repudiation of the overriding frameworks that provided guidance for interpretation up to the end of the eighteenth century, such as the doctrine of the fourfold senses of the Bible, the *episteme* of resemblances and correspondences, and the principles of reason. The enterprise launched by Schleiermacher became all the more pertinent as all the agencies mentioned guaranteed comprehension of whatever appeared to be in dispute.

———

4. As Gadamer, *Truth and Method*, 187f., has stressed, there is a difference for Schleiermacher between grasping the subject matter (*Sachen*) of a text and understanding what the author may have meant by the way he has slanted the subject matter. Schleiermacher considered the author's understanding of how he has related to the subject matter as a surplus of cognition.

As long as the doctrine of the fourfold senses set the guidelines for interpretation of the Bible, "the dogmatic point of view" prevailed, "proceeding from the conviction that the Holy Spirit as a definite personality is the author of the Scriptures" (138).[5] However, "the dogmatic point of view goes beyond its own requirements when it rejects individualistic development . . . and thus destroys itself" (139). It has to be combined with the "philological view" that takes into account the several authors of the New Testament, "because the individuality of the writers was itself a product of their relationship to Christ . . . (Paul is distinctive because of his dialectics, John because of his sensitivity)" (139). As a consequence, there is no given schema according to which the Bible has to be understood, as claimed by the dogmatic view; instead, the two extremes of authorship have to be interrelated, not least since "the New Testament has to be constructed from a group of things that are not yet exactly known to us" (122). In other words, understanding became of paramount concern for Schleiermacher, as it was an indispensable prerequisite for any kind of application. Understanding, however, could not be decreed but had to be worked out by construing the meaning of the text.

Why had understanding, which is a precondition for any application, never been such a major issue before? The reason was largely what Foucault has termed the *episteme* of resemblances, similarities, and correspondences that had grown out of the chain of being and held sway long into the eighteenth century.[6] The dominance of such a world picture meant that resemblances and correspondences had to be discovered and not understood: Because they were preordained, their hiddenness had to be drawn out. Resemblances between things, correspondences among planes, levels, and strata were considered as givens, so there was no need to construe them. Discovering meant perceiving them in their concealed existence. But when such a network of relationships was on the wane, the necessity for understanding became pertinent. If relationships were no longer predetermined, they had to be established, and, in this respect,

5. Schleiermacher's opposition to the biblical exegesis based on the doctrine of the fourfold senses has been adequately dealt with by Hendrik Birus, "Zwischen den Zeiten: Friedrich Schleiermacher als Klassiker der neuzeitlichen Hermeneutik," in *Hermeneutische Positionen: Schleiermacher—Dilthey—Heidegger—Gadamer*, ed. Henrik Birus (Göttingen: Vandenhoeck und Ruprecht, 1982), 19f.

6. See Michel Foucault, *The Order of Things* (New York: Vintage, 1973), 67–77, 200–214.

understanding as a construal of the interconnections among data was Schleiermacher's epoch-making response to the decline of a world picture.

Another reason was that throughout the Age of Enlightenment there was still an unquestioned belief that whatever had been organized according to the rules and categories of reason presented either a state of affairs or an object as it really was. For instance, sentences construed by and therefore corresponding to the principles of reason were truthful, because human beings could not help taking sentences formed according to the principles of reason as axiomatic. Axioms as offshoots of reason do not require mediation in order to be comprehended; instead, they are automatically understood by virtue of participation in their fountainhead: the power of reason shared by all human beings.[7] There is a trace of a medieval concept still to be found in such a view: when Thomas Aquinas referred to meaning, he used the word *participatio*;[8] thus sharability and not understanding was at issue. As we have seen, something similar also applies to the commentary, which gains its authority primarily by participation in that of the canon. At the historical juncture, however, when reason as the structuring principle of truth was no longer taken for granted, reason itself had to be understood. And the need for this became all the more urgent because misunderstanding of speech and language in general was no longer the exception but the rule. Consequently, Schleiermacher writes: "We could formulate the task of hermeneutics in negative terms: to avoid misunderstanding at every point" (218).

Speech uttered or written produces meaning or is at least intended to be meaningful, but meaning can no longer be grasped on the basis that both author and recipient participate in the truth-providing reason. Instead, the meaning of a sentence uttered by someone other than ourselves is basically something foreign, which poses the problem of how it is to be taken. More often than not, misunderstanding ensues. What followed from the situation with which Schleiermacher found himself confronted was the necessity to establish procedures that would grasp the intended meaning of written or spoken utterances. In this respect, the hermeneutical procedures to be developed had to fill the gaps opened up after the loss of the guarantees provided by the network of resemblances

---

7. See Manfred Frank, "Einleitung," in Schleiermacher, *Hermeneutik und Kritik*, 13.
8. See Sancti Thomae Aquinatis, *Summa Theologiae*, vol. 1, Biblioteca de Autores Cristianos (Matriti, Spain: Editorial Catolica, 1961), 508–510.

and participation in human reason. And as neither the dogmatic doctrine of biblical exegesis nor the specific legal or philological subject matter to be interpreted could govern understanding, interpretation had to be reconceived.

It was Schleiermacher's prime objective "to understand an author better than he understood himself" (191). Privileging the author, however, does not mean foregrounding a personality but rather focusing on the author as the originator of the individual and hence not immediately graspable meaning of a foreign or strange speech. "Since we have no direct knowledge," Schleiermacher maintains, "of what was in the author's mind, we must try to become aware of many things of which he himself may have been unconscious, except insofar as he reflects on his own work and becomes his own reader" (112). Therefore striving for a better understanding does not imply that the interpreter will reveal the objective meaning of the foreign or strange speech; instead, a better understanding implies bringing to light the author's sign usage, a usage that he is never fully aware of when producing his texts. In this respect, Schleiermacher's basic formula marks the point of departure for the later hermeneutics of suspicion that guided psychoanalysis. If the individuality of sign usage has to be scrutinized in such a project, this is due to the fact that no author ever has total command or complete knowledge of all the connotations associated with his words. Bakhtin has alerted us to this basic feature by pointing out that the words of a language have traversed very many different contexts in their history,[9] and what they have accumulated over time in terms of denotations and connotations is never fully in the orbit of the language user. Accordingly, the author of a speech act uttered or written never bears in mind the multiple uses his words may have and does not reflect on the diversified possibilities of usage when he forms his sentences. But even if such reflection on the multiple denotations and connotations did take place, the actual use is bound to be selective, and such selection indicates the author's attitude toward the words concerned. This is one of the reasons that, according to Schleiermacher, there can never be total understanding of the speech act to be grasped; there is only the effort to optimize what an author's sign usage may indicate. "The truth is," Schleiermacher concludes, "that in interpretation the task of clarifying what is vague is never-ending" (117).

---

9. See Michael Bachtin (Mikhail Bakhtin), *Die Ästhetik des Wortes*, trans. Rainer Grübel (Frankfurt/Main: Suhrkamp, 1979), 169f., 185.

What are the parameters that structure the rigorous practice of the art of interpretation? With all the metaphysical guarantees gone, the dogmatic frameworks of exegesis abandoned, and the principles of reason discredited, all that remains is language, which is now elevated by Schleiermacher to the status of be-all and end-all. Language takes the place formerly occupied by authority at the time when the canon had to be made available through interpretation.[10]

Language, Schleiermacher holds, is dually coded by both the grammar and the psychology of the user. In the search for meaning, these two aspects became the focus of attention for Schleiermacher, because he was committed to the late-eighteenth-century idea of the interdependence of language and thinking. There is no thinking without language, and no language without thinking. "Indeed," Schleiermacher contends, "a person thinks by means of speaking. . . . But whenever the thinker finds it necessary to fix what he has thought, there arises the art of speaking, that is, the transformation of original internal speaking, and interpretation becomes necessary" (97). Starting out from this interrelationship, a grammatical interpretation allows us to delineate the salient features of the author's sign usage, and the psychological interpretation allows us to infer from the sign usage the stylistic signature of the author's thinking.[11] In Schleiermacher's own words: "A statement may be of maximum significance for one side of interpretation or the other. It is maximally significant for the grammatical side when it is linguistically creative to an exceptional degree and minimally repetitive: classical texts. A statement is maximally significant for the psychological side when it is highly individualized and minimally commonplace: original texts" (102). These two sides depend on one another, and from "this dual relation it is evident that the two tasks are completely equal" (99).

Duality or double-sidedness now becomes the hallmark of hermeneutic interpretation. The duality arises out of the fundamental gap between "all foreign and strange speech" (175) and its understanding, which in the final analysis may be narrowed down but never eliminated. "Since each person, as an individual, is the not-being of the other, it is never possible to eliminate non-understanding completely" (195). Such a residual "non-understanding" inscribes a duality into understanding itself, which is

---

10. See also Frank, "Einleitung," 36.
11. Concerning the interrelationship between these two aspects, see Jean Greisch, *Hermeneutik und Metaphysik* (Munich: Fink, 1993), 143.

meant to diminish misunderstanding. Thus concepts are paired right from the beginning of Schleiermacher's exposition of interpretation. This basic duality spawns further dualities or pairings, all of which provide frames of interpretation for the purpose of optimizing understanding. They are indicative of the liminal space opened up by interpretation, reveal the interpreter's awareness of a fundamental difference, and replace all over-riding orientations such as authority. Instead of authority there is *"brisur"* (Derrida), which is groundless and so causes continual transitions within the pairings established,[12] thereby generating new ones. All these pairings pivot around the liminal space out of which they have arisen and that inscribes itself into them, as the grammatical and the psychological aspects of language are in turn split up into further dualities. The liminal space, one might say, causes a nesting of dualities, all of which are drafted to overcome the *brisur* they have emerged from.[13] Such a countervailing tendency indicates that understanding, in the final analysis, is achieved only approximately. It is Schleiermacher's awareness of the liminal space that induces him to arrange the register as a nesting of dualities into which a "foreign or strange speech" (175) has to be translated for the purpose of understanding.

Therefore Schleiermacher maintains "that whatever efforts can be legitimately called interpretation, there are no other types except those based on the different relationships between the two sides we have noted" (108). Regarding the grammatical side, the focus on an author's language is again dual in character. The meaning of a word is established by two closely interrelated operations, namely, determination and exclusion. No linguistic sign can ever have, or lay claim to, a universal meaning inde-pendent of context. The same holds true for the application of signs. Thus Schleiermacher argues that each sign is to be determined by what it excludes, that is, what it does not mean or signify. What it means or signi-fies is determined by its position in the sentence, which is primarily a syn-tagmatic determination. Schleiermacher considered such a determination the first canon;[14] the second canon he defines as follows: "The meaning

---

12. See Frank, "Einleitung," 27.

13. Schleiermacher, *Hermeneutics*, 216, therefore maintains: "The interpreter must then establish the same relationship between himself and the author as existed between the author and his original audience."

14. For a critique of Schleiermacher's conception of canon, see E. D. Hirsch, *Validity in Interpretation* (New Haven: Yale University Press, 1967), 200ff.

of each word of a passage must be determined by the context in which it occurs. The first canon serves only to exclude certain possibilities. This second canon, however, seems to be determinative, a 'jump' which must be justified" (127). Although the two canons almost make Schleiermacher into a Wittgensteinian *avant la lettre*, it is the duality of the syntactical position and the contextual location that is highlighted as the indispensable criterion for ascertaining the meaning intended by the author. Neither canon would in itself be sufficient for the grammatical interpretation to be successful, and although the two canons form the frame in which meaning is to be grasped, the latter never rests in any given or identifiable unit of language use, as Schleiermacher has emphasized: "Since meaning is not vested in the individual parts of speech but in their connection, the closest parallels are those in which the parts of speech have been combined in the same way" (141). Meaning, then, is produced by varying degrees of differentiation brought about by the connections established among clauses, sequence of sentences, and their contextual location. If similarities between connections enhance the certainty of what the author may have meant, such similarity in turn points to the fact that meaning is not a graspable entity but something that can only be shaped approximately. This approximation is again indicative of the liminal space, whose character makes itself felt insofar as the contours of what is determined by exclusion as well as by syntactical and contextual location keep shifting. This shifting occurs because the positions (syntax and context) are subjected to changing applicability, there being no rules regarding their application. Thus liminality does not confine itself to marking off positions from one another but also blurs the salient features of syntactical and contextual determination, as these features continually shade into one another without losing their identity.

The psychological aspect of interpretation links up with the grammatical aspect in kaleidoscopically shifting relationships. If the focus in grammatical interpretation is on the language system as actualized by the author, the psychological one spotlights the way in which the tools provided by grammar are used; this enables us to find out how the author thinks. The psychological interpretation is basically technically oriented, which is borne out by Schleiermacher's interchangeable use of technical and psychological designations for tracing the author's thinking. Again this is a dual task: "Grammatical interpretation is divided into two contrasting tasks. So is technical interpretation. The first task is to discover the individuality of an author, and the other is to recognize with definiteness how this individuality is expressed" (162). What, though, are the means for identifying the author's individuality and the motives that have "moved the author to communicate" (147)? Although the grammatical and the psychological interpretation are designed to dovetail, the usage of language may furnish salient features of the author's way of thinking only to a certain extent, because the findings of the sign usage have to be evaluated. This holds true even for what one might consider psychological indicators of an author's language, such as the alternation between "pleonasm" and "emphasis" (142). The latter marks an interstice between the two aspects of interpretation without fully establishing the author's individuality, although it may serve to delineate the salience of what the author wanted to express. If language provides the parameter for grammatical usage, what is the parameter for psychological interpretation, apart from the interdependence of the two aspects?

Again Schleiermacher proposes two interlinking procedures as a framework for bringing the psychological aspect of interpretation to full fruition: comparison and divination.

[The] divinatory method seeks to gain an immediate comprehension of the author as an individual. The comparative method proceeds by subsuming the author under a general type. It then tries to find his distinctive traits by comparing him with the others of the same type. Divinatory knowledge is the feminine strength in knowing people; comparative knowledge, the masculine.[15] Each method refers back to the other. The divinatory is based on the assumption that each person is not only a unique individual in his own right, but that he has a receptivity to the uniqueness of every other person. This assumption in turn seems to presuppose that each person contains a minimum of everyone else, and so divination is aroused by comparison with

_____

15. Hirsch, *Validity in Interpretation*, 205, elaborates on this duality, which he considers as

two principle forces not only in interpretation but in human knowledge generally. The implications of that insight stretch beyond the currently fashionable discussion of the opposition between scientific and humanistic cultures in their respective "methods." What is at stake is not some ideal fusion of the separate cultures and their modes of thought, but the right of interpretation (and implicitly all humanistic disciplines) to claim as its object genuine knowledge. The two forces that Schleiermacher perceived in interpretation and in human thinking generally are versions of two processes that are indeed comprised in every realm of thought that can lay claim to knowledge.

oneself. . . . The two methods should never be separated. Divination becomes certain only when it is corroborated by comparisons. . . . But comparison does not provide a distinctive unity. The general and the particular must interpenetrate, and only divination allows this to happen.[16]   (150f)

The divinatory method grasps the individuality of an author, as expressed in what is alien for the interpreter, through a kind of hunch, and the comparative method controls the hunch insofar as the author, representing a certain type, can be compared to others of the same type.

It may seem strange that Schleiermacher calls these two interrelated operations "methods." However, the very terminology points to the fact that they are an offshoot of contemporary philology, which more often than not required informed guesses for the purpose of emending corrupted manuscripts by interpolating what the faulty text might have originally contained. The comparative method was closely linked to this kind of divination, as comparing, collating, and sifting were basic activities for underpinning the conjectures made in the course of restoring flawed or fragmentary manuscripts. This interlinking, then, was a stock-in-trade of early-nineteenth-century editing practice. Hence Schleiermacher's use of the term "method."

Divination, however, is also guided, as Manfred Frank writes, by Schleiermacher's insight that the language system does not contain within itself a prefigured "interpretand" for its actual use, which would set guidelines for the recipient as to how the foreign or strange speech is to be understood.[17] Furthermore, the liminal space, as I have shown, marks a decisive difference that cannot be overcome by any form of decoding the foreign or strange speech, so that divination becomes an indispensable necessity.[18]

The intertwining of divination and comparison functions as a frame of reference for the psychological interpretation, which has to fathom the author's overall use of language and check its salient features by comparing them with other samples of stylistic signatures in the text. This means

---

16. Gadamer, *Truth and Method*, 187, has elucidated the implications of this statement and what the transposition of the interpreter into the author entails.
17. Frank, "Einleitung," 49f.
18. Hans Ineichen, *Philosophische Hermeneutik* (Freiburg: Karl Alber, 1991), 127, goes as far as saying that Schleiermacher considered divination the fountainhead for devising hypotheses of exegesis.

no less than that the act of understanding must simultaneously produce its own framework. Such a framework is again dual in nature, thus bearing the inscription of the liminal space that demands to be bridged. Accordingly, the framework does not contain any rules for narrowing the liminal space. Instead, the latter remains present in the framework, as it makes divination and comparison continually shade into one another in a process of mutual gearing that, as executed by the interpreter, elevates hermeneutics into an art. The purpose of this art is to construe understanding, which, in Schleiermacher's own words, always "constructs something finite and definite from something infinite and indefinite" (100).

The pairings discussed thus far—the grammatical/psychological modes and the divinatory/comparative methods—are not conceived as binary oppositions; on the contrary, they are made to interpenetrate in order to "jump" (Schleiermacher's own word) the space that separates the interpreter from what is to be interpreted. Just as the two canons of syntactical and contextual determination are meant to encircle the author's meaning, so the divinatory and comparative methods are designed to fathom the author's individuality. All these operations proceed in a circular movement. The circularity between grammar and psychology allows us to ascertain the manifestation of an author's individuality; the circularity between the divinatory and the comparative methods allows us to grasp this manifested individuality. The circular movement is thus dual in nature, as it operates not only between grammar and psychology, divination and comparison, but also between the modes and methods. This mutual inscription of circularity gives rise to a network that structures the hermeneutic circle. "Complete knowledge," Schleiermacher maintains, "always involves an apparent circle, that each part can be understood only out of the whole to which it belongs, and vice versa. All knowledge which is scientific must be constructed in this way" (113).

The operation of the circle between parts and whole is the overarching framework of hermeneutics, structuring all the circular movements operative between modes and methods. The part/whole circle governs all interpretive activity insofar "as the whole is understood from the parts, so the parts can be understood only from the whole. This principle is of such consequence for hermeneutics and so incontestable that one cannot even begin to interpret without using it" (196). Such an operative intent prevents the circle from becoming a vicious one. The particular always perspectivizes general knowledge, as there is no general knowledge without the particulars out of which it arises. In turn, the particular would remain ungraspable if it did not endow general knowl-

edge with its significance or did not have a foil against which its specificity becomes discernible.

Thus the circle brings out two things at once: (a) something general is
made ascertainable against the backdrop of a changing array of particulars; (b) the particulars gain salience by being set off from the general, a
distinction that can never be obliterated. Gearing the general to the particular—or, in Schleiermacher's terminology, part to whole—and vice
versa establishes a platform from which to observe the relationships that
structure the interpenetration of modes and methods. The circle makes
part and whole into shifting foils for one another, thereby converting
grammar/psychology as well as divination/comparison into mutually mirroring viewpoints. These circular operations are powered by the drive to
cope with the liminal space, whose presence becomes tangible in the
multiple divisions through which it inscribes itself in the register devised
by Schleiermacher in order to translate alien speech into understanding.
Instead of superimposing a register onto the text, as in the tradition of the
commentary, the liminal space splits up the register into a graduated duality of mutually controlling positions whose circular concatenation is
meant to bridge the difference between them.

The circle of interlinking part/whole, grammar/psychology, and divina-
tion/comparison is the hallmark of hermeneutics. It highlights the fact that
there is no longer a given authority that can validate what interpretation
sets out to achieve. Furthermore, there is no authority dwelling in the text
itself; therefore understanding is to be arrived at from within the text by
means of manifold circular operations that provide a way of correcting and
monitoring understanding. It is the circle that runs both inside modes and
methods and between them, bringing about a to-and-fro movement
between part and whole that maps out the trajectory in each individual
text along which we are able to clarify "what is vague" in order to arrive at
an understanding of a foreign or strange speech (117). This circular procedure alerts us to the fact that neither word, nor sentence, nor mode, nor
method has any definite meaning in itself. Instead, the meaning to be
ascertained and understood arises out of and is situated in relationships,
the fine-tuning of which is produced through a mutual inscription of
circles into the multiple dualities of the register.

This means that understanding realizes itself through a continual circular movement, which finally reveals why hermeneutics has privileged
the circle as its operational device for the act of interpretation. The circle
initiates an ever-widening coupling between parts and whole, not least as
the whole is not given prior to the parts but has to be visualized through

them. The notion of the whole is always relative and is expanded by the circle through multiple interconnections with ever-new features of the parts, and this expansion in turn throws new light on the understanding of the parts involved. It is this broadening out of the circular movement that permits a controlled approximation to understanding.

The circular to-and-fro movement cannot eliminate the liminal space, however, as there always remains a final resistance to the transposition of modes and methods into one another, just as there is always a difference between part and whole. This final resistance not only causes the differentiation of the register but also induces interpretation to become self-reflective, which means that it has to thematize its own procedures, which now have to function as a frame of reference. Thus interpretation as a self-monitoring form of translatability—as Schleiermacher conceived of it—turns out to be a replacement of authority by the hermeneutic circle. One might even go so far as to say that an awareness of the liminal space between the subject matter and its interpretation dawned only at the historical moment when the text to be interpreted had lost its authority. In this respect, the emptiness of that space might be considered as a trace of the vanished authority that had previously determined the relationship between the text and its reader. When there is nothing to be shared anymore, the gap between the text and its understanding becomes apparent, calling for negotiation through an elaborate register whose workings have continually to be monitored.

The hermeneutic circle points to the fact that the vanished authority has left behind a blank that unmistakably separates the text from its interpretation. And yet there remains a blind spot even in the circularity itself that Schleiermacher proposed as a means of coping with this blank. He did not specify what actually happens in the circular movement between the different dualities. Are the dual modes, dual methods, and the duality between part/whole just interlinked, related, mutually imposed on, or are they mutually controlled by one another, made to overlap, to be telescoped, realigned, or intertwined? These questions mark the blind spot in Schleiermacher's concept of circularity. The circle highlights the operative intent but not the strategies of its workings. Thus the circular movement remains abstract, because there is no transcendental stance that would allow us to determine the operations of this steering device.

This blind spot is important for three different though interconnected reasons. In replacing authority by the hermeneutic circle, interpretation is no longer controlled by any overarching third dimension that would bracket the text with its exegesis, and so it has to become self-reflective. Furthermore, the blind spot is indicative of a residual untranslatability produced by interpretation itself, thus implying that untranslatability is bound to vary according to what is interpreted. Finally, the blind spot provides an impetus for continual self-monitoring, because interpretation has both to produce and to change its own frameworks. Such a necessity is largely due to the fact that interpretation is not only a translation of what is given but also a translation of oneself into what one seeks to grasp.

There is a final point that Schleiermacher allows us to see. The register of dual modes, dual methods, and the duality of part and whole is a neatly geared assembly of viewpoints brought to bear on the "foreign or strange speech" for the purpose of achieving understanding. The function exercised by the register is again dual in nature: on the one hand, it is a structured form of perception that penetrates the text; on the other, it provides parameters for translating the text into understanding. As a means of effecting such an operation, the register is identical neither to the text nor to understanding. Rather, by invading the text through its viewpoints, it rearranges the text in such a manner that understanding may emerge. At best the register functions as a mediator, in that its guided perception translates the text into terms of reference that allow understanding to emerge. Whatever emerges by an intervention of something into something else is never definitively to be determined, as it exceeds referentiality; therefore understanding can only be achieved approximately.

Johann Gustav Droysen: The Nesting of Circles

The basic aim of hermeneutics is to achieve understanding; however, the nature of this understanding and the procedures that govern its production will change in relation to what is to be understood. Schleiermacher set out to achieve an understanding of what he had termed the "strange or foreign speech" of an author, the ultimate objective being to understand the "author better than he has understood himself." Such an approach is basically text oriented, and this holds true irrespective of whether the utterance concerned is spoken or written. But what happens when the matter to be understood is not a text produced by an author for comprehension by its recipient? Such a question posed itself for Johann Gustav Droysen (1808–1884) some forty years after Schleiermacher, when he tried to achieve an understanding of history, which for him was no longer a text written by an author but only "faded traces and suppressed gleams" of a past.[19] Data of this kind "are not past things, for these have disappeared, but things which are still present here and now, whether recollections of what was done, or remnants of things that have existed and of events that have occurred" (11). Such a fragmented past extends into the present and is graspable not as a past but only as "Remains," "Sources," and "Monuments" (18). Whatever the specific character of such "historical material" may be like, it is certainly not a text, and even when there are texts, more often than not these too are nothing but traces. The historical material itself—scattered throughout the present—consists of different categories. The remnants may be just isolated facts or traces whose origin has been lost, and thus at best they are contingent fragments of a past. The sources, in contradistinction, already reflect "past events as human understanding has apprehended them" (19) and consequently are slanted by either subjective views or pragmatic exigencies. "The apprehension will obviously vary according as it was intended to aid the author's own memory, or for others, for one person, or a few, or all, for contemporaries or for posterity, for instruction, for entertainment, or for purposes of business" (20). Such a range of possibilities highlights the nature of sources insofar as they *translate* historical occurrences into diversified conceptions. Droysen uses this very term in his lecture course, maintaining that sources translate external events into a form of memory.[20] The framing of facts discernible in sources is a deliberate ploy in monuments, which translate a whole course of events either symbolically or artistically into modes of perception, thus channeling their remembrance for posterity. Monuments themselves already present an understanding of how historical

----

19. Johann Gustav Droysen, *Outline of the Principles of History* (*Grundriss der Historik*), trans. E. Benjamin Andrews (New York: Howard Fertig, 1967), 11. The sources of all other quotations from this volume are given in in-text references to the appropriate pages. Droysen himself prepared this abstract of what has come to be called *Historik*, which was a lecture course on "the Encyclopedia and Methodology of History," delivered, as he put it "from time to time, beginning with 1857." Requests from his students, "led me," as he says in the "Author's Preface," "to write out the skeleton in the same order to give my auditors a basis for my oral amplification." And as this "skeleton" appeared to be very much in demand through numerous "requests, some of them from foreign lands," he decided "to give it to the public" (ix). It was first translated into English in 1893 and reprinted in 1967.
20. See Johann Gustav Droysen, "Textausgabe," in *Historik*, ed. Peter Leyh (Stuttgart: frommann-holzboog, 1977), 79.

facts are to be conceived, so that almost all the historical material is manifestly fashioned. The historian is therefore confronted not only with contingent fragments of a past but also to a large extent with a past that has already been mediated in the event of its occurrence.

Such a state of affairs poses a rather different challenge to understanding than that with which Schleiermacher found himself confronted. A text to be understood at least has a certain coherence, whereas historical material is nothing but a welter of disconnected data. "Always, or nearly always, we have before us only single points out of the facts as they originally were; only individual views of what existed or occurred. Any historical material has gaps in it" (25). If even the facts themselves are punctured by gaps, the latter are bound to multiply owing to the disconnectedness of the historical material through which a past extends into the present.[21] Gaps of this kind are due to a lack of documentation as well as to the faults and distortions that have occurred during their transfer in the passage of time. Such a mixture of punctured facts, disjointed texts, and cryptic encodings presents itself as the subject matter, which requires an elaborate method of interpretation if it is to be understood. Therefore, Droysen maintains, "the point of departure in investigation is historical interrogation. Invention puts us in possession of the materials for historical work. It is the miner's art, that of finding and bringing to the light, 'the underground work' " (18). But how does one delve into the depths of such material, and what is the invention that guides the interrogation? Droysen writes: "Historical Interrogation results in our ascertaining what Remains, Monuments and Sources are to be brought forward for the 'reply' " (21). This means no less than that the remains of the past are indications of a response to a problem, and so they will allow us to reconstitute the situation to which they were a "reply." This is Collingwood's "question and answer logic" *avant la lettre.*[22] Historical facts have to be read as answers to questions that must have posed themselves at a particular time, and "interrogation" of these relic responses calls for the "miner's art" that Droysen is advocating.

---

21. Droysen, *Historik*, 51, elaborates on this issue later on by stating: "And with the discovery of the immeasurable gaps in our historical knowledge, which investigation has not yet filled up and perhaps now can never fill up, investigation espies ever wider breadths to the domains with which it has to do, and anticipates one day filling them with life."

22. See R. G. Collingwood, *An Autobiography* (Oxford: Oxford University Press, Clarendon, 1939).

A basic reason for such a heuristics, which sends the historian into the darkling depths of the past, is the insight that neither beginnings nor ends of history are fathomable. "Beginnings are neither sought by criticism nor demanded by interpretation. In the moral world nothing is without medial antecedents. Yet historical investigation does not propose to explain, in the sense of deriving as mere effects and developments, the latter from the earlier, or phenomena from law" (26). "To the finite eye beginning and end are veiled, but the direction of the streaming movement it can by investigation detect. Condemned to the narrow limit of the here and the now, it yet dimly espies the whence and the whither" (48f.). Both a beginning and a supposed end of history are at best blanks, not least as they cannot be interrogated, because they are not a "reply" to anything in the course of the "streaming movement." Furthermore, explaining a beginning would imply going beyond it, owing to its inherent duality: on the one hand, it entails the launch of something, which now unfolds itself; on the other, it presupposes, as the cause of such a launch, something that is bound to be outside the beginning, just as an assumed *telos* of history is outside the actual happening of the historical process. Whenever beginnings and ends are postulated, history turns into a testimony for preconceived notions, which are supposed to reveal themselves through history but cannot be identical with it. Moreover, understanding facts would be of minor importance if history were considered as a process of unfolding something existing prior to itself or as a march to a goal that by definition would lie outside itself. Instead of going beyond history, Droysen proposed to plumb the depths of the historical material. The "miner's art" is implicitly juxtaposed with a Hegelian transcendentalism. In accordance with this anti-Hegelian thrust of Droysen's *Principles of History*—although not insensitive to Hegel's achievement[23]—interrogation of historical material can only be conducted from inside history. This is the reason that Droysen had to fall back on hermeneutics in order to explore the remains of the past, as hermeneutical procedures can operate out of the midst of the very material that is to be fathomed.[24] Schleiermacher replaced authority with his own hermeneutic perspective, while Droysen replaced all transcendental viewpoints of historical material by an increasingly complex hermeneutical procedure. This was necessary precisely because

---

23. See Droysen, *Historik*, 257.
24. For Droysen's place in the unfolding of history during the nineteenth century, see Ineichen, *Philosophische Hermeneutik*, 118, 137ff., 145, 151.

there was no longer any overriding reference to guide interpretation and because the operation of such a method had to be monitored and controlled by continual self-reflection if the operational intent was to be achieved.

This heightened complexity is all the more essential because history has no identifiable, given existence but has to be constituted[25] by "bringing to light" the hidden interrelationships of the "remnants," "sources," and "monuments" through which a past projects itself into the present. The task of interpretation is thus twofold: it has to constitute its subject matter, and it has to furnish understanding of what has been constituted. What may not have been obvious in Schleiermacher's conception now emerges fully into the open: the inherent duality of interpretation. In Schleiermacher's case, the text to be understood was a given, although the modes and methods he brought to bear for grasping the author's meaning constituted the very subject matter he was concerned with. In Droysen's case, the subject matter—history—cannot be ascertained prior to interpretation, although the latter sets out to understand what it has brought to light. Droysen appears to be aware of such a difference when he writes:

> Certainly these state documents do not as a rule, like those narrations, lay before us an already formed idea of the case, a preliminary historical picture of what has just happened. They are remnants of that which happened; they are pieces of the transaction and of the course it pursued, which still lie directly before our eyes. And if I may give the expression so wide an application, it is as a "transaction," in the broad maze of the present, conditioned and conditioning in a thousand ways, that those events come to pass which we afterwards apprehend successively as History. We thus look at them in a quite different way from that in which they occurred, and which they had in the wishes and deeds of those who enacted them. So it is not a paradox to ask how History (*Geschichte*) comes out of transactions (*Geschäften*), and what it is which with this transfer into another medium, as it were, is added or lost.[26]   (113f)

---

25. See also Peter Leyh, "Vorwort des Herausgebers," in Droysen, *Historik*, xii. See also Droysen, *Outline of the Principles of History*, 95.
26. See also Klaus E. Müller and Jörn Rüsen, "Einleitung," in *Historische Sinnbildung: Problemstellungen, Zeitkonzepte, Wahrnehmungshorizonte, Darstellungsstrategien*, Rowohlts Enzyklopädie, ed. Klaus E. Müller and Jörn Rüsen (Reinbek: Rowohlt, 1997), 11.

This is an important statement in several respects. First of all interpretation of historical transactions 'creates' history by transposing past occurrences into a different "medium." History, however, is not a pure invention
of interpretation either, though it arises out of the translation of the
remains still "before our eyes" into a register that did not belong to the situations within which those observable transactions took place. Therefore
history is a contemporary understanding of past transactions that did not
have understanding as an ingredient when they happened, and this makes
it into a construct for the purpose of understanding the fragments of the
past that are scattered throughout the present.

What does this reveal about interpretation? Above all, that it is marked
by an ineluctable duality. The subject matter to be interpreted is always
shaped by the approach brought to bear, and yet the approach is not just a
superimposition but a register into which the slanted subject matter is
translated. Shaping indicates an act of grasping, whereas translation is
meant to facilitate an understanding of what has been grasped. This dual
operation is indispensable insofar as there is no given frame of reference
for assessing the subject matter prior to interpretation. Fashioning the subject matter, however, points to a difference between what is to be interpreted and the register into which it is transposed. What appears
paradoxical—namely, that the subject matter is simultaneously shaped by
the register and yet taken for something independent of it—is due to the
liminal space that is opened up by interpretation itself.

This basic duality is the hallmark of all interpretation, which is bound
to become more complicated when the subject matter to be interpreted
has to be constituted by interpretation itself. Droysen was aware that in this
case something might get lost and something would be added, not least as
such a construal of history must in turn be dually coded. On the one hand,
it is the "miner's art" to ferret out the contents of the remnants of the past,
and, on the other, such a revelation is intimately linked to the present,
which provides the angle for assessment. History therefore is not a mar-
shaling of events into a progressive order so much as a refraction of past
occurrences in the mirror of the present. This mirroring is caused neither
by the past events themselves nor by anything in the present, and if such
mutual interdependence is called history, the latter is a form of mediation
that is constituted for the purpose of understanding. History, then, is not to
be identified with contingent facts that are given, nor is it a pure invention.
Instead, it turns out to be a construct allowing for dual mediation: between
the given facts and between past and present. The concept of history as
mediation between past and present inevitably entails a circular move-

ment, because past and present are not encompassed by any overarching third dimension that might regulate their interplay.

In this respect, Droysen adopted hermeneutical circularity for his enterprise. The circle gears historical facts to a whole of which they are remnants, while the whole in turn assumes tangibility through what the facts reveal about it. In Droysen's own words: "The individual is understood in the total, and the total from the individual. . . . The process of understanding is as truly synthetic as analytic, as truly inductive as deductive" (14). However, such circularity between part and whole—as developed by Schleiermacher—only serves as a basis for structuring another circle—more important for Droysen—between past and present, in consequence of which a nesting of circles develops. This doubling-up of circularity points to the growing complexity of interpretation, caused by the fact that it has to constitute its own subject matter. This procedure becomes all the more obvious through the method of interpretation that Droysen devised and that he considered necessary for the mediation between past and present. His method turns out to be a diversified register into which the historical material is transposed with the intent of conceiving history.

Droysen advances four methodological viewpoints, which he qualifies as "The Doctrine of Method": namely, "Pragmatic Interpretation," "Interpretation of Conditions," "Psychological Interpretation," and "Interpretation of Ideas." " 'Pragmatic' interpretation takes up the body of criticised facts according to the causal nexus naturally binding together the original events in their course, in order to re-construct this course of events as it once actually was. By 'body of criticised facts' is meant those remains and those views of the once actual course of events which have been verified and arranged in the work of criticism" (27). Pragmatic interpretation is meant to make inferences from the historical material by trying to find out what must have been the problem that is to be traced in that material. A great many facts are necessary in order to make reliable inferences, and they are processed by means of comparisons and analogies "viz., a comparison between the known quantity and the 'x' in question" (27). This is a faint echo of Schleiermacher's method of comparison/divination. Inferences, however, arise out of and are controlled by a circularity between the comparisons and the "x" that is to be ascertained. Therefore the "pragmatic" approach has to fill the gaps in the punctured facts by establishing connections and thus lays the ground for constituting history.

"The 'interpretation of conditions' proceeds upon the truth that we must think the conditions which made the original fact possible and possible so and so, as a part of the fact itself, and hence as certain to enter, however fragmentarily, into all views and remnants of the fact" (27f.). Time and space provide the parameters according to which the facts are fashioned, and this conditioning is caused by various human agents who in turn were acted upon by what they had sparked off. The reliability of such an interpretation increases in conjunction with the number and variety of conditionings that can be traced.[27] Thus historical facts have to be explored by means of two interrelated circles: the one between time and space, and the other between human agencies that are subjected to what they have wrought. Since these two circles inscribe themselves into one another, we get a further nesting, indicative of the many differences between features of historical facts that have to be interrelated. Thus the "conditions" provide a fashioning of history.

 " 'Psychological interpretation' seeks in the given fact, the acts of will which produced it. Such an interpretation may take cognizance of the subject who willed, and of the energy of his volition so far as this influenced the course of events under survey, and of his intellectual force so far as this determined his will" (28f.). In spite of the fact that the will was considered throughout the nineteenth century as the be-all and end-all, Droysen conceived of it less in terms of a substance than as something to be explored through its manifestations in the course of events. But why does the will become an object of investigation? This is due to the insight that the nature of human beings is impenetrable and thus sealed off from knowledge and cognition. If human beings are unfathomable, a contextual specification of their various manifestations is the only way to learn something of what Droysen called the impermeable "circle of its own" (29) by which human beings are distinguished. Under these auspices, historical facts assume a dual aspect: they are conditioned by the human will, and they are also windows allowing a glimpse of the human being's innermost "circle of its own." Now it is no longer the gaps of the punctured facts that have to be remedied by the circularity undertaken by pragmatic interpretation but another "x," which is permeated by the double-sidedness of historical facts as both products and elucidations of human volition. In this respect, the historical facts themselves appear to have a circular structure. Thus the "psychological" approach permits us to reflect on the human agents who reveal themselves through the history they have produced.

---

27. See Droysen, *Historik*, 186.

Finally,

> The "interpretation of ideas" fills the gap which psychological interpre-
> tation leaves. For the individual builds a world for himself in that meas-
> ure in which he has part in the moral potencies. And the more
> diligently and successfully he builds, in his place and for the brief space
> in his life, the more he has furthered those partnerships in which he
> lived and which lived in him; and the more has he on his part served
> the moral potencies which survive him. Without them man were not
> man; but they develop, grow and rise only in the united work of men,
> of peoples, of times, only in the progressive history whose development
> and growth is their unfolding.   (30)

"Ideas" comprise the moral world in which human beings participate,
and they arise out of the way in which the latter redress the conflicts in
their lives by interacting with their fellow human beings. Ideas therefore
are not given but are generated by "the united work of men," who unfold
the moral world by continually exceeding the limitations of the here and
now, as Droysen specified in his extended lecture course.[28] Thus an
"interpretation of ideas" allows history to be conceived as an endless
unfolding of character formation.

These four approaches to processing historical material are closely
interlinked, with each successive method filling a gap left open by the
previous one. This interdependence is necessary, because each of the
interpretive methods offers only a partial interpretation of what is still discernible of the past, and therefore they have to be connected with one
another, as "the exaltation of any of these as by itself essentially determinative of validity, is the source of many theoretical and practical errors"
(27). The concatenation of these four types of interpretation, which Droysen qualifies as "artificial ways,"[29] results in a network through which the
types become foils for one another. Whenever one type becomes the focus
of attention, it is to be perceived against the background of another, which
in turn may become the focus again. Thus the interplay among the four
types is regulated by what later on in phenomenology has been called the
interchange between "theme and horizon."[30] Again, such a reciprocal

---

28. See ibid., 212.
29. Ibid., 164.
30. See Alfred Schütz, *Das Problem der Relevanz*, trans. A. von Baeyer (Frank-
furt/Main: Suhrkamp, 1971), 30f. and 36ff.

shifting of focus and background is circular in nature, not least because a comprehensive interrogation of the historical material requires a multiplication of all imaginable circular interchanges. If one also takes into consideration the fact that the four types in themselves are conceived as circular, the circuit telescopes them into one another, thus fine-tuning the process of constituting history.

Each type of interpretation makes its own specific contribution to this process: the pragmatic interpretation generates the coherence of facts; the interpretation of conditions differentiates among them; the psychological interpretation fashions them; and the interpretation of ideas makes them interact. If circularity, operative in the four "artificial ways," endows the given facts with significance, the network of these interdependent "ways" generates history. Thus history turns out to be an emergent phenomenon produced by the mechanics of the network, which is nothing but a register into which the historical material is transposed. Such a variegated register could be read in two different ways: (a) its diversification indicates that interpretation targets something that is not in the nature of a given but has to be developed out of what there is; (b) its growing complexity highlights the fact that interpretation is also a mode of producing something. This makes interpretation itself into a two-pronged operation. It is no longer confined to exegesis, although each of the four types is primarily exegetical in its thrust. Exegesis can only relate to what is given, whereas the network generates something that is not factual in character. Perhaps interpretation has always been like this, distinguished by its double-sidedness of exegesis and generation, not least as each exegetical move issues into something that does not pertain to what has been interrogated. However, the more interpretation seeks to uncover what lies buried, through what Droysen called the "miner's art," the more prominent the generative aspect of interpretation becomes, to which the exegetical aspect remains subservient.

Why is history made to emerge through interpretation? It has no self-presence and therefore is not a graspable entity but can only gain its presence as a continual unfolding, which the interpretive register brings into focus as history's self-differentiation. Droysen writes:

> It is a continuity, in which everything that precedes transplants itself into what is later, filling it out and extending it as "a contribution to itself"; while the latter presents itself as a result, fulfilment, and enlargement of the earlier. It is not a continuity of a circle that returns into itself, of a period repeating itself, but that of an endless succession, and this in such wise that in every new a further new has its germ and the assurance of

working itself out. . . . In this restless succession, in this continuity advancing upon itself, the general notion of time wins its discreet content, which we designate by the expression "History."   (98f)

Although history is an ever-emerging differentiation of itself, it is nevertheless intimately tied to humans, who set history's continual "contribution" to itself in motion. Thanks to this connection, history can be understood but not encompassed. Whatever human beings are able to make can be understood, yet history seems to exceed human understanding, because what emerges outstrips its cause. Is history more than a mental construct brought about by interpretation? As an emergent phenomenon it seems to be something that actually exists. If it did not, emergence itself would have to be conceived in terms of human understanding, and this is exactly what Droysen proposes. Such a move once more makes history, at least metaphorically, into a text[31] that is to be interpreted, in consequence of which it becomes an object of exegesis. Thus Droysen argues: "History is humanity becoming and being conscious concerning itself. The epochs of History are not the life periods of this 'I' of Humanity—empirically we do not know whether this race 'I' is growing old or renewing its youth, only that it does not continue to be what it was or is,—but they are stages in that ego's self-knowledge, its knowledge of the world and of God" (48). And Droysen concludes his interpretation of emergence by stating somewhat bombastically: "History is Humanity's knowledge of itself, its certainty about itself. It is not 'the light and the truth,' but the search therefor, a sermon thereupon, a consecration thereto. It is like John the Baptist, 'not that Light but sent to bear witness of that Light' " (49).

With such an application, the inherent circularity of Droysen's hermeneutical procedure comes full circle. The construal of history as an emergent phenomenon is not undertaken for its own sake. The mental construct therefore begins to function only when applied to a purpose for which it has been construed. If history emerges as a continual unfolding, then it turns into a mirror for human beings, who are refracted by what they have caused: thus the ceaseless differentiation of history transmutes into a proliferation of humankind's self-grasping. Understanding history would be incomplete if it did not issue into human self-understanding, which in turn is just as unending a process as the very history that humans keep generating.

---

31. See Gadamer, *Truth and Method*, 217f.

This interconnection raises a general problem pertaining to the hermeneutical procedure of interpretation. Achieving understanding as the central objective of hermeneutics bears a dual inscription insofar as it is always an understanding *of* something *for* something. This accounts for the fact that when understanding has been achieved, it has to be applied, as demonstrated by Droysen. The exegesis of history as a text can only justify itself in terms of how it is to be applied, and the application in turn is dependent both on what has been understood and on what that understanding may mean. Thus the pairing of understanding and application turns out to be the hallmark of a hermeneutically oriented interpretation. There are several reasons for this coupling. First of all, application provides closure for the process of interpretation, as it highlights the purpose of understanding. In this respect, application turns out to be the pragmatics of interpretation, as only a pragmatic conclusion can terminate the inherent endlessness of interpretation. Droysen states this quite explicitly: " 'Discussive exposition' takes the total result of the investigation, gathers all its rays as in a concave mirror, and turns them upon some definite point of present interest, throwing light upon it thus in order to 'set it clear' " (55).[32] In his extended lecture course, he elaborates on this statement by stressing the aim of its interpretive enterprise as a "political propaedeutic."[33]

There is another reason that understanding has to culminate in a pragmatically oriented application, namely, the impermeability of the ground from which history hails and to which it is heading: "The highest end, which conditions without being conditioned, moving them all, embracing them all, explaining them all, that is, the supreme end . . . , is not to be discovered by empirical investigation" (47).[34] Thus we have to confine ourselves to what we are able to understand and try to apply it to what we are "condemned to": "the narrow limit of the here and the now" (49). Such an insight points to an ulterior question to be discussed later on in my argument: is interpretation triggered by what is withheld from penetration? If so, it would be an indication that we are not prepared to reconcile ourselves to whatever is sealed off from knowing and experiencing.

---

32. For this mode of presentation, see also Eberhard Lämmert, "Dreimal Wallenstein: Differenzen der Sinngebung zwischen Historiographie und Roman," in *Historische Sinnbildung: Problemstellungen, Zeitkonzepte, Wahrnehmungshorizonte, Darstellungsstrategien*, Rowohlts Enzyklopädie, ed. Klaus E. Müller and Jörn Rüsen (Reinbek: Rowohlt, 1997), 585.
33. Droysen, *Historik*, 278 and 280.
34. See also Hans Robert Jauß, *Literaturgeschichte als Provokation*, Edition Suhrkamp 418 (Frankfurt/Main: Suhrkamp, 1970), 219f.

An overall survey of Droysen's form of circularity is pertinent in view of the fact that modern hermeneutics—originally more a technical procedure of interpretation—has turned into a philosophy, of which Heidegger and Gadamer are the main proponents. Droysen's method of interpretation is distinguished by a multiplication of circles. Schleiermacher's overarching circle between part and whole has been taken over and extended into one that links past and present, the mediation of which requires different types of interpretation, and these in turn have a circular structure. Circles are meant to negotiate gaps, which are of a different nature insofar as the gap between past and present is given, just like those in the available historical material. The gap, however, between the historical material and the register is opened by the "artificial ways" themselves into which, for the purpose of processing, the historical material is translated. Moreover, as each of the four types also leaves a gap to be filled by the subsequent one, another kind of gap appears, the resolution of which results in a network that endows each type with an additional function. The register therefore is not just a set of conditions into which the historical material is transposed but a sort of dynamic machinery reflecting the multiplicity of differently qualified gaps that have to be negotiated for the purpose of understanding an emergent history. Finally, the constitution of history through understanding requires application of such an understanding, thus triggering another circularity between history's unfolding differentiation and humankind's increasing knowledge of itself.

The manifold circles are closely interlinked, owing to the different types of gaps they have to deal with. The mode of such interlinkage is best

---

35. This is not Droysen's term, though it characterizes the overall structure of his interpretive methodology. It is worth noting that Droysen has a distinct liking for "circle" as a term, which he uses to conceptualize the function of history: "And indeed the fact that the great movements of History complete themselves in a small circle of typical formations, the greatest in a still smaller circle, makes it possible valuably to apply History in a didactic way" (*Outline*, 54). This holds equally true when he identifies certain 'typical formations' such as the state: "The Federal State, the confederation of States, the system of States, the world-system of States,—These are ever further wave-circles of this movement" (43). Even methodologically, he privileges the idea of the circle: "The circle of conceptions belonging to it our own science will have to seek for itself, in its own, that is, in an empirical manner. It will be permitted to attempt this because its method is the method of understanding" (91). One can observe a wide semantic range in his use of this favored term, which also recurs very frequently in the *Historik*.

described as a nesting of circles,[35] which makes the overall circularity operative. Such nesting allows for reciprocal control, which is all the more necessary as there is no overarching frame of reference for negotiation of the space between the conditions of history and the procedures unfolded for its interpretation. Simultaneously, the nesting of circles reveals that the space opened up in any act of interpretation can never be totally bridged, which, however, translates into a potentially endless fine-tuning of interpretive procedures. Ultimately, the nesting of circles is a conceptual response to the unfathomableness of history's beginnings and ends and thus represents a counterconcept to any transcendental stance that would marshal the historical material into a premeditated order.

And yet the question remains: is circularity just an operational mode brought to bear by the observer in the act of interpretation, or is it an inherent structure of what is to be grasped? We do not get a definitive answer from Droysen, although at certain junctures of his argument he seems inclined to assume a circularity in the very subject matter to be interpreted: "Our methodological reproduction of the facts must by its correctness enable the thought to make good its character as underlying the course of events, and the course of events to justify the thought. For that thought is to us true to which an existence corresponds, and that existence true which corresponds to a thought" (32). This mutuality that "underlies the course of events" appears to back up the nesting of circles that structures Droysen's operational intent of interpretation. If so, then the methodological framework would find its ultimate grounding in the nature of the subject matter itself, thus eliminating the liminal space that interpretation itself can never overcome, because it has caused it.

This is the point at which modern hermeneutics changes from a method of interpretation into a philosophy. In contradistinction to the nineteenth-century conception of the hermeneutic circle, Gadamer writes:

> According to this theory, the circular movement of understanding runs backward and forward along the text, and ceases when the text is perfectly understood. . . . In contrast to this approach, Heidegger describes the circle in such a way that the understanding of the text remains permanently determined by the anticipatory movement of fore-understanding. . . . The circle, then, is not formal in nature. It is neither subjective nor objective, but describes understanding as the interplay of the movement of tradition and the movement of the interpreter. The anticipation of meaning that governs our understanding of a text is not

an act of subjectivity, but proceeds from the commonality that binds us to the tradition. . . . Thus the circle of understanding is not a "method-ological" circle, but describes an element of the ontological structure of understanding. The circle, which is fundamental to all understand-ing, has a further hermeneutic implication which I call the "fore-con-ception" of completeness.[36]

Irrespective of how we might be inclined to evaluate such a conception of the hermeneutic circle, when the latter is made to change from a formal structure that facilitates understanding to an ontological one that under-lies understanding, it appears to have voided the liminal space. And in doing so, hermeneutics is almost bound to develop into a philosophy, accounting for its definitive bridging of what separates understanding from what is to be understood. Moreover, the application of understand-ing as "fore-conception of completeness" reveals that application always endows understanding—the basic goal of hermeneutics—with a different meaning, in consequence of which application turns into a specifying semantics of understanding.

Paul Ricœur: Transactional Loops

If circularity in interpretation is dependent on the subject matter to be interpreted, the hermeneutic circle is bound to be conceived differently when the concern is no longer with something given but with something hidden that is to be translated into understanding. This is the case with psychoanalysis. Droysen had already advocated the "miner's art," because only delving into the darkling depths of the historical material allows its erstwhile significance to be restored. However, as the material of the past that is still available in the present is not a deliberate distortion of what it

---

36. Gadamer, *Truth and Method*, 293f. For a critical assessment of Gadamer's conception of the hermeneutic circle, see Karlheinz Stierle, "Für eine Erweiterung des hermeneutischen Zirkels," in Karlheinz Stierle, *Ästhetische Rationalität: Kunstwerk und Werkbegriff* (Munich: Fink 1996), 65–77, where Stierle argues convincingly for the methodological importance of the hermeneutic circle, which a philosophy of hermeneutics tends to neglect. Hirsch even contends that Gadamer with his "new hermeneutics . . . offers to replace the tradition of Schleiermacher, Humboldt, Droysen, Boeckh, Steinthal, Dilthey" (*Validity in Interpretation*, 247).

indicates, interpretation can rely on observable facts in order to detect their eclipsed interrelationships. This is no longer the case when something hidden, which only shows itself in disguise, has to be brought to light.

Paul Ricœur (b. 1912) writes: "strictly speaking, there are no 'facts' in psychoanalysis, for the analyst does not observe, he interprets."[37] But if there are no "facts," the question arises as to what is actually to be interpreted by "an interpretation, more comparable to history than to psychology," whose intervention, moreover, in a domain "where one can neither observe nor measure," resists being fully "translated into observational language" (357).

Intervention as the hallmark of psychoanalytical interpretation highlights a prominent feature of what interpretation has always been, namely, the fashioning of a given subject matter. The more elusive and the less coherent the subject matter turns out to be, the more obvious becomes the interventionist thrust of interpretation. Intervention, however, indicates that there is something to be penetrated. The subject matter to be invaded by psychoanalytical interpretation is no longer an author to be understood and no longer history to be constituted for the purpose of applying what has been understood, although psychoanalytical interpretation does contain certain aspects of both of these. It is first and foremost the human subject that is now focused on, both as a patient to be cured and as a subject destined to become conscious of itself in order to develop into its own being. Uncovering something hidden is the main objective of this interventionist interpretation.

So far I have considered the hermeneutic circle only in terms of its manifold applications and the various shapes it assumes in relation to what it is meant to achieve. Now Ricœur's analysis of Freud takes hermeneutic circularity into new areas, and therefore I shall be focusing on his insight into Freud's structure of interpretation and not on Freud's actual interpretive practice. Such an approach has a dual legitimation. First, in the original French version, Ricœur's title for his enterprise is *De*

---

37. Paul Ricœur, *Freud and Philosophy: An Essay in Interpretation*, trans. Denis Savage (New Haven: Yale University Press, 1970), 365. The sources of all other quotations from this volume are given in in-text references to the appropriate pages. It is not my intention to give a critical account of Ricœur's interpretation of Freud but rather to trace the deep structure of Ricœur's own interpretation, which is guided by what he has called a philosophy of reflection.

l'Interprétation: Essai sur Freud, indicating that he intends to thematize the workings of interpretive procedures as epitomized by psychoanalysis. This anatomy of interpretation is more than just self-monitoring; it tries to plumb the deep structure of a hermeneutically oriented interpretation. Such an undertaking, however, is not an attempt at "interpreting interpretation,"[38] for this would presuppose a transcendental vantage point that in turn is either an offshoot of a belief system or itself the result of an interpretation. Scrutinizing interpretation requires an actual interpretation whose operations are subjected to investigation.

Second, Ricœur therefore does not confine himself to a reading of Freud; instead, he gives an assessment of Freud's interpretive practice and, in doing so, he 'relocates' "the architectonic reconstitution of the work [in a] new discourse [i.e.] that of the philosopher."[39] In this way he can spotlight differences and similarities between a psychoanalytical and a reflective hermeneutics that, when arranged as foils for one another, throw into relief the many-sidedness of their common concern: namely, the otherwise hidden infrastructure of the human subject.

Why is this infrastructure concealed? A preliminary answer would be: because it is both "infra- and supralinguistic" (399)[40] by nature, which means that it shifts between failing to reach and going beyond the level of language. This is because the unconscious is sealed off from language

---

38. See William Elford Rogers, *Interpreting Interpretation: Textual Hermeneutics as an Ascetic Discipline* (University Park: Pennsylvania State University Press, 1994), where the author does exactly that, which means he has to fall back on a system that provides a vantage point for interpreting interpretation. Therefore he states right at the beginning that it is "the decisive step of this book . . . to interpret interpretation by thinking about *signs* and, in particular, by thinking through the semiotic of Charles Sanders Peirce" (9).
39. Paul Ricœur, *The Conflict of Interpretations*, ed. Don Ihde (Evanston, Ill.: Northwestern University Press, 1974), 160.
40. Ricœur has taken over this terminology from Émile Benveniste, whom he quotes in order to make clear what these terms imply: "The analyst operates with what the subject tells him, he views the subject in the discourses that the latter makes, he examines him in his locutory and 'story-making' behavior, and through these discourses there is slowly shaped for him another discourse that he must make explicit, that of the complex buried within the unconscious. The analyst, therefore, will take the discourse as a stand-in for another 'language' which has its own rules, symbols, syntax and which refers back to underlying structures of the psychism" (*Freud and Philosophy*, 396).

and the conscious is beyond the denotative character of language, insofar as the subject that reflects on itself can express its growing self-awareness only figuratively through the tropes of rhetoric. "Rhetoric, however, with its metaphors, its metonymies, its synecdoches, its euphemisms, its allusions, its antiphrases, its litotes, is concerned not with the phenomena of language but with procedures of subjectivity that are manifested in discourse" (400). Interpretation, faced at this level with the duality of the subject's infrastructure, cannot gloss over the split between the subject's conscious and unconscious but has to intervene in this intangible relationship by translating it into terms of comprehension. As it does so, the split must be inscribed into the interpretive procedures, in consequence of which to "interpret is to understand a double meaning" (8). Double meaning arises out of dissimulation, as there is always a hiding in the showing: the unconscious shows itself in the disguise of its derivatives, and the conscious in its inevitable self-deceptions. Whatever is present is marked by an absence: in the derivatives the unconscious is absent, and in the deceptions the self-reflection of consciousness is absent. The task of interpretation is thus dual in nature: First, it is a reading of double meaning. "By this I designate a certain meaning effect, according to which one expression, of variable dimensions, while signifying one thing at the same time signifies *another* thing without ceasing to signify the first".[41] Thus the absent and the present are made continually to point at each other. Second, such a reading is designed " 'to translate' the unconscious into the conscious" (408), which both psychoanalysis and the philosophy of reflection consider a necessary mediation for launching the human subject on its way toward its self. The interpretive strategy of double meaning acknowledges the inherent split of the subject's infrastructure and tries to elucidate why the revelation is also a concealment. "Interpretation is lucidity's answer to ruse" (159).

Thus interpretation turns into a "movement from the manifest to the latent" meaning (91). Although meant to telescope what is separated in the interchange between veiling and revealing, such a back-and-forth movement is initially circular. Double meaning allows us to translate the basic disposition of the subject into language by taking over the split for the purpose of negotiating the gap between the unconscious and the conscious. Such a register in turn transmutes the infrastructure into "something like a text" (401) that, as an assembly of representatives of what is hidden, calls for deciphering.

----

41. Ricœur, *The Conflict of Interpretations*, 63.

Now the question arises as to what extent this overriding orientation of Ricœur's method of interpretation can be put into practice in order to bring to light what has hitherto been hidden. Again Ricœur starts out from basic conceptions regarding the ego that both psychoanalysis and the philosophy of reflection share. He uses these to demonstrate how the interpretive register of double meaning draws the human subject out of its hiddenness.

"The first truth—*I am, I think*—remains as abstract and empty as it is invincible; it has to be 'mediated' by the ideas, actions, works, institutions, and monuments that objectify it. It is in these objects, in the widest sense of the word, that the Ego must lose and find itself" (43). Hence "the positing of self is not given, it is a task, it is not *gegeben*, but *aufgegeben*" (45). "And the very term 'self'—*Selbst*—proclaims that self-identity continues to be carried by this self-difference, by this ever-recurring otherness residing in life. It is life that becomes the other, in and through which the self ceaselessly achieves itself" (472). Such a process finally culminates in Freud's well-known dictum: "Where id was, there ego shall be" (492). Becoming conscious provides the overarching guideline for the subject's endeavor to achieve its own self. As consciousness, however, is not given in immediacy, it has to be acquired, which raises the question: how can consciousness conceive of itself, not least as it is not in control of its own origin? It does so by going outside itself into what it is not, in order to experience "that a given consciousness 'has' an unconscious; but this relation becomes manifest only in the dispossession of the consciousness which has that unconscious" (438). If "the dispossession of consciousness is its path" (439) on which it has to lose itself to the 'objects of the world' in order to become conscious of itself, then consciousness has to integrate otherness into itself. This stage marks the point of convergence between psychoanalysis and the philosophy of reflection, which Ricœur stresses by saying that "the unique task of becoming conscious . . . defines the finality of analysis" (492). This finality finds its parallel in the circular movement of Hegel's dialectic, through which consciousness develops into self-consciousness; the latter is to be acquired by acknowledging and finally accepting the displacements and defeats it has suffered on the road to itself. "The dispossession comes first, the reaffirmation only at the end; what is essential occurs between the two, namely, the whole movement through the constellation of figures; master and slave, the stoic exile of thought, skeptical indifference, the unhappy consciousness, the service of the devoted mind, the observation of nature, the spirit as light, etc." (463).

In psychoanalytical understanding, the subject tends to become deformed when it is frozen into a definite shape, thus being arrested on the way to itself. Whenever this happens, the subject is identified with something that it cannot be, because it can only be identified with itself: namely, with its *archê* and its *telos*. The *archê* is both a beginning and an indication of what has been displaced in the effort to realize the subject's *telos*. The *telos* is in turn both an unconscious aim embedded in the *archê* and an inducement to go on striving. Although *archê* and *telos* are closely interrelated, they are hidden from the view of both the subject and the therapist. Moreover, there is a hiatus in what has to be coped with, which Ricœur—in providing an analysis of what happens in psychoanalytical interpretation—tries to tackle through what he called an intertwining of "archeology and teleology" (460). This duality forms the basic assumption of the interpretive register designed to translate into observational language how the subject is to become its own self.

It is worth noting that the two foci posited by Ricœur are marked by a duality themselves: *archê* is both an origin and a repository of displacement, and *telos* is both an unconscious striving and a return to beginnings; owing to this duality the two poles of the subject enfold each other, and such an enfolding has repercussions on the interpretive procedures. As there is a hidden *archê* in the *telos* and vice versa, the coupling of archeology and teleology does not develop along a linear trajectory but in a circular, back-and-forth movement in order to bring out the hidden *telos* in the *archê* and the hidden *archê* in the *telos*. Such a coupling distinguishes Ricœur's project from both Freudian psychoanalysis and Hegelian phenomenology.

"It seems to me," Ricœur contends, "that the concept of archeology of the subject remains very abstract so long as it has not been set in a relationship of dialectical opposition to the complementary concept of teleology. . . . What I wish to demonstrate, then, is that Freudianism is an explicit and thematized archeology, it relates to itself, by the dialectical nature of its concepts, to an implicit and unthematized teleology" (459, 461).[42] In Hegel's case, Ricœur maintains, it is just the opposite. Thus Ricœur marks the point of departure for his own strategy of interpretation. "Whereas Hegel links an explicit teleology of mind or spirit to an implicit archeology of life and desire, Freud links a thematized archeology of

---

42. The archeological dimension of Freud's hermeneutics has been lucidly set out by Ulla Haselstein, *Entziffernde Hermeneutik: Zum Begriff der Lektüre in der psychoanalytischen Theorie des Unbewußten*, Theorie und Geschichte der Literatur und der Schönen Künste 84 (Munich: Fink, 1991), 22–55.

the unconscious to an unthematized teleology of the process of becoming conscious. I do not confuse Hegel with Freud, but I seek to find in Freud an inverted image of Hegel, in order to discern, with the help of this schema, certain dialectical features which, though obviously operative in analytic practice, have not found in a theory a complete systematic elaboration" (461f.). Although Freudianism is, according to Ricœur, "a revelation of the archaic, a manifestation of the ever prior" (440), "the concept of an archeology . . . is not one of Freud's concepts" (419) but is introduced by the philosophy of reflection as a means of excavating the subject's hidden teleology. Ricœur continues by asking: "But of what subject? What must the subject of reflection be if it is likewise to be the subject of psychoanalysis?" (420). Freud looked for the ever-prior, leaving the teleology unthematized, and phenomenology gave "primacy of the intentional over the reflective" (380), leaving the "unconsciousness or unawareness" of intentionality unthematized, which can be pinpointed in "the implicit, the co-intended" of any intentional act (378). Now it becomes obvious what Ricœur originally meant by saying that it was his endeavor to wrap Freudian psychoanalysis in philosophical discourse, which he reiterates before detailing the interpretive register that he proposes: "It must be kept in mind that our enterprise is strictly philosophical and in no way binding on the psychoanalyst as such" (419).

What is the register that Ricœur advances for an interpretation of the subject, and how does he conceive of it?

An archeology remains abstract so long as it is not integrated by way of "complementary opposition" with *teleology*, with a progressive synthesizing of figures or categories, where the meaning of each is clarified by the meaning of further figures or categories. . . . It is at this level that the possibility of interrelating two opposed hermeneutics comes into view; regression and progression are henceforth understood as two possible directions of interpretation, opposed but complementary. This level of thought is sufficiently important to give its name to the third book [i.e., one of the divisions of Ricœur's *De l'Interprétation*]— "Dialectic." . . . The point presented at this level is indeed central, but it is only a transition; the function of a dialectic between regression and progression, between archeology and teleology, is to lead from a reflection that understands its archeology to a symbolic understanding that would grasp the indivisible unity of its archeology and its teleology in the very origin of speech.   (342f.)

This statement contains two different, though closely interrelated levels, which must be separated for the purpose of analyzing Ricœur's mode of interpretation. There is the subject that is focused on, and the technique according to which the subject's way to itself is grasped. The subject "is never the subject one supposes. But if the subject is to attain its true being, it is not enough for it to discover the inadequacy of its self-awareness, or even to discover the power of desire that posits it in existence" (459). Instead, it has to become aware of what is concealed from view: namely, its *archê* and its *telos*. Such a situation creates a problem for interpretation insofar as the latter has to start out from hidden components. What is to be interpreted is neither given in evidence nor to be constituted; it is there, though eclipsed, and hence need not be constituted.

Ferreting out what lies concealed, however, only marks the point of departure for interpretation. This may account for the strange terminology Ricœur brings to bear at this juncture, when calling his modus operandi "dialectic," yoking together "regression and progression," which, though countervailing movements, are nevertheless considered "complementary." Furthermore, there are continual "transitions" between what heads in different "directions," and yet "archeology and teleology" appear to sublate what is opposed into "indivisible unity." Ricœur does not elaborate on the connotations of these terms but demonstrates through his actual interpretation how they are to be conceived.

He starts out by outlining what one might call an anatomy of desire. At the beginning of his book, he reproduces the Freudian version of desire: "As a man desires I go forth in disguise—*larvatus prodeo*" (7). When focusing on desire from the vantage point of his own discourse, Ricœur writes: "Desire is revealed as *human* desire only when it is desire for the desire of another consciousness. . . . The desire of self disengages itself from the desire of things by seeking itself in the other" (466). In this respect, Ricœur believes that he is only drawing out what is already implicit in Freud, namely, "desire is in an intersubjective situation from the very start" (477). Ricœur's whole assessment of Freud is guided by the idea of making the implied explicit, which induces him "to place the structure of the Hegelian self-consciousness at the very center of the Freudian desire" (481).[43] If, from the outset, desire is always in an intersubjective situation,

43. This applies in equal measure to the changing topologies of the psychical apparatus that Freud had developed, which Ricœur perceives as a sequence through which the subsequent topology elucidates what the previous one seems to have implied.

it unleashes a craving for identification with what it desires. Hence "identification is not something added on from without but is rather the dialectic of desire itself" (481). Consequently, there is always a hidden *telos* in desire, which to a large extent is nonthematic and can only be deduced from what the subject tries to identify with. Moreover, desire needs recognition by what it longs to have or be; whenever recognition is denied, a dispossession occurs, turning the progressive impulse of desire into regression. Regression, then, arises out of an unfulfilled *telos*, from which is to be inferred that there would be no regression if there were not a concealed teleology structuring the desire. Such a situation allows two conclusions: (a) desire entails the human subject's need to overstep itself; (b) the subject's hidden *archê* and *telos* can only be extrapolated from human desire. Desire thus bears a double inscription: it designates the status of the human being as something to be exceeded, and it points to the fact that the human subject wants to be become its own other, which poises the human being between what it is in its beginnings and what it wants to be by way of becoming its own self.

The desire to be one's own other manifests itself in two different ways. It functions either as idealization in relation to what the desiring subject wants to be or as sublimation whenever the idealization concerned is denied. Becoming the idealized other reveals something of the hidden *telos* that is embedded in the subject's *archê* and simultaneously allows a glimpse of the *archê* that contains the program of a *telos*. Thus the attainment of self-consciousness gets under way by continual "interplay" between *telos* and *archê*. The two-pronged operation of archeology and teleology brings the concealed components of the subject out into the open, as neither *telos* nor *archê* presents itself as what it is, and each can only be ascertained through interpretation. The nature of the interplay between the gradually graspable components is left as an open question, though, of course, a degree of circularity structures their interlocking. This circularity as interplay between hidden areas of the human subject requires further qualification, however, in order to make the reciprocal translation of *archê* and *telos* tangible, not least as the hiatus between the two has to be negotiated. The reciprocal translation develops as a transposition of something transparent in the desire into what remains concealed and equally of what has revealed itself back into the concealed.

But this mutual interplay needs to be grasped, not least because its operation is to bring about the talking cure, with the subject becoming its own self. For this reason, Ricœur maintains, we have to interpret the symbols that the patient and the human subject respectively produce when they are arrested on the way to their own selves.[44] "We now know," Ricœur contends, "that the key to the solution lies in the dialectic between archeology and teleology. It remains to find the concrete 'mixed texture' in which we see the archeology and teleology. This concrete mixed texture is symbol" (494). The symbol is produced by both the patient and the human subject on the way to its own self. Symbols figure as texts, which the interpreter is given to read, texts, however, that are distinctly different from the written text of an author, on which Schleiermacher had focused, or the punctured historical material from which Droysen started out. The symbol, according to Ricœur, encapsulates "two functions which are thought to be opposed to one another but which symbols coordinate in a concrete unity. Thus the ambiguity of symbolism is not a lack of univocity but is rather the possibility of carrying and engendering opposed interpretations, each of which is self-consistent" (496).[45] The symbol looks in two directions at once, comprising regression and progression, and thereby revealing a buried past and an intended future. It brings about an imbrication of past and future.[46] Although these two directions may engender intrinsically consistent though opposed interpretations, because the archaic and the teleological are not independent spheres, "remembrance gives rise to anticipation; archaism gives rise to prophecy" (497). The dual direction of the symbol makes it into an epitome of double meaning that, owing to its indivisibility, allows the archaic to be read through the teleological and vice versa.

---

44. Ricœur highlights the importance of the symbol for the kind of interpretation that he proposes: "The term symbol stands for all double-meaning expressions and is the pivotal point of interpretation" (Freud, 96). In other words, archeology and teleology both pivot around and are powered by an inherent moment of untranslatability that is constitutive of double meaning.
45. In an earlier essay, Ricœur suggests that in such a situation one "must quit the position, or better, the exile, of the remote and disinterested spectator in order to appropriate in each case an individual symbolism. Then is discovered what may be called the circle of hermeneutics, which the simple amateur of myths unfailingly misses" (The Conflict of Interpretations, 298).
46. In a later book, Interpretation Theory: Discourse and the Surplus Meaning (Fort Worth: Texas Christian University Press, 1976), Ricœur expands his conception of symbol, "which brings together two dimensions, we might even say, two universes, of discourse, one linguistic and the other of a non-linguistic order" (53f.). It brackets "bios" and "logos" together and "testifies to the primordial rootedness of Discourse in Life" (59).

In view of such interdependence, sublimation becomes a prominent symbol for both psychoanalysis and the philosophy of reflection. "Insofar as revealing and disguising coincide in it, we might say that sublimation is the symbolic function itself" (497).[47] Because sublimation is dually coded, it is a process for constituting the sublime, and the sublime is an overpowering force to which the human being responds by unfolding the desire to identify with it, thus bringing out its highest quality. Sublimation, however, is equally a subspecies of suppression and repression and hence an indication of displacement. Again the operational mode of this symbol develops as revelation through disguise, for it shows the *telos* of desire in the trappings of the ideal the subject identifies with, and equally it shows displacements in the manifest distortions. "Thus we should say that symbols carry two vectors. On the one hand, symbols repeat our childhood in all the senses, chronological and nonchronological, of that childhood. On the other hand, they explore our adult life" (496).

Because the symbol figures as the epitome of the interchange between revealing and concealing, it marks the point of intersection between *archê* and *telos*. However, the symbol would collapse if the space between the two psychic components could ever be eliminated. Consequently, the inherent opposition of the symbol unfolds in a circular movement, through which the interconnection of *archê* and *telos* becomes tangible. Ricœur qualified the intertwining of archeology and teleology as "dialectic." It is certainly not a dialectic movement in the received sense of the term; the interchange does not unfold in terms of a thesis-antithesis-synthesis structure. Instead, the very method proposed proceeds by feeding the oppositional directions inherent in the symbol into one another, as only such reciprocity makes it possible to ferret out the teleological thrust hidden in the *archê* and the buried past in the emerging transparency of the *telos*. This kind of interchange is not dialectical in nature, and if Ricœur uses this term, it would seem to signal that the intertwining of archeology and teleology can no longer be adequately conceptualized in terms of the hermeneutic circle.

---

47. Ricœur considers Freud's "theory of sublimation" one-sided and therefore a "failure," as only "the relationship between sublimation and identification enables us to relate the unresolved enigma of sublimation to the origin of self-consciousness in the dialectic of desire" (*Freud*, 490). "Freud accounts very well for the functional unity of dreams and artistic creation, but the qualitative difference, the difference in 'aim' which renders instincts dialectical, escapes him; this is why the question of sublimation remains unresolved" (521). See also Haselstein, *Entziffernde Hermeneutik*, 52.

If there are still traces of circularity to be discerned in Ricœur's proposed means of interpreting the human subject, the familiar back-and-forth movement of the circle now operates in transactional loops. This is because what is to be transposed into an other is never fully in view but masked by symbols, and the oppositional directions inherent in the symbol are not dialectically sublated but telescoped into one another, thus spotlighting what has been split off from the subject and displaced on the way to consciousness of the self. The interpretation of symbols proceeds in transactional loops, because looping as an operational mode becomes necessary when the points of departure for the hermeneutic circle are no longer given, in the sense in which a written or spoken text or historical facts are given. The transmutation of the hermeneutic circle into transactional loops is due to the fact that not only the difference between *archê* and *telos* but also their very concealment has to be coped with. Furthermore, the looping operation is designed to regain what is lost; by making the repressed return, it clears blockages, thus uncovering what the subject had been striving for when losing itself to the otherness of life. What is to be glimpsed of the hidden *archê* is to be fed forward into a surmised *telos*, from which a feedback will be received. Therefore the talking cure takes time, as the transactional loops have to translate what the patient says into the patient's remembrance. The memory's resistance to revealing its fixations has to be overcome in order to activate the patient's self-reflection,[48] as a way to resume the path to the patient's own self. Something similar holds true for the philosophy of reflection, which interprets the human subject as the history of becoming conscious of itself: "For man, to become conscious is to be drawn away from his archaisms by the series of figures that institute and constitute him as man" (544). The archaisms are dual in nature; they can be extrapolated from what the subject identifies with and also from the manifest dispossessions the subject has suffered. Identification reveals the hidden *telos*, and the distorted symbols reveal the displacements in the hidden *archê*. Both instances reveal the subject's own otherness, the awareness of which, by inducing self-reflection, feeds its own otherness back into the subject's consciousness. Through such reciprocity a history develops, in the course of which the subject regains what it has lost on the way to becoming its own self.

---

48. Jürgen Habermas, *Erkenntnis und Interesse* (Frankfurt/Main: Suhrkamp, 1968), 280, 286, 296, 302, 306, 314, 316, and 325, has stressed the importance of self-reflection in psychoanalysis and delineates the process through which it is acquired.

By way of summing up, we might say that archeology and teleology, as a register into which the human subject is translated, allow both excavation of what the distorted manifestations intend to veil and a clear focus on what the idealizations intend to express. The mechanics of such a register unfold in transactional loops, whose operations introject the subject's intangible components—that is, the unconscious and the conscious—into one another, thus drawing the hidden interconnection between *archê* and *telos* out into the open. As there is no external reference for such a procedure, the looping can only be fine-tuned by continually scrutinizing what the transactional loops render tangible. Thus interpretation becomes self-correcting owing to the trial and error pattern that structures transactional looping. Such a built-in mechanism of self-correction becomes all the more necessary for interpretation when there are no definitive references for its procedures. There is no final reference for the talking cure, just as there is none for becoming self-conscious, because, Ricœur maintains, "I do not think that absolute knowledge is possible."[49] However, the self-correcting transactional loops allow the human subject to be grasped as a potentially unending process *ad se ipsum*.

---

49. Ricœur, *The Conflict of Interpretations*, 332.

CHAPTER FOUR
The Recursive Loop

Recursion in Ethnographic Discourse

The methodology of the hermeneutic tradition shows how interpretive procedures change according to the subject matter to be interpreted. The subject matter is tailored to a degree by the interpretive register into which it is translated, and it simultaneously calls for a retooling of the mechanics brought to bear, as evinced by the continual modification through which the hermeneutic circle is reconceived. Moreover, this reconception is preconditioned by the way in which the subject matter is offered to the interpretive act. It makes all the difference if the subject matter is present, or has to be constituted, or must be teased out of its hiddenness. In each of these instances, the gap between what is to be interpreted and the register into which it is translated is of a different dimension, which has repercussions on the methods designed for bridging it. The circle functions as a relay when the subject matter is given (Schleiermacher); it changes into a nesting of circles when the subject matter has to be constituted (Droysen); and it turns into transactional looping when the subject matter has to be brought out into the open (Ricœur). The wider the gap, the more complicated the circle tends to be become.

Furthermore, subject matter and register are themselves bracketed together by a circular movement. Although the different quality of the subject matter calls for a retooling of techniques, it does not totally determine the interpretive procedure, and the register, despite its partial fashioning of the subject matter, does not super-impose itself on what is to be interpreted. Both participate in a circular relationship through which the one conditions the other in a recursive movement that brings about an elucidation of the subject matter and a fine-tuning of the interpretive strategies. Thus there seems to be a recursive undercurrent in the very process of interpretation itself, and so it is recursion that is the focal point of the paradigm I am now going to inspect. I shall call it, in view of its basic operational mode, the cybernetic loop.

If it is true that interpretation—primarily a form of translatability—is dependent on what is translated, it is bound to be different when it concerns itself with: (a) how entropy is translated into control; (b) how randomness is translated into what is central; (c) how the largely intangible reciprocity of hominization and the rise of culture is translated into conceptual language; and (d) how cultures or cultural levels are translated into terms that allow an interchange between what is foreign and what is familiar.

Before I discuss the diversified operations of recursive looping, it seems pertinent to recall the basic features of cybernetics that are applicable to this enterprise. The term "cybernetics" was coined in 1947 by Norbert Wiener, who derived it from the Greek "χυβεϛνήτηϛ or *steersman*," in other words, the man who controls.[1] Wiener combined this designation with what Clerk Maxwell called the "governor," a feedback device on a machine or engine used to provide automatic control for speed, pressure, or temperature. "To control entropy through feedback" is Wiener's formulation of his basic principle.[2] What exactly is feedback, and how does it establish control? An early answer of Wiener's reads as follows: "It is enough to say here that when we desire a motion to follow a given pattern the difference between this pattern and the actually performed motion is used as a new input to cause the part regulated to move in such a way as to bring its motion closer to that given by the pattern."[3] Later on, Wiener elaborated on this basic definition by stating: "*Feedback* [is] the property of being able to adjust future conduct to past performance. Feedback may be as simple as that of a common reflex, or it may be a higher order feedback,

———

1. Norbert Wiener, *Cybernetics; or, Control and Communication in the Animal and the Machine* (Cambridge, Mass.: MIT Press, 1961), 11.

2. Norbert Wiener, *The Human Use of Human Beings* (Garden City, N.Y.: Doubleday, 1954), 26.

3. Wiener, *Cybernetics*, 6f.

in which past experience is used not only to regulate specific movements, but also whole policies of behavior. The nervous system and the automatic machine are fundamentally alike in that they are devices which make decisions on the basis of decisions they have made in the past."[4] The mode according to which feedback works is one of recursion, which is the basic principle of all kinds of servomechanisms that Wiener considered the overriding signature of our age: "The present age is as truly the age of servomechanisms as the nineteenth century was the age of the steam engine or the eighteenth century the age of the clock."[5]

Recursive looping develops as an interchange between input and output, in the course of which a prediction, anticipation, or even projection is corrected insofar as it has failed to square with what it has targeted. Consequently there is—at least potentially—a dual correction: the forward feed returns as an altered feedback loop that in turn feeds into a revised input. This applies to the whole range of learning, from machines to human behavior, all of which are regulated according to Wiener's basic formula that recursive looping "adjusts future conduct to past performance." Effective behavior must be informed by some kind of feedback process, telling it whether it has met requirements or fallen short of them. Wiener details the reason for such recursive looping as follows:

> Certain kinds of machines and some living organisms—particularly the higher living organisms—can, as we have seen, modify their patterns of behavior on the basis of past experience so as to achieve specific anti-entropic ends. In these higher forms of communicative organisms the environment, considered as the past experience of the individual, can modify the pattern of behavior into one which in some sense or other will deal more effectively with the future environment. In other words, the organism is not like the clockwork monad of Leibniz with its pre-established harmony with the universe, but actually seeks a new equilibrium with the universe and its future contingencies. Its present is unlike its past and its future unlike its present. In the living organism as in the universe itself, exact repetition is absolutely impossible.[6]

---

4. Wiener, Human Use, 33.
5. Wiener, *Cybernetics*, 43.
6. Wiener, *Human Use*, 48.

Such a description of recursive looping informs ethnographic discourse when one tries to interpret the reciprocity between the evolution of Homo sapiens and the rise of culture. Although Wiener does not concern himself with the problems of ethnography, he is nevertheless convinced that the principle of recursive looping has an almost unlimited applicability, so that for him "to check a predicted position against an observed position"[7] even underlies policy making, because "every continuing undertaking must be regulated as to its performance by its results. These results constitute, from the information point of view, something which is strictly analogous to what is called 'feedback' in a control machine. The theory of economic and political behavior which is now in vogue in the United States, and which has received a quasi-official sanction, consists fundamentally in a very definite view as to the nature of a feedback which is regarded as sufficient for all social phenomena, and which is enjoined upon us" (118).

Controlling entropy and coming to grips with contingencies are not comparable to what a text-oriented hermeneutics had to face, even when the text was taken as a metaphor, as in psychoanalysis. Between entropy as a measure of disorder and the attempt to control it, there is a yawning gulf, which can hardly be regarded as parallel to the various gaps bridged by the different versions of the hermeneutic circle. Furthermore, entropy and contingency elude knowledge, so that coping with them requires a continual looping from the known to the unknown in order (a) to make the unknown hark back to what is familiar, (b) to achieve control by splitting entropy into order and contingency,[8] and (c) to explore conditions for establishing an equilibrium between past and future environments. Recursive looping organizes such a transfer by processing the information received, recognizing what the input has failed to achieve, and orienting the correction to be fed into the subsequent input. It is intensified by the fact that each input is an intervention into entropy, contingency, or already ordered systems, as I shall show later. These inroads bounce back as a heightened complexity of information, which increases the rapidity of self-correction, leading in turn to a continual fine-tuning of further inputs.

---

7. Norbert Wiener, *Invention: The Care and Feeding of Ideas*, (Cambridge, Mass.: MIT Press, 1994), 117.
8. See Norbert Bolz, *Die Welt als Chaos und als Simulation* (Munich: Fink, 1992), 11ff.

Cybernetics distinguishes between positive and negative feedback loops. With a negative feedback loop, the discrepancy of information between input and output is minimal, and thus it serves to stabilize the system that initiated the recursion. A positive feedback loop has far-reaching repercussions on the system concerned. It may change the original targets and will tend to unbalance the system by bombarding it with uncontrollable factors, making it impossible to process adequately the received information for fine-tuning further inputs. These two types of recursion mark extreme instances of how feedback loops operate. The direction in which recursion veers will depend largely on the aim to be achieved. For example, if recursive looping is meant to chart a foreign culture in order to bring its foreign elements within reach, then a great deal of information generated by the recursion will be screened off. If, however, the aim is to grasp otherness, then the operation will be powered by a positive feedback loop.

For the time being, the operative structure of recursion described above will suffice as reference for the paradigms I am now going to inspect. Recursive looping governs the first example, namely, the type of interpretation ethnographers apply when trying to elucidate the interconnection between the evolution of Homo sapiens and the rise of culture. For such an enterprise, the hermeneutic circle, for all its sophisticated variations, no longer works. There is no text to be understood, no understanding to be applied, and no hidden text to be deciphered. Instead, we have as a starting point something that lies beyond what hermeneutics is able to cope with—even if some hermeneuticists claim otherwise. That starting point is the human confrontation with entropy. This requires two things: (a) establishing control over entropy; and (b) establishing equilibrium between humans and the contingency of their environment.

These issues are a prime concern of Clifford Geertz as developed in his collection of essays *Interpretation of Cultures*.[9] The title of one of the leading essays, "The Impact of the Concept of Culture on the Concept of Man," points already to a recursive relationship. What we call "culture" and "man" are two mutually interdependent systems that appear to feed into one another, allowing us to grasp the interconnection between the evolution of Homo sapiens and human culture as an artificially built habitat.

---

9. Clifford Geertz, *The Interpretation of Cultures: Selected Essays* (New York: Basic, 1973). The sources of all other quotations from this volume are given in in-text references to the appropriate pages.

In order to spotlight this interconnection a few prejudices must be cleared away. Geertz writes: "The rise of a scientific concept of culture amounted to, or at least was connected with, the overthrow of the view of human nature dominant in the Enlightenment—a view that, whatever else may be said for or against it, was both clear and simple—and its replacement by a view not only more complicated but enormously less clear. The attempt to clarify it, to reconstruct an intelligible account of what man is, has underlain scientific thinking about culture ever since" (34). If interest in culture has arisen directly from the abandonment of what the Enlightenment took human nature to be, explaining culture becomes a problem. This may be one of the reasons that the thematization of culture is of recent vintage and that it is closely allied to a different conception of how Homo sapiens evolved.

A decisive shift in focus underlies Geertz's interpretation. The less we are inclined to define human nature in terms of certain basic qualities— let alone in terms of an assumed constancy, independent of time, place, and circumstance—the more varied will be the modifications to which the wrongly assumed constancy of human nature is subjected. Such a revision leads Geertz to this conclusion: Modern anthropology "is firm in the conviction that men unmodified by the customs of particular places do not in fact exist, have never existed, and most important, could not in the very nature of the case exist. . . . This circumstance makes the drawing of a line between what is natural, universal, and constant in man and what is conventional, local, and variable extraordinarily difficult. In fact, it suggests that to draw such a line is to falsify the human situation, or at least to misrender it seriously" (35f.). The less credence we give to eighteenth-century concepts of humanity, as manifested in philosophy and literature, the greater the focus on culture. Humans are so entangled in their environment, shaped and conditioned by what they have spun out of themselves, and challenged by the very habitat they have built for survival and self-preservation, that inevitably the interest in culture arises in proportion to the decline of a uniformitarian view of human nature. This marks the starting point for a feedback loop between humans and their culture, as "men are pure and simply what their culture makes them" (36), a culture that they have produced for and from themselves.

Even such a dynamic conception, however, is not free from pitfalls to which an ethnographical interpretation of the interchange between humans and their habitat has to be alerted. As long as the notion of the human being as a "stratified animal" prevails (38), the interchange becomes frozen at certain levels; "as one analyzes man, one peels off layer after layer, each such layer being complete and irreducible in itself, revealing another, quite different sort of layer underneath" (37). If each layer marks a hypostatization of the human being, whose equipment is alleged to be geared to stratified levels of culture, then the question poses itself: Why is culture? Or, where does it come from? Geertz exposes the assumed stratification of the human makeup as a serious misconception, arguing that it is based on the equally untenable idea of cultural universals (41). Now, because humankind—instead of being chained to an assumed constancy of human nature—"is as various in its essence as it is in its expression" (37), any generalization does not apply so much to human nature as to the methodology through which the interaction of humans with their environment is meant to be grasped. Hence so-called cultural universals are not substances that form the basis of human nature or underlie the constitution of culture; they are changeable and hence nonuniversal responses of humans to their environment.[10] What have been dubbed "cultural universals" (40), to which the "stratified animal" seems to be tied in a preestablished relationship, are nothing but products of human beings that in turn pose a challenge to their producers.

If there are no cultural universals to elucidate the human makeup, then culture must be understood, according to Geertz, as "extragenetic, outside-the-skin control mechanisms" (44). Such an exteriorization is in line with what André Leroi-Gourhan in his magisterial work *Gesture and Speech* has considered the hallmark of hominization: "The whole of our evolution has been oriented toward placing outside ourselves what in the rest of the animal world is achieved *inside* by species adaptation."[11] Turning the "inside" out is necessary, Leroi-Gourhan writes, because throughout

> our evolution, ever since the reptiles, the human appears as the inheritor of creatures that escaped anatomical specialization. Neither human teeth nor hand, neither human foot nor, when all is said and done, brain has attained the perfection of the mammoth's teeth, the horse's hand and foot, or the brain of certain birds—with the result that humans have remained capable of just about every possible action, can

---

10. Geertz, 99, considers human "response capacities" to be "genetically programmed."

11. André Leroi-Gourhan, *Gesture and Speech*, trans. Anna Bostock Berger (Cambridge, Mass.: MIT Press, 1993), 235. The sources of all other quotations from this volume are given in in-text references to the appropriate pages.

eat practically anything, can run and climb, and can use the unbeliev-
ably archaic part of their skeleton, that is, their hands, to perform operations directed by a brain superspecialized in the skill of generalizing.
(118)

Having escaped organic specialization implies two things: (a) there is no
habitat to which humans are geared; and (b) lacking organic specialization makes the human, as Geertz has it, "an incomplete, an unfinished,
animal" (46), which is bound to build its own habitat for survival. Such
an interrelationship is structured by recursive looping. Norbert Wiener,
in pinpointing this interconnection, writes:

> Man like all other organisms lives in a contingent universe, but man's
> advantage over the rest of nature is that he has the physiological and
> hence intellectual equipment to adapt himself to radical changes in his
> environment. . . . We have already indicated that effective behavior
> must be informed by some sort of feedback process, telling it whether it
> has equalled its goal or fallen short. The simplest feedbacks deal with
> gross success or failures of performance. . . . However, there are many
> other forms of feedback of a more subtle nature.[12]

Whatever forms the feedback may take in each of its individual instances,
a basic principle is operative in all of them, namely, writes Wiener, "feedback is a method of controlling a system by reinserting into it the results
of its past performance" (61).

If culture consists of an assembly of "outside-the-skin control mechanisms" for guiding and structuring human behavior, as well as for controlling an entropic environment, then culture is not something added on
to the "unfinished animal" but rather a central ingredient of human self-
production in the endless quest to complete the unfinished animal itself.
This interrelationship is the point of departure for the ethnographical
interpretation that Geertz describes as follows: "In short, we need to look
for systematic relationships among diverse phenomena, not for substan-
tive identities among similar ones. And to do that with any effectiveness,
we need to replace the 'stratigraphic' conception of the relations between
the various aspects of human existence with a synthetic one; that is, one
in which biological, psychological, sociological, and cultural factors can
be treated as variables within unitary systems of analysis" (44). And he

---

12. Wiener, *Human Use*, 58.

adds that such a methodological procedure is by no means new, but applies equally to "a number of recent developments . . . in other sciences," such as "cybernetics" (45). Looking for systematic relationships among diverse phenomena requires a feedback loop that will enable variable factors to be integrated into a unitary system of analysis, since the diverse phenomena to be unfolded have no essence of their own. They change in relation to the unfinished animal that stabilizes and finally creates itself through culture. Therefore Geertz argues as follows:

> Between the cultural pattern, the body, and the brain, a positive feedback system was created in which each shaped the progress of the other, a system in which the interaction among increasing tool use, the changing anatomy of the hand, and the expanding representation of the thumb on the cortex is only one of the more graphic examples. By submitting himself to governance by symbolically mediated programs for producing artifacts, organizing social life, or expressing emotions, man determined, if unwittingly, the culminating stages of his own biological destiny. Quite literally, though quite inadvertently, he created himself . . . . Without men, no culture, certainly; but equally, and more significantly, without culture, no men. (48f)

Thus recursive looping takes place on various levels, and each of these in turn functions by way of feedback loops. This is equally true of the brain itself, whose nervous system operates in a circuit of loops, "i.e., closed loops, the superposition of higher level loops on lower ones, and so on" (72).[13] What happens inside the brain occurs between brain and body,

---

13. For corroboration of such a statement, Geertz enlists the support of neurophysiologists by quoting some of their findings:

> The working of the central nervous system is a hierarchic affair in which functions at a higher level do not deal directly with the ultimate structural units, such as neurons or motor units, but operate by activating lower patterns that have their own relatively autonomous structural unity. The same is true for the sensory input, which does not project itself down to the last final path of motor neurons, but operates by affecting, distorting, and somehow modifying the pre-existing, preformed patterns of central coordination, which, in turn, then confer their distortions upon the lower patterns of effection and so on. . . . The structure of the input does not produce the structure of the output, but merely modifies intrinsic nervous activities that have a structural organization of their own. (70f.)

gesture and speech, and in the overall interaction between the "plasticity" (49) of the unfinished animal and the artificially created habitat. Of
course, there is no proof that recursive looping is a built-in structure
ranging from the functioning of the brain to the patterning of human
plasticity by the "outside-the-skin control mechanisms" that, as a human
product, control both human behavior and the entropic environment
(44). What may appear as an inherent property of the phenomena concerned is, in the final analysis, nothing but a strategy of interpretation.
Such a strategy seems more plausible whenever the dividing line between
the subject matter and the register of interpretation becomes blurred, so
that the method of grasping is taken for the inherent pattern of the subject matter itself.

Why is the interpretive strategy of recursive looping so indispensable
when we seek to elucidate the rise of Homo sapiens? Geertz answers as
follows: "We live, as one writer has neatly put it, in an 'information gap.'
Between what our body tells us and what we have to know in order to
function, there is a vacuum we must fill ourselves, and we fill it with information (or misinformation) provided by our culture. The boundary
between what is innately controlled and what is culturally controlled in
human behavior is an ill-defined and wavering one" (50). Breathing, for
instance, is genetically controlled and requires no cultural guidance,
whereas our "ideas, our values, our acts, even our emotions, are, like our
nervous system itself, cultural products—products manufactured, indeed,
out of tendencies, capacities, and dispositions with which we were born,
but manufactured nonetheless" (50). What, however, is even more important than marking these distinctions is the "information gap" itself, which
not only triggers recursive looping but also reveals why recursion is the
operation best suited to dealing with it. The information gap has a dual
reference: it applies to both humans and their environment. There is a
vacuum in the unfinished animal itself, highlighted by its plasticity, that
needs to be patterned for the sake of self-preservation; and there is the
vacuum of an entropic universe to which humans are exposed. The inception of culture presents itself as an effort to split entropy into order and
contingency, and such an act provides information insofar as information
is "a measure of organization,"[14] thus allowing for differentiation. Differentiating is the first step toward establishing "outside-the-skin control
mechanisms" that, though initially extrapolated from humans, begin

---

14. Wiener, *Human Use*, 21.

recursively to pattern human plasticity, the outcome of which is again fed forward into charting the environment. If dwelling in the information gap originally means that the unfinished animal is exposed to entropy, the filling of the gap is achieved by human culture, which still reflects the dual reference of the vacuum. Entropy is transformed into order, and order in turn shapes human plasticity, through which all human beings are transformed into "cultural artifacts" (51).

It is due to this vacuum that we have culture, which, of course, implies that the latter has no origins outside the human skin. If the information gap were ever done away with, human self-production through culture would come to an end. Its continued presence can be gauged by its repercussions on culture, which is constantly exposed to change. Consequently, we can never identify specific features of culture with culture itself, as all its features seem destined to issue into their own otherness.

In the final analysis, the information gap is a challenge to interpretation itself. It has to be met by the concept of recursive looping, whose explanatory power makes it possible to grasp the process of hominization as well as the interchange between the rise of Homo sapiens and human culture; this in turn conditions humankind by what it has fed forward. The less tangible the subject matter for interpretation, the more versatile the interpretive procedures have to become. Increased versatility distinguishes the recursive loop insofar as the forward feed and the backward feed develop through reciprocal correction, whose continuation is determined by the extent to which the subject matter has been brought under control.

The built-in fine-tuning between input and output through failure and success that guides the recursion has repercussions on the register of interpretation into which the subject matter is to be translated. This can be observed in the assessment of two important constitutive components of culture: the manufacturing of tools and the production of symbols.

Leroi-Gourhan, who considers "the concept of tools as being a 'secretion' of the anthropoid's body and brain" (91), tries to grasp this "secretion" through what he calls functional aesthetics. "Secretion," of course, is the metonymic description of a blank that cannot be filled by an assertion of what such a secretion is like, not least as the tool appears to be an offshoot of the interaction between brain and hand, an interaction that operates recursively.

The tool is not an implement existing for its own sake but has to fulfill a function. For this reason, it has to have form, which is, however, subservient to its use. The form of the tool ensures the appropriate application, thus integrating the tool with the purpose for which it has been designed. "Function and form, both adrift in time, constantly interact" (300). Again a gap between function and form has to be narrowed in order to perfect the functioning of the tool. Leroi-Gourhan writes: "Most living beings and objects are balanced in a complex interplay between (1) the evolution of each function toward satisfactory forms, (2) a compromise between various functions whereby the forms are maintained at a more or less high level of approximation, and (3) superstructures inherited from the biological or ethnic past, which are reflected in 'decorative' elements" (301). If the gap between form and function allows for a certain latitude of interpretation, the figurative element as the "dialogue between the maker and the material employed" (306) points to an additional effort to achieve suitability in the process of manufacturing tools. Figuration, although it appears to be the signature of the ethnic group marked on the tool, nevertheless represents the relationship between the "maker" and his or her product, which indicates a striving for mastery in the interplay between function and form. "This triple aspect of the aesthetics of products of human industry is to be found in all areas of technology, but in varying proportions that accentuate the ambivalent nature of functionality" (308). Nevertheless, minimal conditions for adequate functionality are always observed. There must be: (a) an ideal mechanical function; (b) a form that ensures functional approximation; and (c) a style that figures ethnic conceptions. Leroi-Gourhan called the intermeshing of these three aspects "a cycle," qualifying it only insofar as each of its aspects is either dominant or subservient: "The predominant element of the cycle depends on the category to which the product belongs, but normally all three elements are present" (309).

The underlying pattern that structures the interpretation of toolmaking has two implications: (a) The cycle interconnects the three aspects, thus forming a circuit. This makes function, form, and figuration continually feed into one another for the purpose of optimizing the adequacy of the tool. The feeding always operates recursively, enabling the tool to evolve toward its necessary perfection. The circuit unfolds the triple aspect of toolmaking as a process set in motion by the interconnected components that, while feeding into one another, are bound to become refined, so that the process produces the individuality of the components. (b) The register into which, for the purpose of comprehension, the manufacturing of tools as a secretion of hand and brain is translated is a highly flexible organization. The secretion is a blank that cannot be filled by any straightforward assertion. Instead, it has to be approached in such a way that the framework brought to bear for translating it must operate recursively. Function, form, and figuration as constitutive components of the register are in themselves empty abstractions and hence in their actual operation are continually exposed to reciprocal individualization as manifested through the specificity of the single tool. Obviously, there is no end to the individualization of the components that go into toolmaking, and it is through this unending specification of the circuit between function, form, and figuration that the intangible secretion is translated into terms of perception.[15]

Something similar is to be observed in the "culture concept" as advanced by Geertz, for whom culture, as the artificial habitat built into a vacuum, is a symbol system (89). Symbols are—according to a consensus prevailing among ethnographers—exteriorizations of the imagination for the purpose of organizing the natural environment of humans, integrating space and time into the human orbit and equally the individual into the group, thereby controlling what humans have been able to establish. These diversified tasks qualify symbols as performatives, from which we may conclude that culture itself is a performance, not least as the artificial habitat is continuously being produced without ever being completed.

Symbols as "extrinsic" (92) cultural programs "are so important . . . only because human behavior is so loosely determined by intrinsic sources of information." The symbol, according to Geertz, is marked by a duality: "It is a model *of* 'reality,' " and "a model *for* 'reality.' " "Unlike genes, and other nonsymbolic information sources, which are only models *for*, not models *of*, culture patterns have an intrinsic double aspect: they give meaning, that is, objective conceptual form, to social and psychological reality both by shaping themselves to it and by shaping it to themselves" (93). This duality makes it possible to grasp the operational intent of the symbol, which is an abstraction from something for the purpose of shaping something. Such a duality can be observed, for instance, in the totem, which bears a dual inscription insofar as it is an abstraction from the animal kingdom for the purpose of creating the identity of a social group.

---

15. It is pertinent to note that Leroi-Gourhan, who describes the process of hominization as a continual 'branching' and 'bifurcation,' nevertheless applies a recursive pattern of interpretation when it comes to detailing specific instances of how hominids have coped with their environment. This pattern may be applied to human technology in general. One might even be inclined to consider branching and bifurcation as the outcome of inputs that hominids have made into their entropic environment.

The dual aspect of the symbol reflects the chasm that separates humans from the environment to which they are exposed, and it is simultaneously an attempt to come to grips with this chasm. Therefore an abstraction from the so-called real world has to be made, though not so much in order to represent it as to make it serve as a pattern for organizing challenging realities. If symbols are considered representative at all, their duality is at best indicative of the chasm, which is featureless and has either to be bridged or encompassed by the dual structure, thus making the symbol into a form of action. The performative impulse of the symbol would not issue into an actual performance, however, if the symbol did not operate in feedback loops. As a model *of*, it is a schematized abstraction from something given; as a model *for*, it is a template for charting something new. Whenever the schema is fed forward (in an attempt to bring order out of disorder) and fails to tally with what has been aimed at, a feedback loop occurs that may result in either a modification of the initial abstraction or a search for other areas from which models can be obtained for the purpose concerned. Geertz is quite explicit about the nature of such an interrelationship; he characterizes the shifts between models *of* and models *for* as "intertransposability," which for him is "the distinctive characteristic of our mentality" (94).

"Intertransposability" describes the type of recursion operative in the symbol's dual structure. The latter points to the fact that "structure is *related* to uncertainty, but not to the lack of it, and to have structure is to have uncertainty." The duality of the symbol thus converts uncertainty into a mapping of culture. However elaborate the dual structure turns out to be, to "increase structure is also to increase uncertainty,"[16] which means culture is not an overcoming of the latter but rather a continual specification by means of this very uncertainty. The chasm separating order from contingency is encompassed by the dual structure of the symbol, which allows it to extend beyond the confines of what has been mastered so far and to provide guidance for what has to be coped with: the entropic environment, the apprehension of human experience, and the challenge exercised by cultural achievements to which humans are exposed. The chasm turns out to be an energizing source for change, and change in turn is uncertainty that feeds into the

---

16. See W. R. Garner, *Uncertainty and Structure as Psychological Concepts* (New York: Wiley, 1962), 339.

dual structure of the symbols, thus diversifying an ever-growing cultural patterning.[17]

Interpreting culture as symbolic action powered by the mutual transposition between a model *of* and a model *for* requires a highly versatile register into which such a conception of culture is translated. The register that Leroi-Gourhan advanced for translating toolmaking into conceptual language already showed a flexible structure by linking three different aspects, whose reciprocal interaction makes it possible to pinpoint individualization as the decisive feature of toolmaking. Transposing the intangible rise and development of culture into an interpretive register poses the question as to whether any factors, aspects, or even concepts could be postulated for such an interpretation. However, factors, aspects, and concepts are terms of reference that, when applied, would subject culture—conceived as a recursively operating symbolic action—to an alien framework. What we have, then, is less a cognition of culture than a reading of it, as Geertz has proposed. Reading signs "is sorting out the structure of signification" (9), where the latter consists of "piled-up structures of inference and implication through which an ethnographer is continually trying to pick his way" (7). And yet Geertz seeks to provide "a treatise in cultural theory" (viii), which calls for a certain coherence that is to be achieved by what he terms "thick description," roughly outlined as follows: "Cultural analysis is (or should be) guessing at meanings, assessing the guesses, and drawing explanatory conclusions from the better guesses, not discovering the Continent of Meaning and mapping out its bodiless landscape" (20). Such guessing and assessing of guesses cannot appeal for verification to any given frame of reference but has to produce one for itself through thick description.

How is this to be done? Initially by invoking a negative reference from which thick description is to be distinguished: that is, "thin description,"

---

17. Potentially, such a recursive movement between humans and their culture will never come to an end. This applies equally to the symbolic action according to which culture is charted, and as humans are patterned by what they have charted, the recursive looping will never achieve a final homeostasis. On the contrary, although there may be intermittent states of homeostasis, they will be unbalanced by new challenges to which humans have to respond. This is due to the fact that culture, as we know it, is an assembly of human responses, whose variability arises out of what Geertz called the "genetically programmed . . . response capacities." (99)

which is primarily a reification of abstract concepts that are superimposed on culture. Hence, instead of sweeping abstractions, "the delicacy of . . . distinctions" is the prime concern of observation (25), not least as ethnographic interpretation must take "other peoples' symbol systems [i.e., their culture]" as "actor-oriented" (14). Reading such symbol systems is a matter not so much of grasping what they may represent as bringing out what they imply. There is a gap between what is manifest and what is implied. Thick description therefore strives to unfold the implications that the manifest sign appears to have; whereas thin description amounts to a taxonomical listing of perceivable phenomena, taking the obvious for a self-explanatory fact.

Geertz provides a rather telling example of how thick description is meant to operate by referring to a Beethoven quartet "as an, admittedly rather special but, for these purposes, nicely illustrative, sample of culture." He continues:

No one would, I think, identify it with its score, with the skills and knowledge needed to play it, with the understanding of it possessed by its performers or auditors, nor, to take care, en passant, of the reductionists and reifiers, with a particular performance of it or with some mysterious entity transcending material existence. . . . But that a Beethoven quartet is a temporally developed tonal structure, a coherent sequence of modeled sound — in a word, music — and not anybody's knowledge of or belief about anything, including how to play it, is a proposition to which most people are, upon reflection, likely to assent.

(11–12)

Whatever components are to be observed, they have to be interrelated, thus allowing us to sense what they adumbrate: the music. Bringing to light what the observable signs appear to indicate proceeds by means of a reciprocal intertransposability.

Through intertransposability, signs as signifiers are made to read one another. Reading signs is a matter less of grasping what they represent than of spotlighting what they imply. There is always a gap between what is manifest and what is implied. Thick description is therefore first and foremost an unfolding of the implications of the manifest, which thus becomes all the more richly orchestrated. When signs are made to read one another, they begin to unfold their implications, which bounce back on what they initially seemed to have manifested. Thus there begins a recursive movement between the manifest and the implied, out of which a continually self-refining semiotic web evolves as a register into which culture as symbolic action is translated. Because there is no given reference for such a mutual transposition of the manifest and the implied, recursively operating intertransposability realizes itself in a continual iteration between input and output. Iteration is always the same operation, whose repetition, however, feeds changing inputs and outputs into one another, thereby fine-tuning the semiotic web through continued interaction. In this respect, iteration functions as the reference for recursive looping, which issues into an ever-expanding range of thick description. It is, however, also an indication that "cultural analysis is intrinsically incomplete. And, worse than that, the more deeply it goes the less complete it is" (29). And yet this makes intertransposability operating in loops no less adequate as a method for translating culture, because culture, which generates its organizations as well as the shifts within its network, finds its appropriate interpretation through the iterative intertransposability of the sign.

Systemic Recursion

Recursive looping as an operational strategy is of equal importance for charting the salient features of culture. Interpreting the latter no longer seeks to control entropy but sets out to show how culture works, and this requires a retooling of interpretive procedures. Just as the hermeneutic circle was reconceived for the changing tasks it had to perform, something similar happens to the feedback loop of input/output when the subject to be grasped differs from that which the ethnographers are concerned with.

Such a paradigm switch is to be observed in what has been called the Santiago school of systems theory, of which Francisco Varela is a major proponent. Although the structure of feedback loops that he proposes is not meant as a strategy for interpreting culture but serves to elucidate the principles of biology, it nevertheless lends itself to generalizations, as Varela himself suggests. His emphasis on recursion is intimately tied to what is basic for him, that is, the fact that "the act of distinction lies at the foundation of any description. The most fundamental operation is that of distinguishing the 'it' to be studied from its background. A distinction emerges out of the observer-community that decides the sense in which a distinction is performed. Thus we have physical boundaries, functional groupings, conceptual categorizations, and so on, in an infinitely variegated museum of possible distinctions."[18] Because these distinctions demarcate boundaries, they become an object of observation insofar as one has to find out what is entailed if these boundaries are crossed. Distinctions allow us to conceive as unities what they have separated, and these tend to become reciprocal foils for one another. Varela calls these unities systems, whose internal structure and external relations present themselves as targets for exploration. This is all the more expedient as the "world does not present itself to us neatly divided into systems, subsystems, environments, and so on. These are divisions we make ourselves for various purposes" (83).[19] One of Varela's central purposes is to find out how to handle these distinctions, and the strategy of interpretation that he adopts is "the basic philosophy that animates cybernetics and systems theory" (7).

Living systems such as the immune system or the nervous system are Varela's principal paradigms, which he describes as autonomous and autopoietic. But simultaneously he makes it quite clear that "the autonomy of living systems is a case of, and not synonymous with, autonomy in general" (57); this applies equally to social systems (58).[20] We might extend his analogy by saying that the living systems to be distinguished from one another work together, thus building up the human organism, just as the different social systems interact, thus giving rise to more comprehensive systems, such as society or culture.[21] In each of these instances boundaries are crossed and differences imbricated, and recursion becomes a fundamental strategy for grasping these, "because nothing that, in our culture, is consensually accepted as an effective procedure has ever been found not to be reducible to a recursive function" (58).

It is particularly enlightening in the present context that the subject matter to be interpreted is living systems, which are categorically different from those I have focused on thus far. Distinctions are already present in the internal structure of autonomous systems, which Varela terms

18. Francisco J. Varela, *Principles of Biological Autonomy* (New York: Elsevier North Holland, 1979), 107. The sources of all other quotations from this volume are given in in-text references to the appropriate pages.

19. For a specification of distinctions, see also Humberto R. Maturana and Francisco J. Varela, *The Tree of Knowledge: The Biological Roots of Human Understanding*, trans. Robert Paolucci, rev. ed. (Boston: Shambhala, 1992), 40.

20. For further details, see ibid., 193.

21. For cultural phenomena, see ibid., 194–201.

"autopoietic machines" and whose basic definition reads: "*An autopoietic system is organized (defined as a unity) as a network of processes of production (transformation and destruction) of components that produces the components that: (1) through their interactions and transformations continuously regenerate and realize the network of processes (relations) that produced them; and (2) constitute it (the machine) as a concrete unity in the space in which they exist by specifying the topological domain of its realization as such a network*" (13). Living systems are autopoietic insofar as they have no essence that they could appeal to or draw from in order to function. An essence would inevitably lie outside and thus be structurally different from the inner workings of the living system. Instead, systems of this kind are more or less complex organizations, within which transmittal of information, reception of information, and equally interruption of these exchanges take place on all levels. Such a concatenation of communicative interactions, which Varela likens to "conversation" (267–269),[22] proceeds recursively through a continual feed forward and feed backward between the levels of the system. Consequently, the system does not consist simply of an assembly of components but operates as a process that produces its own components, which, through their reciprocal interpenetration, bring forth a dynamic network. "A network of feedback loops mutually interconnected is organizationally closed . . . , and the representation of such coherence is generalized to any form of indefinite recursion of defining processes such that they generate the unitary character of the system" (56). This makes the system into a self-regulating organization, which simultaneously reveals the dual aspect of the feedback loop: (a) The recursive interactions between levels, components, and processes of the system result in a network of "mutual interconnectedness" (86) that keeps specifying their

---

22. Varela specifies conversation as follows:

In fact, a *conversation* has been a basic image throughout this presentation as a paradigm for interactions among autonomous systems. It is a paradigm as well as a particular instance of an autonomous system, and these two sides of it go together. Its role as exemplary case of autonomous interaction comes from the fact that a conversation is *direct* experience, human experience *par excellence*—we live and breathe in dialogue and language. And from this direct experience we know that one cannot find a firm reference point for the content of a dialogue.   (*Principles*, 268)

"A conversation . . . embodies a direct prototype of the way in which autonomous units interact" (270).

function by making them reciprocally select from and impinge on one another. This two-way traffic proceeds as conversation through which the exchange of information is continually differentiated. (b) Such an incessant internal recursion provides the closure of the system, not least as there is no external agency that might do it, and thus the system's "recursivity [is] its closure" (235). Moreover, the "indefinite recursion" is also instrumental in generating what is absolutely vital to the living system: its self-maintenance. Thus the dual aspect of the feedback loop allows us to conceive the servomechanism through which an autonomous system sustains itself.

Such an interpretation of the living system's basic structure calls for differentiation insofar as it has to be distinguished from Wiener's model of cybernetics.[23] Therefore Varela writes: "The autopoietic machine has no inputs or outputs" (68). He is fully aware that "this point of view is alien to the Wienerian idea of feedback *simpliciter*" (56). In spite of the fact that he acknowledges the breakthrough Wiener achieved with his "feedback idea" (166), which replaces "cause-effect relationships" (167), he nevertheless maintains that such a type of cybernetics remains committed "to fixed reference points, or finiteness in the recursion" (167). Consequently, "in dealing with natural systems, the whole idea of input-output becomes muddled. Who and how are we to select a fixed set of input and output spaces? It is more accurate to talk about environmental perturbations/compensations" (167f.). This makes the input/output conception of the feedback loop into a special case of recursion, as there are no "fixed reference points" in the autopoietic systems between which such an interchange might take place for the purpose of achieving control. Instead, the indefinite recursion, which organizes the conversation between levels and components in order to generate the system's self-maintenance, has to react to "environmental perturbation," not least because systems have other systems as their surroundings. Such a perturbation, however, is not an input that a living system might need for its self-maintenance. Instead, it triggers a compensating operation within the system itself. This is done by recursively reshuffling the latter's organization, because the perturbation is "noise" in the sense that its randomness has nothing to do with the system's architecture. Noise, however, has to be processed, and this is effected by

---

23. For a similar criticism of the input/output model and the paradigm switch in general systems theory, see also Niklas Luhmann, *Soziale Systeme: Grundriß einer allgemeinen Theorie* (Frankfurt/Main: Suhrkamp, 1984), 275–282.

the system's internal recursion. What happens in such cases has been called by Henri Atlan "self-organization from noise";[24] put another way, in Heinz von Foerster's more vivid metaphor, "self-organizing systems do not only feed upon order, they will also find noise on their menu."[25]

Processing such external noise may, in turn, cause internal noise as well, because there are no fixed trajectories along which the indefinite recursion can travel inside the system. On the contrary, the internal feedback loops do not follow any prestructured pattern; instead, as Gregory Bateson once phrased it, "noise [is] the only possible source of *new* patterns."[26] Thus recursion presents itself as a two-tiered operation: it produces and is simultaneously driven by internal noise, because the processing of noise creates order, the achievement of which requires feedback loops to carve out interconnections between levels in order to counteract the perturbations experienced. Therefore Varela qualifies systemic recursion as indefinite, because the system's self-organization as a process of compensating for perturbations is unpredictable.

There are a few conclusions to be drawn at this juncture of the argument. Recursion as the internally operating agency of living systems turns out to be an interpretive strategy that is able to account for the system's autopoiesis. Consequently, autopoiesis and recursion are interchangeable concepts for describing how the system functions, which makes recursion into an explanatory pattern for the nature of generation. What recursion produces is the identity and self-maintenance of the system: "its behavior will be such that all perturbations and changes will be subordinated to the maintenance of the system's identity" (58). The latter is not a goal, as the living system does not have a purpose outside itself but sustains itself through continuous internal recursions. Self-maintenance therefore emerges incessantly, and the feedback loops as agents of emergence do not issue into a definite product.

This marks a final difference between the input/output model of recursive looping and the model advocated by Varela. The former is purpose-

---

24. See William R. Paulson, *The Noise of Culture: Literary Texts in a World of Information* (Ithaca: Cornell University Press, 1988), 69–75.
25. Heinz von Foerster, "On Self-Organizing Systems and Their Environments," in *Self-Organizing Systems*, ed. M. C. Yovits and S. Cameron (New York: Pergamon, 1960), 43.
26. Gregory Bateson, *Steps to an Ecology of Mind* (New York: Ballantine, 1973), 410.

oriented, for the realization of which the trajectory is basically linear, not least as the overall purpose of the input/output relationship is to achieve control. The unforeseeable processes that develop through internal recursion within a self-referential system, however, make it nonlinear. Self-organization is not a goal to be attained but an ongoing operation that ensures the system's self-maintenance by continually balancing out its threatened homeostasis. Linearity therefore would mean that homeostasis, once achieved, would stagnate, thereby immobilizing the system's compensatory capability. The system would then have to be sustained from a source outside itself, with which it would interact according to the input/output model. The contrast between the achievement of control and the emergence of self-maintenance spotlights the difference between the linear operation of input/output feedback and the nonlinear one of systemic recursion as an internal exchange of information.

Now we must consider the fact that systems do not exist in isolation but have other systems in their environment.

Autopoietic systems may interact with each other under conditions that result in structural (behavioral) coupling. In this coupling, the autopoietic conduct of an organism A becomes a source of deformation of an organism B, and the compensatory behavior of organism B acts, in turn, as a source of deformation of organism A, whose compensatory behavior acts again as a source of deformation of B, and so on recursively until the coupling is interrupted. In this manner, a chain of interlocked interactions develops. In each interaction the conduct of each organism is constitutively independent in its generation of the conduct of the other, because it is internally determined by the structure of the behaving organism only; but it is for the other organism, while the chain lasts, a source of compensable deformations that can be described as meaningful in the context of the coupled behavior. *These are communicative interactions.*[27]   (48f.)

The effect of structural coupling is twofold and may be qualified as intrinsic and extrinsic in relation to the systems that are linked up with one another.

------

27. See also Maturana and Varela, who sum up this relationship by stating: "Structural coupling is always mutual; both organism and environment undergo transformations" (*Tree of Knowledge*, 102).

If the perturbation experienced by a system results in an internal reshuffling of its structure, then the latter will also cause a perturbation for the initiator of the noise. What does this mean for the system's self-organization, and why is it able to face up to such pressures without falling apart when disturbed by something outside itself? The answer lies in the system's "structural plasticity" (33).[28] This plasticity allows specifications of the system's behavioral patterns, because when coupled with other systems, the reciprocal perturbation does not change its structure altogether but causes a modification of behavior in order to ensure self-maintenance. This inherent plasticity makes the changes of the system's behavior viable, and this in turn is indispensable for environmental noise to be converted into functional order. If there were no such plasticity, living systems would perish, as they would be incapable of reacting. And reaction means maintaining their self-organization through their ability to compensate for the deformations suffered.

The structural coupling that constitutes the versatility of the system's behavior, however, is not a purely defensive maneuver; simultaneously it is a continual patterning of the system's plasticity, thus increasing the complexity of the system's behavior. This makes structural coupling into more than an accident for the systems concerned; it sets in motion "the possible diversity of recursive histories" that, as "pathways taken by self-organization," are "astronomical" (235). There is no end to specifying the system's behavioral patterns, and the latter in turn develop recursively by interacting with their previous patterns, which feed into one another. This process of behavioral specification has to hark back to earlier ways of coping with perturbations in order to work out recursively a response to the new challenge. As the system has no essence, it must avail itself of these previous behavioral patterns and process potentially all the efforts it has made to ensure self-maintenance, thus giving rise to its internal "recursive history." It is recursive in a dual sense: it has no goal outside itself, and so it must take up what it has already developed earlier as guidance for maintaining self-organization; in doing so, it converts its structural plasticity into an increasing complexity of specified behavior. Thus the recursive history allows the system to reactivate its own past as "an interlocked history of structural transformations" (33).

---

28. For a more comprehensive discussion of "structural plasticity," see ibid., 166ff.

So far structural coupling as an explanatory concept applies to delineating the intrinsic impact systems experience through their interlinking, which Varela sums up by saying: "Coupling arises as a result of the mutual modifications that interacting unities undergo in the course of their interactions without loss of identity." There is, however, another and no doubt equally important aspect to structural coupling, because in "general . . . coupling leads also to the generation of a new unity that may exist in a *different domain* in which the component coupled unities retain their identity" (50). Therefore systems of a higher order emerge from an interlocking of systems. If "a system is realized through the coupling of autopoietic unities and is defined by relations of production of components that generate these relations and constitute it as a unity in some space . . . then it is called an autopoietic system of *higher order*" (51). Society and culture are composite systems, and Varela emphasizes that they have a "unity that is livinglike" (58); he continues by saying: "I do want to make it clear that the idea of autonomy and its consequences are *not* restricted to biological, natural systems, but can encompass human and social systems *as well*" (59). Such a claim arises out of the assumption that the "understanding of life becomes a mirror of our epistemological choices, which carry over to human actions" (46).

Structural coupling of autopoietic unities proceeds recursively insofar as the interlocking of systems has to cope with the liminal space, which is to be ported over through continued interaction between unities that are separate. These feedback loops turn out to be a mechanism that makes "higher-order autopoietic systems" (53) emerge. Just as internal recursion ensures the self-maintenance of the system, so external recursion between different systems generates more complex unities. We only have to think of society as such a higher-order system arising out of the interlocking of political, economic, cultural, communicative, legal, scientific, and religious systems to recognize that a great many of them are already composite unities themselves.[29] In this respect, culture may serve as an even more vivid illustration. High, popular, and low culture as well as the arts and media are in continual conversation with one another, which more often than not leads to an interchange of components between these unities.

Basically, there are two ways of conceiving this conversation. Depending on the observer who describes culture, the various unities coupled

---

29. See Luhmann, *Soziale Systeme,* 345, for whom society is the most complex and all-encompassing system.

may assume different functions, for instance, when taken as allopoietic systems, meaning that they only play a role within the composite system by representing an aspect necessary for it to function. The conversation, however, could also be described as circulation through which the operational aspect is privileged, making culture into something that is continually emerging and simultaneously highlights circulation as an embodiment of recursion.[30]

The salient features of recursion that guide this paradigm of interpretation now move into sharper focus; it proves to be a strategy of great explanatory power, as it exercises multiple, though interrelated functions. First of all, it allows us to conceive how liminal spaces both inside and outside the systems are coped with. By interlocking intrasystemic levels, recursion spotlights how the system participates in resolving disturbances of its homeostasis. It thus transforms liminal spaces into a circuit of interconnections and, in doing so, provides closure for the system, featuring it as an autonomous autopoietic unity. Just as the feedback loops structure the system's internal organization through a permanent interaction among levels, components, and processes, they also negotiate the liminal space between systems, the coupling of which gives rise to composite systems.

Therefore recursion appears as a generative force. It brings about the emergence of the system's self-maintenance and composite systems of a higher order. By turning into an explanatory concept for emergence, it exposes as mythological the old concept of a generative matrix out of which creative processes are presumed to arise. Simultaneously it qualifies such emergence as a dynamic entity of kaleidoscopically changing features, quite different from a clear-cut product.[31]

Furthermore, recursive looping, both intra- and extrasystemically, operates as a continual specification and differentiation, enhancing the

---

30. The structure of such a circulation develops in "strange loops," which means there is not only a back-and-forth movement but also one of "tangled hierarchies," owing to a "jumping" in this conversation between different levels. For a description of "strange loops" and how they cause "tangled hierarchies," see Douglas R. Hofstadter, *Gödel, Escher, Bach: An Eternal Golden Braid* (New York: Vintage, 1989), 709f. Maturana and Varela characterize the nervous system as "a maze of interconnections" involving "an interaction of the sensory and motor elements that are distant" (*Tree of Knowledge*, 152f.).
31. Varela, *Principles*, 102f., gives a very revealing account regarding music as an emergent phenomenon.

system's complexity and allowing it to compensate for the perturbations experienced by reshuffling itself internally in response to noise. Consequently, recursion elucidates the system's self-reproduction, in the course of which even the interconnections described are generated, revealing the system's structure as nonlinear. This renewal unfolds as a selective "reciprocal connectivity" (91) between levels and components, which function as operators for the system's self-organization. Nonlinear systems maintain themselves through recursive interactions, the concatenations of which issue forth into potentially limitless specifications of their internal patternings.

What makes recursion into such an important interpretive strategy is the fact that the inner workings of the systems so far described are not as tangible as they may seem. Reference to levels, components, and processes that feed into the system's dynamic network is, in the final analysis, a sophisticated assumption, and this holds true in particular for living systems, such as the immune and nervous systems, which are Varela's main paradigms. If the impression is conveyed that the structural items mentioned are really given, this is primarily due to the persuasiveness of the feedback loop as an interpretive strategy. Speaking of levels, components, processes, and networks is at best, according to a term of Douglas Hofstadter's, "junking," which means that such designations are intended for the purpose of interpretation with no certainty that they really exist (287).[32] They provide guidelines, however, and the explanatory power of recursion appears to convert them into tangible realities. For this reason, we might say that recursive looping makes accessible what is otherwise hidden from view; it provides insight into the inner workings of systems that cannot be seen.

Mapping reality in terms of recursively operating systems is pertinent insofar as there is no given reality other than the one made to appear by the systems. If reality as a structured order were to exist, systems as a mode of construing it would be redundant. Therefore Varela states: "All of this boils down, actually, to a realization that although the world *does* look solid and regular, when we come to examine it there is no fixed point of reference to which it can be pinned down; it is nowhere substantial and solid" (275). At best the world can only be disclosed as an emerging phe-

---

32. See Hofstadter, Gödel, Escher, Bach, 287ff., and also chapter 11, "Brains and Thoughts," 337–368, in which he details the different types of "junking" necessary to describe the levels of the brain and its ways of functioning.

nomenon, to be fathomed by recursively operating systems.[33] For this reason, we are bound to reflect on the recursivity of these explanatory con-
structions, and hence what he calls the "observer-community" becomes
of paramount concern.

Varela writes that he wants to "show how the study of autonomy and
system's descriptions in general cannot be distinguished from a study of
the describer's properties, and . . . the system and observer appear as an
inseparable pair" (63). Thus the register, we might say, forms an integral
part of the subject matter that is opened up by observation, which is quite
natural insofar as the system's operative devices, the construction of the
system itself, and the mapping of reality through the structural coupling
of systems are all offshoots of the "observer-community" (276). Therefore
the "describer" is inside the subject matter to be interpreted; in other
words, the register itself is a component part of what otherwise exists as
living systems or autonomous social systems. The very fact that the register penetrates the subject matter highlights what Hofstadter has indicated
by calling the whole internal description a form of "junking," which gains
its plausibility and justification through recursion, allowing the observer
to account for the operability of the system. In this respect, the observer
forms part of the observed.

What prevents the register from collapsing into the subject matter,
however, is the duality inscribed into it, which Varela designates as
"descriptive complementarity" (70) and explains as follows: "What I will
argue now is that an operational explanation for the living phenomenology needs a complementary mode of explanation to be complete, a mode
of explanation that I have referred to as *symbolic*" (71). Consequently, the
register proposed has a two-tiered structure, consisting of an operational
and a symbolic frame into which the subject matter is to be translated.
The observer-community that describes the system operationally belongs
to the system insofar as it construes the latter's dynamic structure, which,
however, is not a pure invention because what are termed living and social
systems have a substratum. This substratum can only be conceived according to the structures proposed, as Varela emphasizes again at the end of
his book by saying that such a model is just "an image," which will help
us "to chart, as an operative process and in a formal fashion, that peculiar
relationship between unities and their cognition" (277). But why must an

---

33. Maturana and Varela state: "What is known is brought forth" (*Tree of
Knowledge*, 255).

operational interpretation be coupled with a symbolic one? Because "an operational explanation . . . says nothing about whether it is *cognitively possible or satisfactory*" (74).[34] And cognition is indispensable, as our lack of knowledge regarding "all the positions and momenta of all the particles in the universe" makes it impossible "to calculate their future trajectories" (74). Symbolic interpretation is thus dual in character; it is caused by gaps in knowledge, and simultaneously it is a takeover of what the operational description fits into a frame external to the system.

Without further specifying the cognitive intent, what this duality of operational and symbolic explanation reveals is that the liminal space that exists both inside and between living and social systems inscribes itself into the very register that is to grasp the subject matter. Although split up by the liminal space into a two-tiered structure, the distinct components of the register are nevertheless made to interlink, because the operational interpretation is guided to a certain degree by symbolic considerations and the former simultaneously has repercussions on the latter. Thus the liminal space recurring in the register triggers a recursive movement that, however, travels along an input/output trajectory, not least as there is a purpose to be achieved.[35] Such a feedback operation inside the register is apposite for this type of interpretation, which conceives of the world as an

---

34. Varela quotes Maturana for an illustration of what these two types of description entail. The situation is as follows: A pilot is landing while his family awaits him. "When the pilot comes out of the plane, however, his wife and friends embrace him with joy and tell him: 'What a wonderful landing you made: we were afraid because of the heavy fog.' But the pilot answers in surprise: 'Flight? Landing? What do you mean? I did not fly or land: I only manipulated certain internal relations of the plane in order to obtain a particular sequence of readings in a set of instruments'" (*Principles*, 250). The pilot's description was an operational one, whereas the family gave a symbolic description.

35. Varela elaborates on this duality by saying:

> A preference for operational explanations seems to be rooted in the understanding that causes are "out there" and reflect a state of affairs independent of the describer. This is, by the very argument used here, untenable . . . . An operational description is no more and no less than a mode of agreement within an inquiring community, and in no way has an intrinsically superior status to a symbolic explanation. . . . It seems to me that there are tremendous advantages to maintaining this duality of explanations in full view. (ibid., 77)

And one of the basic reasons for such a duality is the avoidance "of *methodological monism*."

assembly of autonomous systems whose internal autopoiesis and external coupling are taken for maps that make territories emerge. What the duality of the register thus establishes is an *"epistemology of participation"* (276), as the observer-community is simultaneously inside and outside the systems, whose operations are construed for the purpose of cognition. This makes the register itself into a recursive operation, which assumes—in contradistinction to the types of interpretive paradigms discussed so far—a dynamic quality that is appropriate for conceptualizing the world as an assembly of autopoietic systems. Such a register is much more conditioned by the subject matter than in our previous paradigms, because it is both a component part of the subject matter and a stance outside of it.

This points to a further aspect of the "descriptive complementarity" between operational and symbolic observation: the latter is conceived as an observation of the former, thus bringing the epistemological implications of such a "complementary" to the fore. An operational description makes distinctions by separating levels, components, and networks from one another, without being able to see the distinctions themselves. The symbolic observation focuses on this blind spot, allowing the observer to perceive what cannot be seen in the operational description. Consequently, observation of an observation becomes pertinent in order to spotlight the distinction,[36] whose function as specification and differentiation of systemic recursion is then to be grasped.

It is important to bear in mind that the symbolic description of the two-tiered register is not—as it may seem—a fixed position. Instead, a feedback loop also develops between the symbolic description and its environment, which feeds the purpose of cognition into the description, just as the description may feed operational features back into the context. This makes cognition into a changeable frame of reference, allowing the observer-community to move the coupling and interpenetration of systems into kaleidoscopically shifting constellations.

In order to illustrate how this works, we may take culture as a case in point. Being a composite system, culture has lower-order autonomous systems as its components. Through structural coupling, these are turned into allopoietic roles, thus representing functions necessary to the composite system. The observer-community is able to pinpoint these lower-order systems that, through their coupling, make culture emerge as a system of a higher order. Such a description is at best operational, confining

---

36. See Niklas Luhmann, *Die Wissenschaft der Gesellschaft* (Frankfurt/Main: Suhrkamp, 1990), 79ff.

observation to the distinction of formal features and not touching on questions such as why and how the outcome of coupling is to be conceived. When such questions are addressed, a switch to symbolic description takes place, through which the composite system is transposed into a cognitive frame of reference.

Such a transposition is necessary for several reasons. First of all, the composite system—having emerged out of structural coupling—calls for a conceptualization of emergence, which an operational description is unable to formulate; hence a cognitive effort is required. Such an effort is not independent of the environment of the observer-community. Cognition of the composite system is conditioned by what appears to be relevant for the environment, and simultaneously the conceptualization of this emergent phenomenon is fed back into the environment. Thus cognition, as the hallmark of symbolic description, is set in motion by a looping of input and output, which adjusts the way emergence is to be conceived in terms of environmental demands and into which the outcome of this emergence is fed back.

This basic interrelationship has a further consequence. It is the cognitive intent that decides which of the lower-order systems are to play allopoietic roles[37] or epitomize the salient feature of the composite system. There may well be an observer-community for whom popular culture is the epitome of culture and for whom high culture is a foil, thus functioning in an allopoietic role, and vice versa. Without elaborating on such multifarious interchangeabilities, we may say that the observer-community causes these shifts in perspectives, by means of which operational and symbolic descriptions feed just as permanently into one another as the symbolic description feeds into its environment. Operationally speaking, culture appears as circulation between its assembly of lower-order systems; symbolically speaking, it appears as an interchangeable backgrounding and foregrounding of its coupled unities, out of which the kaleidoscopically shifting panorama of culture emerges.[38]

---

37. Varela details this relationship as follows: An "observer can describe an autopoietic component of a composite system as playing an *allopoietic role* in the realization of the larger system that it contributes to realizing through autopoiesis. In other words, the autopoietic unity functions in the context of the composite system in a manner that the observer would describe as allopoietic" (*Principles*, 52).

38. Paulson, *The Noise of Culture*, 101–185, provides a penetrating analysis of how the text-reader relationship may be conceived along similar lines and, in particular, of how literature functions as a system within the composite system of culture.

CHAPTER FIVE

The Traveling Differential: Franz Rosenzweig, *The Star of Redemption*

"The Birth of the Elements Out of the Somber Foundations of Nought"[1]

Interpretation—as we have seen—is an act of translating something either verbal or nonverbal into a register that is linguistic in nature. This applies not only to the transposition of a text into another type of text but also to the translation of a past into a present or a hidden life into transparency. It applies as well to the control of entropy, the processing of a heritage, all encounters between cultures, and the telescoping of different cultural levels. The various modes investigated thus far have shown that interpretation as translation is not a matter of one language being rendered in terms of another, because transposing a subject into a register does not mean that the latter figures as an equivalent for the former. Instead, the register functions as a means of opening up, providing access, grasping, controlling, and also regulating the observation of the subject. Simultaneously, the nature of the material to be interpreted has repercussions not only on the register but also on the liminal space, which may be negotiated in multiple ways, ranging from the network of the hermeneutic circle through the nesting of circles, transactional loops, recursive loops, and systemic recursion.

---

1. Franz Rosenzweig, *The Star of Redemption*, trans. William W. Hallo (Notre Dame: Notre Dame University Press, 1985), 125. The sources of all other quotations from this volume are given in in-text references to the appropriate pages.

A different problem poses itself when something experienced as immeasurable is to be grasped through an act of interpretation. This situation arises when seemingly incontrovertible facts—such as the existence of the world, of humankind, and above all (for believers) of God—have to be apprehended. For this task, no universal conventions, let alone overarching frames of reference, are available that might regulate or even control such a transposition into terms of knowledge. As interpretation is a cognitive enterprise, transposing something immeasurable into cognition requires a different operational mode from those discussed thus far.

Any act of interpretation opens up a liminal space between the subject matter and the register into which it is to be transposed. Such a space not only results from interpretation but also structures the modes of the interpretive operation. In the case of recursive looping, when control of entropy is at issue, the liminal space triggers a reaction between input and output through which the latter effects readjustments of the former. As a rule, what has been fed forward does not tally exactly with what it has aimed at; something familiar impinges on something foreign that in turn imprints itself on the familiar, giving rise to a negative feedback loop. This recursion realizes itself through a play movement by shuttling back and forth between the familiar and the foreign. The play movement is marked by a duality, which manifests itself in an ongoing interplay between what might be termed free and instrumental play. Instrumental play sets out to achieve its aim in terms of the familiar, whereas free play invalidates the familiar to a certain degree, thus correcting it and highlighting what still appears to be beyond control. The reciprocal inscription of free and instrumental play maps out the trajectory along which recursive looping develops. Recursion, then, as a mode of achieving control, allows us to bring something foreign, something beyond our ken, within a range we are familiar with. Recursion, however, prevents the familiar from superimposing itself onto the foreign. Instead, the familiar is subjected to correction and change when something that is originally beyond its scope is fed back into it.

Recursive looping as a structure of translatability reveals that the liminal space between the foreign and the familiar, between input and output, between the structural coupling of systems, and between the levels of autonomous systems, cannot be eliminated, although recursivity is powered by the drive to eliminate it. Consequently, the liminal space highlights a residual untranslatability, which gives rise to a growing complexity of the procedures operative in interpretation.

Coping with the liminal space is therefore bound to reach new heights of complexity when something immeasurable, such as God, is to be translated into terms of cognition. A translation of this kind cannot subsume God under frames of reference of whatever persuasion, and this applies equally to all existing forms of theology and philosophy. The latter are of no avail for such an undertaking, as they lie outside what they are set to determine, thus conceptualizing God according to existing beliefs or preconceived notions. Consequently, the immeasurable must be unfolded from inside itself in order to convey what it may be like.

This is exactly the task Franz Rosenzweig undertook in *The Star of Redemption* (1921), which will serve as my final paradigm for interpretation as translatability. Whenever we encounter a major shift in the variables of interpretation, we are alerted to a predicament that throws up new questions that can no longer be met by old answers. The waning authority of the canon gave birth to the hermeneutic circle. The necessity to control entropy, to manage open-endedness, and to conceive of the self-organization of autonomous systems marked the rise of recursive looping as an interpretive strategy. What could have been the issue that seemed to have necessitated a translation of something immeasurable, such as God, the world, and humankind into terms of knowledge?

Rosenzweig describes his task as follows: "Theological problems strive to be translated into man's existence and the latter to be driven into a theological dimension."[2] This existential quest was propelled by Rosenzweig's own experience. *The Star of Redemption*[3] was partly conceived and written in the trenches of the Great War, as was another equally revolutionizing

---

2. Franz Rosenzweig, "Das neue Denken: Einige nachträgliche Bemerkungen zum 'Stern der Erlösung' (1925)," in *Kleinere Schriften* (Berlin: Schocken, 1937), 389; see also Gershom Scholem, "Franz Rosenzweig und sein Buch 'Der Stern der Erlösung,' " in Franz Rosenzweig, *Der Stern der Erlösung*, Bibliothek Suhrkamp (Frankfurt/Main: Suhrkamp, 1988), 529ff.
3. Karl Löwith, "M. Heidegger und F. Rosenzweig: Ein Nachtrag zu *Sein und Zeit*," in *Sämtliche Schriften* (Stuttgart: Metzler, 1984), maintains: "If Heidegger ever had a contemporary, not only in the chronological, but in the true sense of the word, it was this German Jew, whose principle work appeared six years before *Being and Time*. The contemporaneous connection of this 'new way of thinking' between Heidegger and Rosenzweig was not generally recognized at the time, although Rosenzweig was aware of it" (8:72). Scholem, "Franz Rosenzweig," 529, considers Rosenzweig's essay "Das neue Denken" one of the most important philosophical statements that Rosenzweig has made.

book, Wittgenstein's *Tractatus*. It was the trauma caused by the historic catastrophe of the war—which marked the nadir of Western civilization—and the dawn of an inconceivable new era[4] that led Rosenzweig to turn away from an intellectual past rooted in German idealism and made him endeavor to translate what is given in immediate evidence—namely, God—into knowledge. Such an undertaking means no less than grasping evidentiary experiences cognitively.

Whatever is given in evidence is beyond doubt, although more often than not it proves hard to translate such experiences into cognition. Doubling an evidentiary experience by attempting to know what it is may run counter to the economy principle of our human makeup. What is experienced in immediacy is taken for truth, so that there is no need to convert such experiences into knowledge. There are, however, quite a few evidentiary experiences in human life—love, for example—which appear to elude cognition yet make us crave to know what they are, as is borne out not least by literature, which is obsessed with a continual enactment of such evidentiary experiences. It is in the nature of such experiences that we are so wrapped up in them whenever they occur that we find it difficult to untangle ourselves from them. Any attempt to grasp them may risk dissolving their natural spontaneity. It may, however, be our very involvement that powers the drive to come to know what we have experienced.

For Rosenzweig, the existence of God, the world, and humankind are experiential realities given in self-evidence, and yet he makes it quite clear from the outset that he intends no less than to obtain knowledge of what is otherwise only available as evidentiary experience. Coming to know what is given in self-evidence is a fundamental problem of modern times. Helmuth Plessner, for example, states: "We are, but we do not have ourselves."[5] There is no doubt in our minds that we exist, although we do not have knowledge of what such an indubitable experience entails. But why are we driven to know what is given in self-evidence, and what accounts for our reluctance to accept the fact that there are experiences that we are aware of without knowing what they are?

---

4. Stéphane Mosès, *Der Engel der Geschichte: Franz Rosenzweig—Walter Benjamin—Gershom Scholem* (Frankfurt/Main: Suhrkamp, 1994), 18.
5. Helmuth Plessner, "Die anthropologische Dimension der Geschichtlichkeit," in *Sozialer Wandel: Zivilisation und Fortschritt als Kategorien der soziologischen Theorie*, ed. Hans Peter Dreitzel (Neuwied: Luchterhand, 1972), 160.

Rosenzweig addresses such a question in the first sentence of his book, which points to a deeper level of the predicament to which he will respond by developing another variable of interpretation, different from those reviewed so far. The sentence reads: "All cognition . . . originates from the fear of death." All kinds of panaceas intended to alleviate this fear have proved ineffective, especially those proffered by philosophy, the very domain of cognition. Rosenzweig maintains, however, that it is not so much the fear of death that has created the predicament, as philosophy itself, because it has been unable to fulfill its promise "to bear us over the grave which yawns at our feet with every step" (3). And as the stronghold of knowledge and cognition has crumbled, the ensuing predicament can only be met, according to Rosenzweig, by replacing philosophy with an enterprise designed to translate the evidentiary experiences of God, the world, and humankind into knowability. In this respect, Rosenzweig's point of departure is almost a total reversal of what Descartes considered the root of knowledge: it is not the ability to doubt that provides certainty but rather what is beyond doubt. Although the latter eludes our grasp, it has to be targeted by cognition.

For such a task, a variable of interpretation has to be conceived that, in Rosenzweig's words, makes the "course of knowledge" proceed "to ever more profound cognition . . . as a re-creation in thought of the uncreated Being" (229). Such an interpretive enterprise implies first and foremost a heightened awareness of the liminal space, which philosophy not only had been unable to cope with but had simply ignored. Therefore Rosenzweig embarks on a ground-clearing operation by deconstructing philosophy altogether. It is pertinent to note that whenever there is a drastic retooling of interpretive procedures, a dismantling of previous approaches appears to be indispensable in order to highlight the importance of what is now to be advanced. This was already evident when hermeneutics entered the stage: Schleiermacher discarded the tradition of commentary, and Droysen rejected any preconceived philosophy of history. Something similar occurred with recursive looping, when Geertz replaced thin with thick description, and general systems theory replaced the input/output pattern with systemic recursivity. Offsetting one's own point of departure from a negatively conceived foil indicates that interpretation as a technical procedure is guided by an operative intent that gains salience by what it turns away from.

Rosenzweig's deconstruction *avant la lettre* was aimed at the blanket concept advanced by philosophy: namely, that everything there is is encompassed by what is called the All. Such an overriding conception of everything there is has basic flaws. If the concept of the All is meant to counteract the fear of death, it merely glosses over the liminal space that yawns between ourselves and our end. The All therefore is meant to eliminate this space, just as the shifting authority in interpretation eliminated the difference between the canonical text and its reading. In either case, the liminal space is colonized. Moreover, the projection of an All is nothing but an abstraction from everything there is, so that anything individual is either ignored or relegated to insignificance. Philosophy, Rosenzweig maintains, deceives the human being "by weaving the blue mist of its idea of the All about the earthly" (4), only to reveal the All as a construct that in itself is nothing because it cannot be substantiated, thus making philosophy lapse into "cruel lying" (5), as it cannot deliver what it has promised.

If philosophy claims to be able to counteract the fear of death and to master the contingency of the world by projecting its holistic notion of the All beyond which there is nothing, the very projection entails a stance outside the All to enable it to be projected. As such a grandstand view can never be established, the umbrella concept is not tenable and hence falls apart. What such a 'fractured totality' leaves behind are God, world, and humankind, which are immeasurable, or multifarious, or particular. They mark the fallout of the logical impossibility in which philosophy has entrapped itself through its transcendental stance posited outside everything there is. And such an entrapment turns philosophy itself into nothing, not least as philosophy maintains that there is nothing beyond the All.

The same impulse that made philosophy superimpose the blanket concept of the All on everything there is is equally operative in the categories that philosophy continually spins out of itself, testifying to its ultimate intent to provide totalizing conceptualizations for what it organizes. Therefore, when categories are applied to God, world, and humankind, they turn out to be unable to encompass what God, world, and humankind may be like, as these outstrip the limitations imposed on them through categorization. Instead of being subsumed under what has been postulated for their cognition, they themselves figure as overarching dimensions, exceeding the classifications applied to them. Categorizing God, world, and humans in terms of metaphysics, logic, or ethics would ultimately remove their multifariousness by elevating one component into each one's respective be-all and end-all.

Rosenzweig is opposed not only to a specific brand of philosophy—

that is, German idealism, the tradition in which he was trained[6]—but to the basic tenets of philosophy itself. He considers it a philosophical super-stition to believe that reason is geared to being and vice versa. Such an assumption marked for him the congenital defect of philosophy that has plagued it ever since. "Philosophy started only when reasoning wedded itself to being. But it is precisely to philosophy, and precisely at this point, that we deny our allegiance. We seek what is everlasting, what does not first require reasoning in order to be" (20). In disputing this intimate cor-relation between reason and being, Rosenzweig dismantles such an inter-twining on logical grounds, simultaneously highlighting how the failure of philosophy furnishes cognitive proof for his own enterprise. He argues as follows:

> Thus the identity of reasoning and being presupposes an inner non-identity. Though reasoning refers throughout to being, it is at the same time a diversity in itself because it also, at the same time, refers to itself. Thus reasoning, itself the unity of its own inner multiplicity, in addition establishes the unity of being, and that insofar as it is mul-tiplicity, not unity. And therewith the unity of reasoning, as concerned directly only with reasoning, not with being, is excluded from the cosmos of being-reasoning. With its intertwining of the two multi-plicities, this cosmos itself thus has now a unity entirely beyond itself. (13)

And as the cosmos—overarching the alleged identity of reasoning and being—is no longer the be-all and the end-all of modern thought, the existence of God as the "beyond" of the cosmos is the logical inference that Rosenzweig is able to establish by taking apart philosophy's basic tenet of thinking.

With such an argument, Rosenzweig turns into neither a skeptic nor a theologian in his attempt to remedy the deficiencies of philosophy. If he had become a skeptic, he would still have remained a philosopher of a certain traditional persuasion. If he had turned theologian, he would have had to commit himself to a specific religious doctrine. As neither option was an alternative for him, he had to come up with a solution of his own, epitomized by his attempt to translate God and what is dependent on him into cognition.

---

6. See Scholem, "Franz Rosenzweig," 527.

Having thrown down "the gauntlet to the whole honorable company of philosophers from Iona to Jena" (12),[7] Rosenzweig embarks on his enterprise, which sails under the motto: "Our voyage of exploration advances from the Noughts of knowledge to the Aught of knowledge" (19). The pairing of Nought and Aught structures the argument of his entire undertaking and provides the conceptual tools for translating the immeasurable into knowing. The pair of concepts is well chosen: neither of them is a loaded term, and hence they do not carry manifold connotations in their wake, such as often mar the clarity of conceptual language.[8] In order to find out what these words may mean, we need to consult the dictionary, as they have not as yet solidified into terminology. One might even be inclined to say that the words are deliberately not meant to be concepts, because they function as shifters, indicating the transfer of something intangible into perception. Rosenzweig's whole argument pivots around these terms, if one can call them terms at all. For this reason he avails himself of almost all the dictionary meanings these words carry. The entries for "Nought" in *The American Heritage Dictionary* are as follows: (a) nothing, (b) the symbol o, (c) zero, (d) not in the least, (e) no more.

Nought, then, is not nothingness in the sense of an absolute Nothing. And as God, world, and humankind are given in indisputable self-evidence, Nought for Rosenzweig—although indicating initially "the Noughts of knowledge" (19)—is bound to be more complex. Running through the list of dictionary entries, we can already see how the semantic

---

7. See also Mosès, *Engel der Geschichte*, 28.
8. In the German original, the pairing reads "Nichts" (Nought) and "Etwas" (Aught). But as "Nichts" is a loaded term, Rosenzweig elaborates on what is meant by "Nichts": "Wohlgemerkt, wir sprechen nicht wie die frühere Philosophie, die nur das All als ihren Gegenstand anerkannte, von einem Nichts überhaupt. Wir kennen kein eines und allgemeines Nichts, weil wir uns der Voraussetzung des einen und allgemeinen All entschlagen haben. Wir kennen nur das einzelne (deswegen aber nicht etwa bestimmte, sondern nur bestimmungserzeugende) Nichts des einzelnen Problems" (*Stern der Erlösung*, 27). For this reason, Rosenzweig occasionally uses a plural form of "Nichts," which does not exist in German, when he speaks of the "Nichtsen des Wissens" (22). In this respect, the English rendering of "Nichts" by "Nought" avoids all the terminological connotations that the German concept drags in its wake. Even "Aught" for "Etwas" brings out more pointedly the quality that Rosenzweig wanted to convey by "Etwas."

range of Nought can be instrumentalized: (a) as *nothing*, it designates the absence of something; (b) as *symbol* o, it indicates blanks and gaps, which suggest that there is something on either side of them; (c) as *zero*, it signifies nothing and marks the beginning of a series of numbers; (d) as *not in the least*, it points to exclusions; (e) as *no more*, it highlights something that has vanished.

Thus the Nought of knowledge, even when it designates the not-knowing of the immeasurable, appears right from the beginning in Rosenzweig's argument as the opportunity for a manifold demarcation rather than an ultimate limit beyond which there is nothing. Lines of demarcation are bound to vary according to the shades of meaning that Nought assumes in the course of its differential employment. This changeability points to the fact that Nought is not to be mistaken for, or even meant to function as, a concept; instead, metaphorically speaking, it is a chameleon that takes on the hue of its conditional applications, and these are basically modes of transposition.

Something similar applies to the word that Rosenzweig pairs with Nought, outlined right at the beginning in a basic statement that indicates his interpretive thrust: "The Nought is not Nothing, it is Aught" (5). "Aught" also carries a great many meanings. Its dictionary entries are as follows: (a) anything whatever, (b) at all, (c) in any respect, (d) anything, (e) not yet, (f) symbol o, (g) zero.

If the Nought is not nothing but adumbrates an Aught, it highlights one connotation that the two words have in common, namely, zero. If zero marks the point of intersection, we might say that Nought indicates a shift toward zero, whereas Aught indicates an advance from zero. Thus their interlinking results in a sliding scale, which turns the Nought into an operation that reveals something, a something, however, that is still hidden as long as the Nought dominates, although it is contained in it just as any negation harbors a potential affirmation that motivates the negation. Hence Nought is to be translated into an Aught, which means no less than that Nought is of an enabling nature. At this juncture of the argument, a dual coding of Nought already comes to the fore, which is best perceived when viewed within the context from which it has arisen. According to Rosenzweig, as we have seen, philosophy is the Nought of knowledge, evinced by the fact that the All projected by philosophy as a blanket concept makes everything dissolve into abstractions. In this respect, Nought designates zero, because the All as an incomprehensible postulate is nothing. Such a Nought, however, is double-edged insofar as its designation of the All as nothing results in a cancellation of this overriding philosophical concept and thus frees the whole range of what is immeasurable (God), multifarious (world), and particular (humankind), which in turn are the "Noughts of knowledge" as far as philosophy is concerned.[9] Such a Nought is bound to trigger an Aught, thereby propelling an advance from philosophy's Nought of knowledge to an enabling comprehension of 'anything whatever' and thus translating itself into its Aught.

This pairing is fundamental to Rosenzweig's argument, in that it activates a traveling differential between the two terms that turns out to be the hallmark of the interpretive paradigm that he advances. Hence Rosenzweig advocates thinking in terms of relationships instead of positions, postulates, categories, or even concepts. The terms employed for his undertaking are adequate insofar as they do not carry the burden of any traditional meanings in their wake. As terms, they are rather opaque and by no means strictly defined, which, however, enables them to unfold more and more nuances and allows them to spotlight developments in the relationship between them. Therefore Nought and Aught may be conceived first and foremost as operators, and as such they prove to be adequate for the task of converting into knowledge God's immeasurability and what has sprung from it, that is, the world and humans.

My task here is to trace the pattern of interpretation that structures Rosenzweig's attempt to translate the immeasurable into cognition. I am not concerned with the religious dimension of his argument, which issues into a fundamental exposition of Judaism. Instead, I shall confine myself to tracing the architectonics of his argument. As I have done with the interpretive paradigms reviewed so far, I shall focus on the structure according to which a subject matter is transposed into a register and on the extent to which the latter intervenes into the former, with a resultant burgeoning of ramifications. Although the modes of interpretation are always conditioned by the subject matter that they are intended to tackle, they are definitively different from what they are meant to open up. This is particularly true in Rosenzweig's case, as he approaches a religious question in terms not so much of doctrinal belief as of an intricate intertwining between belief and knowledge: "We make belief wholly the content of knowledge, but of a knowledge which itself lays its foundation on a

---

9. Rosenzweig contends: "Of man too we therefore know nothing. And this nothing too is but a beginning, is indeed the beginning of a beginning" (*Star of Redemption*, 63).

fundamental concept of belief. This can only become apparent in the course of the procedure itself, for the fundamental concept of belief cannot be recognized as such until knowledge has arrived at the exposition of belief" (103). Such a distinction makes it possible to separate Rosenzweig's operational mode of interpretation from his commitment to Judaism. Although this is highlighted in *The Star of Redemption*, the strategy of its presentation is not derived from a belief system, but—as Rosenzweig himself claims—from mathematics in the first book, grammar in the second, and ritual in the third (294f.), all of them being structurally unfolded by a traveling differential.

As Nought and Aught are the basic parameters for this undertaking, the first project is to examine how they function and what makes them dovetail. It is Rosenzweig himself who describes the mode operative between them as a traveling differential:

> The differential combines in itself the characteristics of the Nought and the Aught. It is a Nought which points to an Aught, its Aught; at the same time it is an Aught that still slumbers in the lap of the Nought. It is on the one hand the dimension as this loses itself in the immeasurable, and then again it borrows, as the "infinitesimal," all the characteristics of finite magnitude with the sole exception of finite magnitude itself. Thus it draws its power to establish reality on the one hand from the forcible negation with which it breaks the lap of the Nought, and on the other hand equally from the calm affirmation of whatever borders on the Nought to which, as itself infinitesimal, it still and all remains attached. Thus it opens two paths from the Nought to the Aught—the path of affirmation of what is not Nought, and the path of the negation of the Nought. Mathematics is the guide for the sake of these two paths. It teaches us to recognize the origin of the Aught in the Nought. Thus even if Cohen, the master, would be far from admitting it, we are continuing to build on the great scientific achievement of his logic of origins, the new concept of the Nought. (20f)

Now, before elaborating on the operational mode of the differential and the way in which Rosenzweig conceived of its workings, let us once more consider the dictionary entries, not least because Rosenzweig again availed himself of almost all the functions exercised by the differential. This is all the more pertinent as Rosenzweig explicitly took over the differential as a strategy of interpretation from his teacher, Hermann

Cohen, though his use of it was not exactly the same as Cohen's.[10] The word "differential" is defined in the dictionary as: (a) pertaining to or showing difference, (b) constituting or making a difference, (c) dependent on or making use of a difference or a distinction, (d) of or pertaining to differentiation, (e) an infinitesimal increment in a variable. In simultaneously making and using a difference, the differential operates by continually distinguishing and interlinking the Nought as a no-more and the Aught as a not-yet. It draws out into the open the affirmation that each negation harbors as its motivation for the negating act, thus making the negation slide into its Aught, which, in Rosenzweig's words, is "slumbering in the lap of the Nought." In and of itself the differential is neither an entity nor a quantity but rather a "no-thing" (21), just as the "no-more" and the "not-yet" are in and of themselves no-things. The differential only maps out a path along which the Nought is made to reveal the non-Nought that is contained within itself, featured as something still to come.

In order to grasp the operational intent of the differential, we should have a look at Cohen's work, in which he investigated the method of the infinitesimal increment by reviewing it in the light of its history.[11] The differential is fundamentally a realizing operation, which proves to be particularly apt when it comes to conceiving of reality, continuity, or even infinity. These cannot be conceptualized from stances outside themselves, as such an act would imply conferring predicates on them with which they could not be identical. Therefore reality may be nothing but the realization of its existence, which, however, has to be "objectified," as Cohen maintains (98), in order to be apprehended. The differential therefore proves to be the operational mode for unfolding reality as realization. This applies equally to continuity and infinity. Instead of determining what continuity is or might be, the differential realizes continuity insofar as it splits up what is continuous by marking off ever-varying shapes from one another, which in their respective specificity turn into foils for the following shape, thus unfolding continuity through an individually graduated

---

10. Rosenzweig has written extensively on the work of Cohen; see Franz Rosenzweig, "Zum Werk Hermann Cohens," in Der Mensch und sein Werk, Gesammelte Schriften 3, ed. Reinhold Mayer and Annamarie Mayer (Dordrecht: Martinus Nijhoff, 1984), 165–240.
11. Hermann Cohen, Das Prinzip der Infinitesimal-Methode und seine Geschichte: Ein Kapitel zur Grundlegung der Erkenntniskritik (1883; reprint, Frankfurt/Main: Suhrkamp, 1968).

sequence of profiles. Therefore the infinitesimal increment is first and foremost a "principle of movement" (78f.) that splits continuity into a sequence of limited segments, thereby unfurling it as a transition between its discrete divisions. The operational mode of the differential is thus dual in character: it segments continuity and, as it passes between the segments, unfolds continuity as realization, thereby giving presence to a continuum. Something similar applies to infinity, as Cohen has shown (128). Here as elsewhere the movement of the infinitesimal increment dissects infinity into an ever-emerging series of finite scissions (88), thus presenting it as the transition between its divisions or—as Rosenzweig phrased the insight of his "master"—the "infinitesimal" borrows "all the characteristics of finite magnitude with the sole exception of finite magnitude itself." Because the "infinitesimal calculus" operates as "the principle of realization" (209) it cannot be conceived as an entity; instead, as a dissecting movement, the infinitesimal increment replaces all a priori concepts for grasping reality, continuity, and infinity as it travels inside what it draws out into realization. By initiating and driving a movement, the differential functions as a realizing agency or, in Cohen's words, "The differential is distinguished from all kinds of abstractions in that it marks the fundamental beginning and the final competent instance for all those operations, which are united in the objective to generate cognition of whatever is real" (207).[12]

Whereas Cohen intended to 'objectify' cognition by means of the "infinitesimal calculus," Rosenzweig employs the differential as an operative mode for translating God into cognition. Such an interpretive approach prevents him from falling into the trap of philosophy, as he does not have to postulate any conceptualization of God; instead, he uses the traveling differential as a means of grasping God as his own realization. He starts out by maintaining: "Of God we know nothing. But this ignorance is ignorance of God. As such it is the beginning of our knowledge of him—the beginning and not the end" (23). Therefore God cannot be defined as "indefinability," because such an assertion would imply, as Rosenzweig puts it, that atheism and mysticism are to "shake hands" (23). Something similar applies to negative theology, which essentializes

---

12. In reviewing the changing conception of the infinitesimal method, Cohen himself used it in order to unfold the relationship between thinking and perceiving as a process of realization, for which the principle of continuity—basic to the different conceptions of the infinitesimal calculus—provides the central orientation. In this respect, Rosenzweig follows Cohen, though with a shift in emphasis.

ignorance insofar as it identifies God with the Nought of knowledge, resulting in the fatal consequence of turning an Aught, in the sense of "at all," into a Nought.

Therefore another line of reasoning has to be adopted for ascertaining God's essence. The Nought of knowledge is to be taken in its connotation as zero, which ties in with the same connotation of zero in Aught; thus the duality of zero becomes apparent: namely, zero is something not yet defined but enabling definability. Or, in mathematical terms, zero is the number that allows for counting, and counting is the differential unfolding of what numbers are. Counting presupposes the differential—as Cohen has amply demonstrated—and thus converts the number into its realization, which implies not stopping at any point in the process of counting.[13]

As God cannot be nothing, he is bound to be a non-Nought from which an Aught, his Aught, is to "well forth" (28). Rosenzweig thus draws a different logical conclusion from those of atheism, mysticism, negative theology, and philosophy, by uncoupling their Nought of knowledge from the "immeasurable" in order to prevent their ignorance from being conferred on God as his basic attribute. Consequently, the Nought of knowledge cannot be made into God's central qualification. As an ultimate reference, the Nought of knowledge would convert God into nothing, thus phasing him out of existence altogether, although his very existence is experienced by humans as certainty. Therefore the evidentiary experience undercuts the Nought of knowledge and simultaneously demands that what is evident should be grasped. Such a split is the first differentiation according to which God is adumbrated in differential terms.

-----

13. See Cohen, *Das Prinzip*, 87f. Mosès, *Engel der Geschichte*, 72f., quotes portions of a letter that Rosenzweig had written on May 10/11, 1918, to Hans Ehrenberg, at a time when he was already working on *The Star of Redemption*. In the letter he elaborates on the distinction between irrational and rational numbers. For the rational numbers, infinity marks an unreachable limit owing to their linear progression, whereas the irrational numbers create a spatial, nonlinear all-embracing whole. Rosenzweig expands this statement by saying: "Infinity is, as an infinitesimal number, the hidden drive of the rational numbers, which unfold reality into tangibility. Through irrational numbers infinity becomes apparent . . . and yet remains forever alien." What appears as a groping speculation at this juncture of Rosenzweig's thinking is later on conceived as a special operation of the differential that, as a geometric point, unfolds realization of infinity by means of conversion, thus allowing us to conceive of the differential as a nonlinear movement.

The differential, as Rosenzweig has noted, "loses itself in the immeasurable"; however, in doing so, it invades the immeasurable, thus making it into the subject matter of interpretation. "Losing itself" is a delicate expression for the penetration of what the register is meant to make available, and it also reveals that the differential operation tries to open up the immeasurable for cognition from inside itself. The first step for such an undertaking is the distinction between "Yea" and "Nay," which feature as "root words" (126f.) for God's differential unfolding (28).

> The Nay is just as original as the Yea. . . . The original Nay presupposes nothing but the Nought. It is the Nay of Nought. Now of course it is true that it bursts forth directly from the Nought, bursts forth, that is, as its negation, and no Yea precedes it; but an affirmation does precede it. In other words: while it presupposes only the Nought, the Nought it presupposes is a Nought from which the Yea had to well forth, not a Nought with which it could have let the matter rest. . . . Therefore the affirmation of the non-Nought circumscribes as inner limit the infinity of all that is not Nought. An infinity is affirmed: God's infinite essence.
>
> (28, 26f.)

The infinite essence is disclosed as a Yea, which arises out of the Nay of Nought, and thus makes the Nay and the Yea coeval, not least because God's essence could not be the one or the other. However, the dovetailing of Nay and Yea nonetheless establishes a distinction, and this proliferates into infinite differentiations, in the sense once detailed by Gregory Bateson, who stated in another context that "it is the difference that makes a difference."[14] As self-differentiation, God's essence is translated into "his infinite actuality, his Physis" (27), which manifests itself by issuing into an array of multifarious possibilities.

The differential operative between the Nay and the Yea keeps God clear from any particular human projection and allows us to unfold his infinity as realization. The latter becomes tangible through the operative drive of the differential, which "loses itself in the immeasurable" and simultaneously "borrows as the infinitesimal all the characteristics of finite magnitude with the sole exception of finite magnitude itself" (20). Every possibility emerging from the "infinite actuality" of God's Physis appears

---

14. Gregory Bateson, *Steps to an Ecology of Mind* (New York: Ballantine, 1972), 315.

to be determinate and finite, and yet the infinity is operative in the potentially endless differentiation. Thus the differential permits us to perceive how God's "arch-nay . . . now emerges anew no longer as Nay but as Yea," for "God can have no attributes at all prior to his emergence from himself" (113).

In order to grasp this emergence, language is of paramount importance for Rosenzweig, as thought and language are intimately wedded. Therefore he makes it quite clear that cognition of the immeasurable can only be achieved through "the real employment of language [which is] the center-piece as it were of this entire book" (174).[15]

God would never have become an experiential reality for humans if he had not affirmed his non-Nought, that is, his not being nothing. Therefore the affirmation of not being nothing is the first differentiation according to which God's immeasurability is adumbrated in differential terms. However, the non-Nought requires an act in order to become apparent. Such an act is to be conceived as God's freedom, because the affirmation of his not being nothing made him abandon his concealment. Still, the question remains why he did it. Stepping out of his hiddenness can only be qualified as God's "infinite caprice" (30). "For there is caprice, not in the creator's act of creation, but prior to it in the self-configuration of God

---

15. On language, Rosenzweig writes: "Though language is rooted in the subterranean foundations of being with the arch-words, it already shoots upward into the light of the terrestrial life in these root-words, and in this light it blossoms forth into colorful multiplicity. . . . Yet it is distinguished from this life precisely because it does not move capriciously over the surface, but rather sinks roots into the dark foundations beneath life" (145f.). For Rosenzweig's conception of language, see Klaus Reichert, " 'It Is Time': The Buber-Rosenzweig Bible Translation in Context," in *The Translatability of Cultures: Figurations of the Space Between*, ed. Sanford Budick and Wolfgang Iser (Stanford: Stanford University Press, 1996), 169–185. Reichert places both Buber's and Rosenzweig's language in the cultural environment of the twenties and concludes by characterizing their Bible translation as follows: "The paradox remains . . . to invent a language that is at one and the same time thoroughly Hebrew and the embodiment of a German that never existed, but might come into existence, be revealed, in the act of creation. A veritable utopian design: to be a Jew *and* a German, self and other, without appropriation" (185). See also Löwith, "M. Heidegger und F. Rosenzweig," 76f., where the author elaborates on the importance of language, which Rosenzweig shares with Heidegger; both of them practice in their principal works a "grammatical thinking."

which precedes his act of creation" (115). In terms of a differential interpretation, caprice is the originary event, which resists translatability but
sets the differential in motion. If the originary differentiation is unfathomable, it nevertheless converts its untranslatability into an unceasing
drive that produces multifarious translations.

God's abandonment of his hiddenness through the exercise of his freedom turns the negation of his concealment into a revelation of his essence
through which his self-negating Nought issues forth into an Aught of infinite configurations. "That which had struggled to the surface out of God's
'Nought' as self-negation of this Nought, re-emerged from its immersion in
God's living 'Aught,' no longer as self-negation, but rather as world-affir-
mation" (157). Thus God's Aught presents itself as emergence, articulated
by an endlessly proliferating sequence of ever-new profiles of his essence
through which the concealed God, by abandoning his hiddenness, unveils
the "vitality" of his Physis (157). The latter becomes manifest in the creation. Consequently, the creation is not an unfathomable fiat but is God's
transmutation of his hiddenness into his "infinite actuality" by making his
self-negating Nought spawn his Aught as limitless possibilities.

The differential may facilitate such a translation of God's essence into
his Physis, as manifested in the unforeseeable diversity of the creation,
and thus enables the initial phase of his realization to be conceived. It is
the basic operative drive of the differential "to lose itself in the immeasurable" and by making inroads convert the immeasurable into the graspable idea of God's self-negating Nought. In doing so, it simultaneously
"borrows as an infinitesimally operating variable all the characteristics of
finite magnitude," thus segmenting God's immeasurable essence into
infinitesimal increments of ever-varying shapes, which can be grasped,
although none of them is representative of the creation and each of them
remains enigmatic in its singularity. Therefore every possibility that
unfolds the infinite actuality of God's Physis is determinate and finite,
and yet infinity is operative in the potentially limitless differentiation of
what has become manifest.

Thus the differential draws out God's essence into a sliding scale, allowing us to ascertain how his self-negating of not being nothing—his non-
Nought—shifts into his being "at all": his Aught. Only such an unending
sequence permits God to be translated into perception, which means, as
Rosenzweig puts it, "gingerly [making] our way along the tightrope of the
consciousness of cognition" (88). As the differential is only a mode of translation, it must not be mistaken for an ontological qualification of God's
essence; instead, as an operating agent it is meant to give presence to

essence. In order to achieve such conceivability, the Aught that "wells forth" from the non-Nought has to be presented in terms of performance. Only when the Aught is performed is it not determined by anything outside itself; rather, it gains presence as realization of itself. For this reason, the traveling differential is nothing but a shifter for setting such realization in motion; as an infinitesimal increment it is not an entity but only functions as the unfolding operator that turns the Aught into performance.

In this respect, Rosenzweig is in harmony with Hermann Cohen, who qualified the differential—in spite of the fact that it is called an infinitesimal increment—not as a unit but as "a principle of movement" that, by continually dissecting what it unfurls, proceeds as a "delimiting movement."[16]

Thus far the differential as an interpretive mode permits us to translate God's essence into a realizing performance, but this does not as yet indicate the mode of operation according to which the realization develops. In addressing this problem, Rosenzweig introduces a conception of the differential that, as he says earlier on, might not have met with the "master's" approval. The differential is now further detailed as the point of conversion (*Umkehr* in the German original) between the concealed and the revealed God. It is the "geometric point . . . of the two segments of the divine Nought, the arch-yea, and the arch-nay; and the conversion can only be comprehended as the reversal of the directions, which, then, converged in the one case and diverged in the other" (157). This additional qualification of the differential as a geometric point still functions as a "principle of movement" that, however, assumes its specificity by separating "the two segments of the divine Nought" and simultaneously feeding them into one another. The duality of differentiating and intertwining makes the geometric point look "like the point (x y) within a system of co-ordinates, . . . which is defined only as the point of departure of directions," whereas it "is not defined" as "the end point (o) of a system of co-ordinates" (157f.). In other words, it is determinate through its separation of the two segments but indeterminate as regards the outcome of its intertwining. Now Rosenzweig's specification of the differential becomes apparent. As the "principle of movement" (Cohen), the differential does not proceed in a linear direction; its specification as a geometric point turns it into a countervailing movement by interlinking what it has separated. Thus the principle of movement operates as a principle of conversion: The Nay converts through

16. Cohen, *Das Prinzip*, 78f.

its negation into God's non-Nought, and the Yea converts through its affirmation into God's abandoning his concealment.

What does such a geometric point allow us to perceive in terms of cognition? Nay and Yea will not stay the same whenever such a conversion occurs. Rosenzweig contends: "This conversion, however, lacks a name; it is no more than, as it were, the geometric point out of which the emergence takes place" (157). Emergence is the decisive word, because it indicates that something is always brought about whenever different systems are coupled with one another, as is the case with the Yea and Nay. Thus the differential unfolding of God's essence proceeds as his realization but simultaneously structures the latter as a continual *Umkehr* of those systems that it has marked off from one another. Such a conversion is necessary, because whatever the differential unfolds of God's essence bears the inscription of finite magnitude, whose inherent limitations call for reversals.

As a principle of movement, the infinitesimal increment functions as a delimiting operation, allowing Rosenzweig to translate God's essence into a self-performing realization. As a geometric point, it marks the interstice between segments, which it converts both into their reverse side and into one another, thus allowing Rosenzweig to spell out realization as boundless emergence. What the differential as a principle of movement proceeding as a principle of conversion highlights is a differentiation of the differential itself. The basic reason for this is that the immeasurable cannot be qualified in terms of predicates, which would have to be conferred from the outside.[17] Thus the differential turns out to be the counterconcept to predication when the immeasurable is to be brought within comprehension.

Emergence requires specification, if the realization of God's Physis is to be made tangible. Therefore the differential must again be differentiated in order to permit the translation of God's infinite actuality into cognitive terms. The necessary shift in the differential occurs when the world—just as "incommensurable" as God and man (398)—has to be made comprehensible in terms of its differential realization. What Rosenzweig calls the being of the world is its "Everywhere and Ever" (43), and we as humans are in the world just as the world is within us. What prevents the "Everywhere and Ever" from being locked up in "the nocturnal prison of the Nought" is "the plenitude of visions." "But the emergence of

---

17. Rosenzweig therefore maintains: "God can have no attributes at all prior to his emergence from himself" (113).

plenitude from Nought is here again something different from the previous emergence of the world-logos," which issued from God as an actuality of his Physis. Consequently, the wall of this prison is continually penetrated by the fact that

> everything new is a new negation of the Nought, a never-before, a new start unto itself, something unheard of, something "new under the sun." Here the force of the negation of Nought is infinite, but every individual effect of this force is finite; the fulness is infinite, the vision finite. The individual phenomena emerge from the night, baseless and aimless. Whence they are coming or whither going has not been inscribed on their foreheads: they simply exist. But in existing they are individual, each a one against all others, each distinguished from all others, "particular," "not-otherwise."   (45)

What is it that makes the "Everywhere and Ever" continually unfold and emerge with a new distinctiveness of this and not otherwise? It is the logos that demonstrates "a new side of the effectiveness of the original Yea" (44) as its application to the world converts the featurelessness of the "Everywhere and Ever" into specificity. Thus the application of the logos gives birth to the world's plenitude that "bursts forth in its individual result as a thoroughgoing miracle, with the overwhelming force of the unpredicted, the unpredictable" (49). Such an operation in turn translates the logos into a vivid perception, allowing us to grasp its seminal character, which is indicative of God's Physis as manifested in the creation. Furthermore, God's infinite actuality thus translates into the self-specification of the world, which therefore features the "Everywhere and Ever" in its unforeseeably emerging individuality.

This differential self-specification of the world is a further step toward making perceivable the otherwise abstract character of God's essence as realization. Such perception in turn is indispensable insofar as grasping God in cognitive terms prohibits any conferral of predicates on him. Consequently, Rosenzweig even refrains from equating God with truth (390), which, as a predication, presupposes an overarching view that is bound to be beyond this attribution. God's essence can only be conceived as a graduated sequence of ever-new shapes of its realization, drawn out through the world into terms of a comprehensible self-differentiation. Therefore Rosenzweig writes of the world: "God's essence has vanished in his deed, a deed wholly in-essential, wholly real, wholly proximate, in his love. And this his wholly manifest act of loving now enters

space, freed as that is from the rigidity of essence, and fills it to every far-
thest corner." (390)

Again the function of the differential changes when man is moved into
focus. "Of man too," Rosenzweig contends, " we . . . know nothing. And
this nothing too is but a beginning, is indeed but the beginning of a beginning. In him too the primeval words awaken; the Yea of the creation, the
Nay of generation, and the And of configuration" (63). The existence of
man vis-à-vis God and the world is, according to Rosenzweig, ephemeral,
which he illustrates by a quotation from Goethe: "What distinguishes
gods from men? That many waves walk before the former—us the wave
lifts, the wave swallows, and we sink away" (63). This turns ephemerality
into the hallmark of man, which, however, as the And between the Yea
and the Nay, links him up with what he is distinguished from, and this
intermediate position between Nay and Yea takes him into endless configurations of himself. Being ephemeral marks human existence as one of
total isolation, and the essence of humans can only be unfolded by negating this ephemerality—just as God negated his essence of being hidden—
and such a self-negating Nought manifests itself as volition through which
humans exercise their freedom. The latter, however, is limited: "Human
freedom in contrast to divine freedom is denied capability in its very origin, but its volition is as unconditional, as boundless, as the capacity of
God" (66).

What direction is taken by this boundless and unconditional volition
that has sprung from the non-Nought of human essence? Its main thrust
is defiance of its own particularity. In this respect, it is marked by a duality insofar as it reaches out toward an otherness but simultaneously remains
inextricably tied to its isolated individuality, which can never be left
behind.

The differential has to present human essence as its realization, and so
it begins to travel as the delimiting movement between "a no more" and
"a not yet," thus highlighting its apparent destination, which is every
human being's aim: to become "his self" (68). However, the self never
consolidates into an identifiable, let alone ultimate, shape. Instead, it
passes through endless configurations of itself. None of "them becomes
its property. Even what is its very own, its character, its peculiarity, it
retains in name only. In truth no recognizable portion of it remains to it
in its passage through the configurations" (79). Thus the " 'selfication' of
his self" (78), as Rosenzweig calls it, proliferates into a continual recon-
figuration. Each individual manifestation of such an unfolding sequence
of 'selfing' is nothing but a transition, leading to another shape of the self

that 'man' is set to become. Because each individual shape of these configurations remains transient, the non-Nought of man's essence is drawn
out into ever-new configurations. This course on which 'man' has
launched himself turns him, grammatically speaking, into the 'copula'
that interlinks the Nay and the Yea; by making them shade into one another, the self is highlighted as forever dispersing into a differential of itself.
Such a differential makes tangible the sense that man was created in God's
image (155).

Proliferating Translatability

The differential operations demonstrated thus far allow us to perceive
how incommensurabilities are translated into cognitive terms. God's
Physis became apparent through the differential as a geometric point,
which converted the Arch-Nay into a negation of the non-Nought, and
the Arch-Yea into an affirmation of abandoning concealment. Thus the
differential unfolds the inherent duality of the root words as an emergence of God's Physis in infinite actuality, which it articulates as realization in terms of performance. Initially, the differential is conceived as an
adumbration of an Aught in a Nought, thus opening up an interplay
between what it simultaneously separates. As an operative agent it is
bound to become differentiated itself when the switch is made from the
differential unfolding of God's essence to those of world and man, not
least as the differential is dependent on what it separates and interlinks.
If God's essence is differentiated into his infinite actuality, such a self-
differentiation translates into a continual self-specification of the world's
distinctness that, in its individuality of this and not otherwise, unfurls
finite distinctness into ever-new variations. This process is endless.
Hence the differential realization of the world's essence allows us to conceive infinity as spawning unforeseeable specifications of itself. Once
again, the differential is made to operate differently in the unfolding of
human essence, whose realization appears as an unending sequence of
transient configurations, none of which can ever be identified with the
self, because the shifting shapes "only lead deeper into the silence of the
interior" (80). This graduated differentiation of the differential is in itself
nothing but an operational mode that, however, appears to be the only
mode available when it comes to translating immeasurability into cognition. Ranging from God's infinite actuality through the world's distinctness to the transient configurations of the human self, the differential, in

dissecting essence, converts it into a series of discrete profiles. These profiles, however, are continually telescoped into one another, not least as none of them can be identical to what they segment. The telescoping and the segmenting are simultaneous, which makes the differential operate as a continuously delimiting movement. The infinitesimal increment is therefore not a quantity but an agent of motion, a motion, however, that draws its impetus from the linking of what it has separated, thereby ceaselessly shading one scission into another. God's essence is thus given presence as the realization of itself; this self-realization translates into the continual self-specification of the world and equally into the shifting configurations of the human self.

Such an interrelationship, however, poses a new problem for a differential unfolding of God's essence. So far, God, world, and humankind appear to be only elements of a process. "Not man alone but God too and so too the world are each of them a solitary self, each staring fixedly into itself and knowing of no Without" (84). At first glance, it seems as if Rosenzweig is contradicting himself in view of the argument advanced in the first book of *The Star of Redemption*. After all, God's Physis as infinite actuality has manifested itself in the creation, of which world and humankind provide the most tangible experience. There is still a prevailing tendency to take the three elements as "three Wholes," but this turns out to be unacceptable, as "three Alls are unthinkable. And so the question of their relationship must be asked after all" (84). In so doing, "it is necessary to cure those elements of their subterranean fragmentation, to articulate them, to transport them out of their mutual exclusiveness into a free-flowing interrelationship, to 'emerge' upward once more instead of 'submerging' in the night of positivism" (87). How is one to conceive such an emergence, which overarches the elements that have become tangible in the act of creation? As we have seen, creation arose out of the non-Nought of God's essence, which, as God's Physis, is infinite actuality, but as such it is now there. If taken in isolation, the creation is an event of the past, which would mean, "God threatened to lose himself again behind the infinity of creation. He appeared to become mere 'origin' of creation and therewith once more the concealed God after all, just what he ceased to be by virtue of the creation" (160). This might even be corroborated by an "earthly analogy," as death is "the capstone of creation" that "stamps every created thing with the ineradicable stamp of creatureliness, the word 'has been' " (156). If it were to stay this way, creation would turn into a predicate conferred on God the Creator, who has vanished behind his work and thus is no longer present as an emerging realization of himself.

At best he would have to be qualified as *deus absconditus*, which again points to an assumed stance outside God for the purpose of defining him. In order to cognize creation as a tangible stage in the process of realizing God's essence, creation itself has to be made conceivable in differential terms. Therefore Rosenzweig contends: "The created death of the creature portends the revelation of a life which is above the creaturely level. For each created thing, death is the very consummator of its entire materiality. It removes creation imperceptibly into the past, and thus turns it into the tacit, permanent prediction of the miracle of its renewal" (155). And Rosenzweig details the miracle again in differential terms by saying: "Prediction, the expectation of a miracle, always remains the actual constitutive factor, while the miracle itself is but the factor of realization" (96). In other words, the "miracle of renewal" marks out the space between "a no more" and "a not yet," which unfolds the creation as prophecy, thus turning it into a continual presence of God, as God the Creator realizes himself as God the Revealer (165). "In its groundless presentness, revelation must now permanently touch the ground. This ground lies beyond its presentness, that is, in the past, but revelation itself renders it visible only from out the presentness of experience. . . . The creation which becomes visible in revelation is creation of the revelation" (182f.). By being grounded in a past, the presentness of revelation gains its tangible reality.

Creation itself is now to be unfolded through a geometric point, which, as I have indicated, operates by way of conversion: the death of creatureliness converts into a prediction of what is to come, and its pastness into a ground for revelation. Rosenzweig goes to great lengths in order to detail the emergence of revelation out of creation, which proceeds by ever-new translations of God's presence into human experience, especially through love. "It is love which meets all the demands here made on the concept of the revealer, the love of the lover, not that of the beloved. Only the love of the lover is such a continually renewed self-sacrifice; it is only he who gives himself away in love" (162). Such a statement is undeniably a *theologoumenon*. However, Rosenzweig does not posit it as a religious conviction but extrapolates it from God's initial Nay of his non-Nought, which in human terms can only be grasped as "a continually renewed self-sacrifice" through which God's "caprice"—in itself an incommensurable act of divine freedom—is translated into the human orbit. Such a translation in turn has repercussions on the human situation. In being loved, the "soul awakes" and "makes acknowledgement before God's countenance and thereby acknowledges and attests God's being; therewith God too, the manifest God, first attains being" (182). If revelation, in the first instance, sprang from a conversion of creation's pastness into an ever-renewed differentiation of the world's individuality and equally into an ever-shifting configuration of the self, it now gains its experiential reality through the acknowledgment of God's self-sacrifice, which, in turn, caused the "soul" to emerge "from the seclusion of the self into the open" (206).

Revelation thus assumes a threefold qualification: It is the negation of God's concealment, which, as a self-sacrifice, can only be an act of love through which God attains reality for the human soul. Revelation is again unfolded through the differential operating in terms of geometric points that convert what they have separated into their reverse side: God's concealment into self-sacrifice, the human self into the awakening of the soul, and God's self-imposed confinement through the assumption of his Physis (178) into an experiential reality for the soul.

If creation was an occurrence of the past and revelation is the manifestation of God's presence, then redemption will be God's future. Just as revelation emerged out of creation by converting death into renewal, redemption will emerge out of revelation. "God is a Redeemer in a much graver sense than he is Creator or Revealer. For he is not only the one who redeems, but also the one who is redeemed. In the redemption of the world by man, of man by means of the world, God redeems himself. Man and world disappear in the redemption, but God perfects himself. Only in redemption, God becomes the One and All" (238). Redemption converts revelation into its reverse side insofar as revelation manifests God's presence in terms of evidentiary experience, whereas redemption configures God's reality as plenitude.

Now Rosenzweig's polemics against philosophy comes full circle. The All as plenitude emerges at the end and could never have been present amid the world's diversity. On the contrary, the diversification of what there is, which the philosophically postulated All was supposed to encompass, had to be redeemed of its singularity by making it disappear into plenitude.

Rosenzweig conceived of the sequence of creation—revelation—redemption as "*Bahn*," thus pointing out both their distinction and their interlinkage. The English translation of the German *Bahn* is "course," but this term screens off important connotations that are pertinent for Rosenzweig's differential articulation of God. *Bahn* does not mean "course" in the sense of "cursus." As such, it would indicate something that runs full circle, which would imply a hidden telos. Instead, it highlights an unfolding that does not head in a specific direction. Although creation, revelation, and redemption provide God with a shifting salience, God himself does not run a course; *Bahn* is rather a differential articulation of what the immeasurable has always been but that has to be translated into conceivable terms. *Bahn* is itself a translation insofar as it provides a concretization of what the immeasurable—which is only to be perceived in terms of its realization—may entail.

God is plenitude; however, the sheer postulation of this is ungraspable, so that only a differential unfolding offers access to it. The sequence of creation, revelation, and redemption translates plenitude as its realization into human terms. Therefore redemption, as an act through which God redeems himself, is a return into his beginning, through which the differential also articulates redemption as a geometric point. If the concept of *Bahn* is meant to draw out plenitude into a sequence of stages, which inevitably transpose God into terms of temporality, then each of these stages must itself be marked by conversion (*Umkehr*), otherwise God would assume the characteristics of a developing Hegelian Spirit. Therefore the differential as geometric point dissects each of these stages into a countervailing movement. If *Bahn* initially suggests a course, as the English rendering has it, then a Hegelian qualification of God tends to become prominent, whereas *Bahn* presents itself in all its strangeness as an unfolding that proceeds in reversals. These reversals highlight the fact that plenitude cannot be conceived as temporal development but has to be inscribed into such a sequence by an inherent conversion that is operative at each stage. Thus the differential as a principle of movement exercises a dual function: it unfolds God's essence as its realization and simultaneously unfolds each of these stages as self-conversion, thus erasing their apparent temporality and giving plenitude its experiential presence.

If the All appears to become present at the end, this seemingly temporal qualification of its occurrence bears witness to the fact that God could not be identified with its realization, which, as a differential unfolding, is only a mode of translation and not a predicate. Plenitude is ever present, and dating its happening marks the final difference between the immeasurable and its conceivability in human terms. In other words, it indicates the residual untranslatability of Rosenzweig's effort to translate God into cognition.

Here as elsewhere untranslatability powers the drive to overcome it, even if this can only be done symbolically, as expressed in Rosenzweig's understanding of the Star of David. The two triangles of the star make the trajectory mapped out so far intersect:

[If] the first three points correspond to the elements God, world, man, then the three new points would have to stand for the trajectories creation, revelation, redemption, and the triangle which they formed would have to be so situated as not to end up with the first triangle. . . . The connection from one point to the other two must cross in its own turn the line of the original triangle so that the two triangles intersect . . . . Thus there arises a structure in the form of a star which now retroactively transforms the geometric elements of which it is constituted into configurations as well. (256)

The Star of David thus becomes an embodiment of manifold functions. First of all, the star is the symbolic diagram of the register that is to open up access to God and translate him into cognition. It is symbolically conceived insofar as no pragmatic decision guides the interpretation of God's essence; instead, it has to be given presence as realization. Therefore the two structures employed for such an enterprise have to be coupled, not least as the one separates the immeasurable into its elements, which the other has to interlink. Both, however, operate by dissecting a potential in order to be able to feature it as realization. What is thus unfolded has to be folded back on itself, without undoing the function exercised by the traveling differential. This makes the "figures," as Rosenzweig contends, into a "configuration," and the latter can no longer be presented in terms of "geometric elements" but is bound to become a "demathematized configuration" (256).

The configuration, however, can only be symbolically rendered in order to assume tangibility. Moreover, the symbolic quality of the register marks a final stand against the translation of God's essence into cognition. Thus the liminal space between God and cognition of him—caused by the effort of interpretation—inscribes itself into the register by transforming it into a symbol that, in the final analysis, indicates its insurmountable separation from what it appears to make present.

As a configuration, the Star of David embodies the interpretive register as a means of access to God's essence and simultaneously transposes that essence into human terms. It comprises the multifarious levels of translatability, whose proliferations indicate that there is no conceivable end to the transmutation of the matter in hand. Therefore Rosenzweig states: "The protocosmos contained only the mute elements of which the course of the Star was built. The course itself was a reality but at no moment to be seen by the eyes. For the Star which runs this course never stands still even for the batting of an eye. Only what endures more than one batting can be seen by the eyes, and only that moment which has been arrested by its eternalization permits the eyes to perceive the structure in it. Structure is thus more than elemental, more than real; it is directly subject to perception" (295). Thus the duality of the star as a representation of the interpretive register becomes apparent. Structure implies the need to cope with uncertainty, and so any interpretive register is bound to have structure. What concerns us here is of a heightened dynamics, which makes both elements and course appear as proliferating self-specifications on which the eye can never rest. What the eye is given to perceive is the structure of this trajectory, however, through which the traveling differential makes the segments it has separated convert into one another. Thus the differential as the operating structure that unfolds both the elements and the course as well as their interconnection renders essence as its realization perceptible to the human eye.

The symbolic substance of the Star runs as an all-pervading feature through Rosenzweig's interpretive paradigm, specifying and ramifying the translation of God into an ever-expanding multiformity of human cognition. As mentioned earlier, each of the three books of *The Star of Redemption* privileges a special mode of translation. Mathematics provides the level for transposing the elements, grammar for transposing the course, and liturgy for transposing the presence of plenitude into cognitive terms. The elements are displayed as an ever-increasing individuation; the course as perpetual translatability; and plenitude as illimitable differentiation. On each of these levels, the respective translation is fine-tuned, thus making the modes themselves proliferate into ramified specifications of what they allow us to grasp. Such a multifarious translatability issues into a continual differentiation of the register, so that one might be inclined to speak of several registers, whose multiplicity is meant to draw out into conceivability what the previous translation did not allow us to see.

Such perpetual translatability is revealing in two respects. First, an interpretive register is bound to increase its structural diversity in proportion to the complexity of the subject matter to be interpreted. If it is designed to open access to something immeasurable, the latter will cause a nuanced sophistication of those terms into which it is to be translated. Thus a traveling differential becomes operative inside the register itself, translating the realization of essence into a continual self-specification of segments brought to bear for cognition. Second, through such a process, cognition can no longer be conceived in terms of unifying conceptualizations that are superimposed on what has to be cognized. Therefore presuppositions, categories, or postulates, let alone encompassing ideas such as the All, as monistic principles are implicitly exposed for what they are: namely, pragmatically oriented intentions that are in themselves situationally and historically conditioned. Cognition has to become multiform if it is to be successful vis-à-vis a subject matter that cannot be subsumed under what has been posited for its comprehension. Translating God into cognition is thus bound to transform cognition into a continually increasing assembly of viewpoints, each of which must give way to another because of its inherent limitations.

In the final analysis, Rosenzweig's discourse itself is permeated with this awareness. Committed though he is to demonstrating how the differential as a principle of movement enables us to conceive of the immeasurable as its realization, he nevertheless appears to be under the ineluctable obligation to provide corroborative evidence for what the traveling differential makes transparent. This is why *The Star of Redemption* is permeated by historical examples, mainly taken from the great world religions, mythology, and idealistic philosophy, in order to spotlight what happens when the differential unfolding of God's essence does not originate from the Nay of his non-Nought and the Yea of abandoning his concealment.

Brahma, Nirvana, or Tao, as the distinguishing prime constituents in Asian religions, "come to a halt in the forecourts of Yea and Nay" (57). The "veil of Maya . . . allowed only the 'self' to count and dissolved this self in turn in the solitude of the Brahmin" (57f.). In "the doctrine of Buddha . . . the entire world generated by . . . cognition and volition, including its gods and its essence, is at last suspended into the Nought. The Nought? No, here too we prefer to avoid a term which yet contains a residuum of positivism, and to speak instead of a realm beyond cognition and noncognition. Again we have reached a point just short of the limit of the Nought and withal far to the rear of the infinite universality of cognition, which negates the Nought and thus infinitely affirms itself" (58). And "Lao-tzu reached behind the all-too-visible, all-too-busy, all-too-industrious, all-too-regulated world of Confucius and, without denying its essential reality, seeks the root and source of all this headlong industry. All the fullness of action springs from this source of in-action" (59). These fundamental concepts of the great Asian religions have one feature in common in that all of them designate a realm that lies beyond God, who is thus dwarfed by what these prime constituents have reified. The world—and what else exists—is either made to pale into nothingness or is generated out of an inconceivable emptiness. Apart from the realms postulated by each of these religions as the be-all and end-all that exists beyond God, cognition of these fundamentals is utterly impossible, not least as cognition is either one of the mundane features to be dissolved or a helpless gesture in the attempt to grasp the elusive emptiness. This in turn testifies to the great importance Rosenzweig attaches to cognition as an effort that allows humans to conceive of the immeasurable, because what is beyond conceivability may either fade into insignificance or lead to an hypostatization of the initial Nought of knowledge into an attribute of God, thus shifting him out of the orbit of human concerns altogether.

Furthermore, what the Asian religions are unable to specify is how self and world dwindle into dissolution or nothingness or how emptiness translates itself into action. In other words, Rosenzweig's prime concern (i.e., how God's translation into the world and humankind and once again into a differential unfolding of creation-revelation-redemption[18] can be made graspable) is bracketed or at best remains concealed.

On the very same ground he challenges the Greek philosophers. "Within the world . . . Plato himself as well as Aristotle teach no emanatory relation, no active relation at all, between idea and phenomenon, between concept and thing, between category and individual or whatever terms may capture the contrast. Rather we have here the odd idea that things 'imitate' the idea, that they 'look out' for it, 'yearn' for it, 'develop' into or toward it, though it is 'purpose' not cause" (53).

The great many negative examples that permeate Rosenzweig's discourse are meant to reveal the reverse side of his own interpretive enterprise. In the various religions and different brands of philosophy he discusses, a specific reification occurs, which is elevated to an overarching principle. In Greek religion, for instance, the gods are nothing but an hypostatization of humans, whose qualities are mirrored by the Olympians. It is somewhat different in Islam: "Mohammed's creator is 'wealthy without any world.' . . . He proves his power, like an Oriental despot, not by creating what is necessary, . . . but in his freedom for the capricious act" (117), thus hypostatizing, according to Rosenzweig, one of God's features that is responsible for setting the differential shift between Nay and Yea in motion.

---

18. Rosenzweig describes this relationship as follows: "In reality creation, revelation, and redemption are not categories. Categories never form a sequence among themselves. At most they can lay the foundations on which such a sequence can be formed in reality. As the sequence creation-revelation-redemption, however, creation, revelation, and redemption are themselves a reality, and it is a concession to the idealistic mode of thinking if we place commas between them instead of hyphens" (189).

Without going into further details, hypostatizations—irrespective of whether they occur in religions, theologies, or philosophies—replace God as the be-all and end-all and move their respective, universally constitutive principles beyond comprehension. Consequently, hypostatization indicates where interpretation ceases. At the same time, it appears to be impossible to account for these multifarious hypostatizations, although they seem to be first and foremost reifications of human urges, desires, experiences, ideas, and aspects or viewpoints elevated to the status of a totalizing explanation. This, however, leaves the reason for the generation of these self-produced hypostatizations inexplicable, and hence the question remains: why do humans create an unfathomableness to which they subordinate themselves?

Such an anthropological question is no longer Rosenzweig's concern; instead, the negative examples, which in the final analysis include Christianity as well as the arts, serve him as analogies for his own enterprise. The reason for invoking them is twofold: First, in spite of their diversity, all of them are marked by the reification of principles, ideas, aspects, or postulates, and thus feature as counterconcepts to the traveling differential. Reification moves the incommensurable beyond comprehension, whereas the differential allows us to unfold it as its realization. Reifications bring the traveling differential to a standstill and in doing so mark the point at which the unfolding of the incommensurable has been arrested. Second, such a decisive contrast turns all the specified reifications into negative foils in order to spotlight how the differential as a principle of movement, operating as a nonlinear movement of conversions, translates the immeasurable into terms of cognition. In negotiating the chasm that yawns between the immeasurable and cognition, the traveling differential is not overarched by any third dimension. Lacking such a referential status, the string of reifications that permeates Rosenzweig's exposition from beginning to end functions as a "route of reference"[19] meant to illuminate what a differential interpretation is able to achieve when it comes to grasping the immeasurable. For this reason, reifications accompany the unending translation effected by the differential, not least as they mark, in each individual case invoked, why and how the movement of the infinitesimal increment has been stalled. The kinds of reifications in which the

---

19. "Routes of reference" is a concept advanced by Nelson Goodman, *Of Mind and Other Matters* (Cambridge: Harvard University Press, 1984), 36, 55–71, 136f., in order to indicate the function of referential criteria and the interchange among their functions.

essence of God, world, and humans has been imprisoned then becomes apparent, as all of them are predications conferred on the immeasurable from stances outside it. Therefore Rosenzweig opts for and develops a differential mode of interpretation, because the differential is never outside what it differentiates, is never a stance from which predications are made, and is never a category to be superimposed on what is to be grasped.

As the differential travels between "a no more" and "a not yet," it belongs to neither of its constituents and therefore is able to turn them into operators for unfolding the immeasurable without conceptualizing it. Making the immeasurable slide into a dawning comprehension features it as an ever-expanding concatenation of acts, thus translating the immeasurable into a self-specification of cognition. In order to promote such a process, the various reifications not only shed light on how the differential converts God into knowledge but are simultaneously deconstructed as conceptualizations that have been superimposed on what they were meant to make accessible.

This duality makes Rosenzweig's discourse itself into a differential that runs through the marked reifications, splitting them up into negative references as well as into targets for deconstruction. Such an effort is guided by the necessity to show what hypostatizations either veil, conceal, or fall short of when it comes to transposing their founding principles into comprehension. The main reason, however, that Rosenzweig's discourse itself develops as a traveling differential is the fact that translatability does not have the character of an object that is to be grasped. Instead, it can only become palpable through its multiformity, which is realized by changing levels of transposition, by their enmeshing, and by the inconclusiveness of all attempts at translation, which highlights the ultimate difference between the immeasurable and its cognition. This ultimate difference preserves the immeasurable and yet makes it knowable through a proliferating translatability brought about by a discourse that itself functions as a differential.

CHAPTER SIX
Configurations of Interpretation: An Epilogue

To sum up, I will highlight the main points that this discussion of interpretation has yielded. Interpretation is an act of translation, the execution of which depends on the subject matter to be interpreted as well as on the context within which the activity takes place. Consequently, there are only variables of interpretation, conceived as iterations of translatability, and there can never be such a thing as *the* interpretation. The major shifts in the variables of interpretation examined are context-bound:

a. Authority was of paramount concern when holy texts had to be translated into the life of the community or when canonized authors were invoked as guidelines for both the production and reception of literature.

b. The hermeneutic circle as a strategy of interpretation entered the stage when the singular authority of the canon could no longer be maintained in the face of its many different readings, which more often than not subjected the authority of the text to situationally conditioned manipulations, in consequence of which the canon became a matter of dispute or even lost much of its erstwhile orientation.

c. The recursive loop became prominent when entropy had to be controlled, or reality was to be conceived in terms of autonomous systems, or composite systems emerged out of a structural coupling of systems, or encounters between cultures or levels of culture made it necessary to negotiate between the familiar and the alien, not least as what is initially beyond reach will respond to an intervention from a standpoint outside itself.

d. The traveling differential—although it had a special history of its own—became a decisive mode of interpretation when holistic conceptualizations, as advanced by philosophy and even theology, proved incapable of converting incommensurabilities into cognition.

In each of these instances, an overall context caused a shift in the procedures of interpretation. It was not only the change in context, however, that necessitated this retooling of interpretive procedures; the prime cause was the subject matter to be coped with.

It must be borne in mind that for the sake of analysis I have emphasized distinctions among hermeneutics, cybernetics, and differential realizations as types of interpretation. The differences between their operational modes, however, are by no means as rigid, and indeed the hermeneutic circle, the recursive loop, and the traveling differential actually shade into one another whenever interpretation occurs. More often than not, though, one of the procedures outlined is dominant. There is an element of looping in the hermeneutic circle, comprising the to-and-fro movement between the text and its understanding, application, or deciphering. A differential also operates within the circle, unfolding the potential of a text by realizing it as a sequence of graduated profiles. Furthermore, there is a circular motion in recursive looping, indicated by the feed forward and the feed backward, just as there is a differential operating in the continual remolding of input and output, spotlighted by the difference between a "no longer" and a "not yet." Finally, the traveling differential contains an element of recursion, because the graduated profiles into which it fans out the potential to be interpreted are made to fold back on the potential, thus allowing us to grasp it. The relative dominance or subservience of these interpretive activities will depend on the purpose to be realized whenever interpretation occurs.

What makes this interplay among circularity, recursion, and the differential so important for interpretation? As demonstrated, each interpretation is an act of translation that opens up a space between the subject matter to be interpreted and what the subject matter is transposed into. The space is to a certain extent independent of what is translated and of what it is translated into. For this reason, I have qualified it as liminal space, because it marks off the subject matter from the register and therefore does not belong to either. In another context, Eco once used the term "space,"[1] conceived as an interval in time, in which a great many selections take place (222). Although Eco had a different type of relationship in mind, his observation nevertheless applies to interpretation as well. These selections decide not only how the transposition of any interpretive act is executed but also how the subject matter to be transposed will be slanted or constituted for apprehension. In view of the many selections that have to take place, modes of coping with the liminal space are of prime importance.

The circle organizes trial runs between the features privileged in order to attain understanding or to apply what has been understood. The recursion feeds the initial shortfall back into the input, thus initiating fine-tuning of further assumptions that are necessary for achieving control. The differential, having dissected the subject matter into a sequence of ever-new scissions, continually makes them fold back on one another, thus allowing us to conceive what initially eludes cognition. Circle, recursion, and differential shift the subject matter into something else, organize this shift as a mode of transfer, and exercise a certain degree of control when cognitive terms are superimposed on the subject matter during the process of interpretation.

At the same time, these modalities point to what resists translation. Because the liminal space is created by the act of interpretation, it cannot be eliminated in its entirety. The residual untranslatability, however, transforms itself into the power that drives the hermeneutic circle, the recursive loop, and the traveling differential.

The ability of these three basic operators to cope with the liminal space is derived from the duality inscribed into each of them. The circle mediates between the given and its understanding, the recursion effects a switch from a stance to entropy and open-endedness, and the differential enables an unbounded potential to achieve conceivability. Each of the operators fulfills its task through these dual references, insofar as the subject matter and the terms into which it is transposed have to be encompassed in each act of interpretation. Thus the potentially manifold combinations of the operational modes structure the liminal space opened up by any interpretation.

Although this space is structured by what it demarcates, it appears to have a dynamics of its own. How may we account for such a dynamics? After all, the liminal space is empty, and yet something seems to arise out

---

1. Umberto Eco, *I Limiti dell' Interpretazione* (Milan: Bompiani, 1990), 227.

of it. Circle, loop, and differential—each with its own particular mode of operation—try to cope with the space between subject matter and register by establishing ever more refined, diversified, and complex connections and relationships. This brings about a dual effect: while circle, loop, and differential are meant to exercise control in the first instance, they succeed to the degree in which they combine through a mutual interplay. Play is the interface of the modes through which the liminal space is negotiated. In this respect, the operational modes themselves endow the empty space with a certain dynamic quality that hails from their interplay. Such play is without rules, although it is guided by the many selections made by the interpreter, which Eco alluded to when describing the space as an interval in time. These selections are responsible for what is combined with what and even for what is dominant within the interplay of circle, loop, and differential. They are made subconsciously, however, just as 'passive syntheses' are, which, according to Husserl, are necessary operations for establishing 'good continuation.'[2] Furthermore, if we take into account that circle, loop, and even differential are not only in themselves differentiated but also assume a growing diversification in relation to the task to be performed, then the interplay among them, guided by subconscious selections underlying their combinations, makes the liminal space into a vortex. When combined, the operational modes struggle with one another, testing which of them might be more capable of negotiating the liminal space; in doing so, their reciprocal inscription turns the circle into a looping movement, the loop into a differential self-correction, and the differential into a circular recombination of what it has separated. This illustration by no means exhausts the potentially unforeseeable moves of such an interplay, but it at least indicates how a variety of processes may be tangled up in a single vortex.

   The liminal space, then, is charged with a dynamism that strives to discharge itself into something. The operational modes are meant to exercise control and in doing so find themselves in play with one another; the selections made for guiding the play are of a subconscious nature and hence not in full command of what they trigger, making them potentially subject to modification. Thus the liminal space itself is not exactly

---

2. See Edmund Husserl, *Analysen zur Passiven Synthesis*, Gesammelte Werke 11, ed. Margot Fleischer (The Hague: Martinus Nijhoff, 1966); and Aron Gurwitsch, *The Field of Consciousness* (Pittsburgh: Duquesne University Press, 1964), 150ff.

autopoietic but assumes such a quality by drawing its dynamism from what is inserted into it from outside.

When the modes begin to negotiate the liminal space by playing with one another, their interrelation may be one of reciprocal telescoping, or mutual inscribing, or interchanging dominance and subservience. Such play is, according to Victor Turner, "the categorically uncategorizable," not least as it is "essentially interstitial, betwixt-and-between all standard taxonomical nodes."[3] Negotiating by playing therefore entails dispensing even with the limited degrees of reference that each of the operational modes possesses. Moreover, the selections that structure the playing occur below the interpreter's threshold of consciousness, thus triggering "a kind of Strange Loop" between the interplay of the modes and the subconscious decision making. A strange loop is, according to Douglas Hofstadter, "an interaction between levels in which the top level reaches back down towards the bottom level and influences it, while at the same time being itself determined by the bottom level,"[4] thus creating "tangled hierarchies" (684ff., esp. 709).

Consequently, the liminal space appears, through its kaleidoscopically shifting forms of strange loops, as if it were organizing itself. Apart from its own inherent dynamism, the liminal space draws both information and energy from what the subject matter is like and from what the register is meant to achieve. The information (subject matter) and the guidelines (register), however, are subjected to processing when interlinked in the liminal space that initially has separated them from one another. Owing to the interplay between the operational modes, their strange loops, and the interpreter's subconscious selections, this processing does not develop solely according to what the subject matter is like and what the register wants it to be but also according to a force that gathers in the liminal space itself, powered by what the interplay among circle, loop, and differential have set in motion.

This force is indefinable and lends itself to description only insofar as the transmutation of information and guidelines converts the liminal space into a nonlinear system. "Force" would then designate the nonlinearity of the processing that occurs in the liminal space. The latter thus functions as a catalyst that is indispensable for transposing a subject

---

3. Victor Turner, *The Anthropology of Performance* (New York: PAJ, 1988), 17.
4. Douglas R. Hofstadter, *Gödel, Escher, Bach: An Eternal Golden Braid* (New York: Vintage, 1989), 709.

matter into a register. As a catalyst it effects what is categorically distinguished, thereby slanting the subject matter and differentiating the register. Simultaneously, nonlinear organizations are distinguished by the fact that they also generate a certain uncontrollability, as evinced by the unforeseeable play movements of the modes. Uncontrollability, however, does not mean that things are always liable to get out of hand; instead, in the final analysis, it proves to be the self-generated fuel for the dynamics that make the liminal space into a self-organizing system through which the complex structure of the liminal space is able to organize itself. If linear systems have a certain telos, the realization of which is intended by the workings of the systems concerned, nonlinear systems, through the strange loops among their factors, levels, and whatever else is fed into them from outside, are a source of emergent phenomena. Thus nonlinearity becomes the wellspring of emergence.

The force that gathers in the liminal space has a poetic quality, as it brings something about that hitherto did not exist. Conceiving of this quality brings to mind the poetic philosophy of Giambattista Vico and his *New Science* intended to chart the world anew. History, Vico maintains, is a process of ever-new beginnings, as it appears to be both linear and cyclical, and such a countervailing movement is intertwined by what he calls the *ricorso*. If the latter forms the infrastructure of this new map of the world, how does it operate? Giuseppe Mazotta has recently given a brilliant exposition of its workings, which succinctly pinpoint the poetic quality generated by the vortex of the liminal space.

> By its interweaving of circle and line, which produces the spiral, the *ricorso*, thus, is the simultaneous figuration of closure and openness of a circle that repeats itself with a difference, is always out of place and is eccentric to the other circles in the series. . . . Together with the *ricorso*, the *cursus* suggests Vico's spiral style of writing and spiral style of thinking, the poetic art of connecting events or words remote from one another. . . . It is a language that leaps over conventional connections, that slides, like a cursor, backward and forward, pursues seemingly random but rigorously elliptical orbits in a series, and creates a special place for a discourse whereby a new, all-encompassing configuration of the past, present, and future can appear before our eyes.[5]

---

5. Giuseppe Mazotta, *The New Map of the World: The Poetic Philosophy of Giambattista Vico* (Princeton: Princeton University Press, 1999), 228.

Thus the *ricorso* is a close-up allowing us to perceive the engendering of poetic qualities that give rise to emergent phenomena in the act of interpretation.

Before detailing these phenomena, a caveat seems to be necessary regarding the elimination of the liminal space by certain types of interpretation. Whenever the presuppositions of the register are superimposed on the subject matter, the liminal space is colonized by the concepts brought to bear. Such a colonization converts interpretation into an act that determines the intended meaning of the subject matter. When this happens, interpretation ceases. The colonization of the liminal space therefore sacrifices translatability and with it the chance to embrace more than was possible before the superimposition. Whenever presuppositions are predominant, interpretation results in a predication of the subject matter concerned. By contrast, the interplay of the modes and their strange loops, with the subconscious selections through which information and guidelines are processed, makes the liminal space into a nonlinear organization, thus unfolding interpretation as production. Understood this way, interpretation produces emergent phenomena or constitutes a source of emergence.

Whenever interpretation occurs, something emerges, and this something is identical neither with the subject matter nor with the register into which the subject matter is to be transposed. Before examining what emerges in the paradigms outlined, attention has to be drawn to a final condition that is responsible for every kind of emergence in the act of interpretation. The register brought to bear in such an act is marked by a basic duality: (a) it is meant to provide a means of access to what is interpreted, but (b) it is also the framework into which the subject matter is translated. These two functions of the register are interdependent, and this holds true—at least up to point—even if the register is more or less superimposed on the subject matter. In this case, the framework nevertheless functions as a means of access.

As a rule, however, there is a sliding scale between extremes, marked, on the one hand, by making the subject matter subservient to the register, and, on the other, by differentiating the register when the subject matter is meant to be perceived in all its complexity. Whatever the position on that sliding scale, there is always a structural coupling between subject matter and register. Through this structural coupling, the register—by opening access—is bound to make inroads into the subject matter, as it is purpose-governed and hence through its very intervention occasions disturbances. These are an inevitable consequence of any structural coupling and manifest themselves as what the theorists of self-organizing systems, such as Heinz von Foerster and Henri Atlan, call "noise," which means that something uncontrollable has emerged.[6]

In relation to the paradigms discussed, the noise may be qualified in a hermeneutically conceived register as misunderstanding; in a cybernetically conceived one as uncontrollability of—or even damage to—the systems coupled; and in a differentially conceived one as ungraspability of the immeasurable. The multiformity of noise that overshadows the intent of the register has to be processed, and the outcome of this is bound to be different from both subject matter and register, because the register functions only as an operational tool, and the subject matter is not identical to the angle from which it is approached. Thus we get a chain reaction: the structural coupling of subject matter and register causes disturbances that produce noise, the processing of which makes something emerge that is different from what has been coupled.

Now we have reached a point at which we can fully appreciate the liminal space as a vortex that is catalytic insofar as it transforms, by means of strange loops, the multiplicity of operational modes and the subconscious selection of their employment into emergent phenomena.

Let us now turn to the paradigms in order to pinpoint what has actually emerged in the cases discussed. In the genre of interpretation represented by the commentary, it is *guidance* for the community. In the genre of interpretation represented by hermeneutics, it is *understanding* and *application* of what has been understood, or the emergence of *history* out of punctured facts, or the *cure* of the patient. In the genre of interpretation represented by cybernetics, it is *control* or *composition* of systems of secondary and tertiary order. And in the genre of interpretation represented by the differential, it is *realization* of the immeasurable.

Emergent phenomena of this kind also have repercussions on the register. Bearing in mind the duality of the register, the side-effects of access, manifest as noise, issue into a differentiation of the framework. This is to be observed in all the paradigms discussed. There is an increasing sophistication of the hermeneutic circle, caused by the subject matter, which is either given, or has to be constituted, or has to be ferreted out of its hiddenness. Consequently, the circle, which operates in Schleiermacher's case as a play structure of toing and froing, changes into a nesting of circles

---

6. For this particular issue, see William R. Paulson, *The Noise of Culture: Literary Texts in a World of Information* (Ithaca: Cornell University Press, 1988), 66–100.

in Droysen's attempt to construe history and into transactional loops in a psychoanalytical register. This applies equally to the cybernetic paradigm. Thick description in Geertz's case is marked by an expanding, countervailing organization of guesses and assessment of guesses. Such dual countering strives for a continual refinement of the register through self-correction. Self-correction also remains basic for the interpretation of the self-maintenance of autonomous systems, in which recursion is conceived as the infrastructure of an ongoing autopoiesis. In Rosenzweig's paradigm, the differential changes into ever-new variants, so that in the final analysis his discourse itself turns out to be differential. Thus emergent phenomena are not only produced by the coupling of subject matter and register, but the coupling also causes a continually emerging self-specification of the register.

A basic reason for the differentiation of the register is the residual untranslatability that—as we have seen—is not a feature of the subject matter to be interpreted but is produced by interpretation itself. This self-produced untranslatability, however, functions as a propellant for a continual fine-tuning operation of the modes brought to bear by the register. It may also cause a change in the modes applied, when a growing refinement will no longer suffice. This is most striking in the psychoanalytic paradigm, in which the transactional loop emerges out of the circle as a new mode of operation. For this reason, we might qualify the self-produced residual untranslatability as autopoietic, because it is the source of (a) the growing complexity of the register, (b) the change of the register, and (c) the emergence of differently organized registers.

Thus interpretation is basically performative in character. It makes something happen, and what arises out of this performance are emergent phenomena. The performative nature of interpretation is brought out by the fact that it generates its own power, that is, the ineliminable residual untranslatability drives the performance.

This emphasis on the technical aspect of interpretation throws up a final question: Why are we as human beings so incessantly engaged in translating something into something else? The techniques focused on thus far let us only see what happens in interpretation, without, however, accounting for its multiplicity or the endlessly ongoing activity of interpretation itself. The question raised points to manifold implications underlying this activity.

One of the most obvious reasons for the variables of interpretation is the fact that more often than not there are pragmatic issues and objectives involved that are only solved pragmatically. If interpretation, however, were only concerned with achieving pragmatic ends—important as they may be—then whatever it came up with would end this activity, whereas in fact it never ends.

Interpretation, as we have seen, always makes something emerge, so that we might be justified in saying that emergence is its hallmark. This applies equally to the solution that arises out of any pragmatic interpretive act. The pragmatic intent is an objective, however, and not the matrix of emergence. There are two sides to emergence as the hallmark of interpretation: (a) it indicates the ever-widening ramification of attempts to bring things about; and (b) whatever comes about is a charting of the reality we live in. As we cannot encompass this reality, we map it out into a plurality of worlds, for which interpretation as emergence is a central activity. This endeavor appears to be an anthropological necessity and is perhaps as close as one can get to answering the final question initially raised. Before addressing it, a further consideration is pertinent.

As translatability, interpretation is basically a two-tiered operation that enables any given subject matter to function. Whatever there is would lie forever dormant if it were not made functional, and this making functional is effected by the structure of the two-tiered interpretation. Translating something into something else is thus an activity that allows us to transform anything given into its functionality. Emergent phenomena are the outcome of this operation, and they point to the fact that interpretation is basically an act intended to enable things to function.

In this respect, it is interesting to note that the functioning of the genetic code can be described in similar terms. "DNA usually comes in double strands—that is, two single strands which are paired up."[7] The dual strands have to be coupled, just like the subject matter and the register. The similarity of the descriptive terms continues when the functioning of the genetic code is detailed: "The process by which the DNA gets copied onto mRNA inside the nucleus is called *transcription*" (517).[8] From "transcription" we

---

7. Hofstadter, *Gödel, Escher, Bach*, 514.
8. Hofstadter comments on mRNA as follows:

> mRNA strands . . . constitute a kind of DNA Rapid Transit Service; by this is meant not that mRNA physically carries DNA anywhere, but rather that it serves to carry the information, or message, stored in the DNA in its nuclear chamber, out to the ribosomes in the cytoplasm. How is this done? The idea is easy: a special kind of enzyme inside the nucleus faithfully copies long stretches of the DNA's base sequence onto a new strand—a strand of messenger RNA. This mRNA then departs from the nucleus and wanders out into the cytoplasm, where it runs into many ribosomes which begin doing their enzyme-creating work on it. (517)

now pass to translation: "Since the DNA contains all the information for construction of proteins, which are the active agents of the cell, DNA can be viewed as a *program* written in a higher-level language, which is subsequently translated (or interpreted) into the 'machine language' of the cell (proteins)" (547). Not only is this two-tiered relationship basic for the functioning of the genetic code, but there is also a great deal of translation going on as a prerequisite for its functionality. Therefore Hofstadter uses terms such as "transcription," "translation," and "interpreter"—though mostly in italics—in order to indicate how the operation of the genetic code is to be conceived. In the imaginary dialogues that introduce each of the chapters in Hofstadter's book, he makes Achilles say to Tortoise: "Molecular biology is filled with peculiar convoluted loops which I can't quite understand, such as the way that folded proteins, which are coded for the DNA, can loop back and manipulate the DNA, which they came from" (231). A multiple translatability appears to be going on in human "hardware," which we can gauge by what it brings about in the "software." The language of translatability appears to lend itself to these processes. I am not suggesting, however, that DNA is an analogue for what happens in interpretation. If translatability enables things to function, it is simply worth noting that the functioning of DNA is described in terms that epitomize interpretation. From this we may conclude that the nature of interpretation is to make functional whatever is given, and this view is supported by the metaphor used to explain the operation of the genetic code.

This basic feature of interpretation leads us back to the question of why we are constantly interpreting. Such a question is all the more pertinent as forms and even genres of interpretation have burgeoned enormously in the last couple of centuries. We have to ask ourselves why this has happened and why there is a growing interest in the structure and achievements of interpretation.

Human beings, at least in our century, are increasingly faced by what is unavailable to them. Two major problems pose themselves: First, the ground from which human beings have sprung is unfathomable and thus appears to be withheld from them.[9] Second, human beings have also

---

9. This situation has been very aptly analyzed by Dieter Henrich, "Selbstbewußtsein: Kritische Einleitung in eine Theorie," in *Hermeneutik und Dialektik*, Festschrift Gadamer (Tübingen: Mohr/Siebeck, 1970), 257–284. Henrich has elaborated on this initial exploration in the following works: *Selbstverhältnisse* (Stuttgart: Reclam, 1982), 83–130; *Fluchtlinien: Philosophische Essays* (Frankfurt/Main: Suhrkamp, 1982), 99–178; and his latest essay "Subjektivität als Prinzip," *Deutsche Zeitschrift für Philosophie* 46 (1998): 31–44.

become unavailable to themselves; we are but do not know what it is to be.[10] In view of these two basic blanks—if one may call these unavailabilities blanks—human beings have to lead conscious lives, which, however, are permeated by the awareness that the fundamentals are unplumbable. The unending activity of interpretation as the production of emergent phenomena could be conceived as a response to these basic unavailabilities. Therefore we might say that human beings seek to achieve understanding, self-understanding, control, system building, and differentiation of difference as a means of reaching the unreachable. What thus emerges are only maps, which chart territories. Mapping is not exactly a compensation for what is unavailable to human beings, because such an activity does not aim to gain ground or to attain self-presence. At best, it draws its vigor from what is forever unavailable, without the intention of ever possessing it. This makes mapping into a performative activity by reversing the map/territory relationship.[11] Instead of denoting a territory, the map enables the contours of a territory to emerge, which will coincide with the map because it has no existence outside this designation. Therefore the map adumbrates the conditions under which the not-yet-existing may be conceived. In this respect, it may be said that the basic unavailabilities power the drive of "worldmaking." This ties in with one of Goodman's remarks, that there is nothing "stolid underneath" in our ways of "worldmaking."[12] Therefore interpretation highlights the fact that human beings live by what they produce, which points to an important facet of the human condition: humans appear to be an unending performance of themselves.

----

10. See Helmuth Plessner, "Die anthropologische Dimension der Geschichtlichkeit," in *Sozialer Wandel: Zivilisation und Fortschritt als Kategorien der soziologischen Theorie*, ed. Hans Peter Dreitzel (Neuwied: Luchterhand, 1972), 160; but especially the penetrating study by Gabriele Schwab, *Subjects Without Selves: Transitional Texts in Modern Fiction* (Cambridge: Harvard University Press, 1994).

11. I have elaborated on the map/territory relationship in connection with play theory in *The Fictive and the Imaginary: Charting Literary Anthropology* (Baltimore: Johns Hopkins University Press, 1993), 247–250, where I have extended what Gregory Bateson, *Steps to an Ecology of Mind* (New York: Ballantine, 1972), 180, had developed by taking up the pairing map/territory from A. Korzybski.

12. Nelson Goodman, *Ways of Worldmaking* (Hassocks: Harvester, 1978), 6 and 96.

In the final analysis, however, interpretation as an activity to make phenomena emerge remains inconclusive. This inconclusiveness may be
viewed in different ways. It seems to be responsible for the fact that there
is no end to the interpretive activity of mapping. Mapping in turn is necessary, because we are always in the midst of life and yet continually seek
to lift ourselves out of our entanglement, which accounts for the illusory
quality inherent in our maps. Such self-lifting may be one of the reasons
that interpretation—though basically a *techné*—tends to become transformed into a philosophy. Thus we have a hermeneutically based philosophy in which understanding, or the application of it, is meant to enhance
our self-understanding.[13] Something similar can be observed in general
systems theory as epitomized by *The Tree of Knowledge*, which tries "to
articulate" "(1) the need for a nonrepresentationist view of knowledge
based on the sense-making capacity of an autonomous living system and
(2) the need to close the circle between what is valid as a mechanism for
animals and machines and what pertains to our experience, including
doing science."[14] Providing closure appears to be the common denomina-
tor for both a hermeneutically and a scientifically oriented philosophy
that, in the final analysis, are also responses to the inconclusiveness inherent in interpretation. Such an attempt is plausible insofar as inconclusiveness calls for a more comprehensive context within which leftover
problems might be resolved. A resolution of this kind, however, implies
that interpretive techniques are elevated to transcendental vantage points,
thus making circularity and recursion into umbrella concepts. The latter
cease to be vehicles of mapping and become the infrastructure of the
philosophies concerned. And yet, in spite of the closure attempted, the
potential open-endedness of interpretation begins to loom large again, as
there is no definitive end to self-understanding, and the *"knowledge of*

---

13. See Hans-Georg Gadamer, *Truth and Method*, 2d ed., trans. rev. by Joel
Weinsheimer and Donald G. Marshall (New York: Crossroad, 1989); Jean
Greisch, *Hermeneutik und Metaphysik: Eine Problemgeschichte* (Munich:
Fink, 1993), 155–223; Hartmut Raguse, *Der Raum des Textes: Elemente einer
transdisziplinären theologischen Hermeneutik* (Stuttgart: Kohlhammer, 1994);
Gerald L. Bruns, *Hermeneutics Ancient and Modern* (New Haven: Yale
University Press, 1992), 213–266; and Gianni Vattimo, *Oltre l'interpretazione:
Il significato dell'ermeneutica per la filosofia* (Rome: Laterza, 1994).
14. Humberto R. Maturana and Francisco J. Varela, *The Tree of Knowledge:
The Biological Roots of Human Understanding*, trans. Robert Paolucci, rev.
ed. (Boston: Shambhala, 1992), 254.

knowledge compels . . . us to adopt an attitude of permanent vigilance against the temptation of certainty" (245) because *"we have only the world that we bring forth with others"* (248).

Acknowledging the open-endedness of all interpretation may allow us to turn our question around, and by deliberately defying any temptation toward closure, we may achieve a position that will enable us to conceive how far basic human unavailabilities translate into a productive mapping of ever-new territories. What thus emerges from interpretation is an insight into the unforeseeable multifariousness of human beings' responses to their constitutive blanks. Viewed from this angle, interpretation indicates what it might mean to lead a conscious life that is permeated by awareness of the unfathomableness out of which it arises. Such a view tends to prevent us from lapsing into another master narrative of the human condition, because unending interpretation unfolds in fleeting figurations, during the course of which each is either modified or canceled by what is to follow. This sequence highlights figuration as a mapping activity, which equally assembles and dismantles territories, thus invalidating any notion that claims to represent human life. Life cannot be frozen into a hypostatization of any of its aspects, for it is basically unrepresentable and can therefore only be conceived in terms of the transient figurations of interpretation.

APPENDIX

The Emergence of a Cross-Cultural Discourse:
Thomas Carlyle's *Sartor Resartus*

The outline of a cross-cultural discourse as advanced
in Carlyle's *Sartor Resartus* is a paradigm but by no
means a blueprint of the telescoping of different cultures. It does, however, provide guidelines as to how
such a telescoping might be conceived. It is paradigmatic insofar as a cross-cultural discourse cannot be
set up as a transcendental stance under which the
relationships between different cultures are subsumed. Instead of an overarching third dimension,
the discourse concerned can only function as an
interlinking network and will assume a shape whose
generic features cannot be equated with any of the
existing genres.

HISTORICAL PRELIMINARIES

Why has the translatability of cultures become an
issue? As long as the interconnection of traditions—
whether in terms of receiving an inheritance or of
recasting a heritage—was taken for granted, the relationship of cultures did not pose a problem. Tradition was either reinterpreted or appropriated in
accordance with prevailing standards or needs. This
holds true up to the eighteenth century and is borne
out, for instance, in the famous criticism Nietzsche
leveled at Shakespeare, that in the Roman plays
Shakespeare depicted his protagonists not as Romans
but as Renaissance heroes.

The "Querelle des Anciens et des Modernes,"

however, is the striking exception to this commonly accepted relationship. It was the perception of a fundamental difference between the *antiqui* and the *moderni* that brought about an awareness of distance between the cultures of antiquity and those of the modern age.[1] The battle was triggered by the question of how to achieve perfection, an aim that both the moderns and the ancients shared. For the latter, perfection was achieved by imitating nature, whereas for the former the ancient models were no longer to be imitated but had to be surpassed. Such a shift was largely due to the fact that the moderns found themselves confronted with an ever-expanding, open-ended world, in contradistinction to the ancients, who entertained the idea of a closed cosmos. Consequently, progress became the guiding light for the moderns, who thus turned the inherited world order completely around by conceiving it as an irreversible advance into a future. The cyclical movement of day and night and the seasons, indicative of an ordered cosmos, was replaced by a linear ascent. Perfection therefore was no longer a given that required contemplation, as exemplified by the Greek *theoria*; instead, it was now something to be achieved, and as a task to be performed it could no longer be an act of imitation.

In his *Parallèle des Anciens et des Modernes* (1688–97), Charles Perrault listed the existing differences between the two cultures.[2] This list, however, was meant to prove the superiority of the moderns, who had exceeded what the ancients had achieved. In order to substantiate such a claim, the passing of time became a frame of reference for both collating and assessing the differences, in the course of which a history began to unfold itself: by discovering difference as the dividing line between cultures, history as a cross-cultural discourse emerged. The moderns were now no longer dwarfs standing on the shoulders of the giants, as John of Salisbury had it; they were different. And as the ancient culture could not be dispensed with—not least as it had to provide a point of comparison for the achievements of the moderns—history as a form of cross-cultural

---

1. For details, see Hans Robert Jauß, "Ästhetische Normen und geschichtliche Reflexion in der *Querelle des Anciens et des Modernes*," in Charles Perrault, *Parallèle des Anciens et des Modernes en ce qui regarde les Arts et les Sciences*, ed. Hans Robert Jauß, Theorie und Geschichte der Literatur und der Schönen Künste 2 (Munich: Eidos, 1964), 8–79.
2. See especially Charles Perrault, *Parallèle des Anciens et des Modernes en ce qui regarde les Arts et les Sciences*, ed. Hans Robert Jauß, Theorie und Geschichte der Literatur und der Schönen Künste 2 (Munich: Eidos, 1964), 103–164.

interrelationship bears the inscription of a dual coding. On the one hand, the difference between the two cultures has to be overcome by a developing sequence, and, on the other, this very difference has to be maintained in order to gauge the superiority achieved. This duality was to remain an incontrovertible structure of all cross-cultural discourse henceforth.

The Querelle, however, remained a "Battle of Books." Questions of how to attain perfection or perfectibility, of how to imitate nature or inherited models, or of how nature as a guiding norm is to be replaced by taste[3] and of how the latter—no longer to be related to nature—is to be conceived turned out to be the overriding concern of the Querelle, which thus confined itself to matters of art in the broadest sense of the term. Moreover, the moderns proved to be rather self-assertive in this process of differentiation, thereby endowing their discourse of history with a teleological direction.

What, however, happens when such optimism wanes? This stage was reached some fifty years after Perrault, when Rousseau responded to the prize competition of the Académie de Dijon in 1750 by stating that the arts and sciences had not, in actual fact, improved morals but had corrupted them. Such a devastating statement marked the beginning of what has since come to be known as cultural critique, sparked off by a crisis of culture that had not been in the orbit of those who had pleaded the superiority of their own culture over the ancients.'

The experience of crisis splits culture itself apart, and this process began to deepen and accelerate with the dawn of the Industrial Revolution. Fundamental differences opened up in individual cultures, not least through the experience of an all-pervading rift that divided culture into an inaccessible past and a helplessly stricken present. A past cut off from the present is pushed back into an irredeemable pastness, thus inverting the very relationship highlighted in the evolving discourse of history as it had grown out of the Querelle. Furthermore, the Industrial Revolution divided the very nation into two nations: one that participated in the growing wealth and another that had to bear the hardships. Crisis as a waning belief in a set of values—a belief indispensable for the stability of a culture—meant a split within the nation that eventually resolved itself into a nation of two cultures.

Thomas Carlyle was one of the first who not only had forebodings of

---

3. See Jauß, "Ästhetische Normen," 47.

such a situation but gave expression to his fears in order to remedy what the crisis had laid bare.[4] The rifts that had opened up in what one had been led to believe was a homogeneous culture could no longer be closed by the discourse of history, for its inherent optimism regarding perfection by progress had been shattered. Consequently, a renegotiation between past and present became an issue for Carlyle, which he tried to solve by translating the past into the present and also by transposing different cultures into his own.

Progress was now placated as a glossing-over of difference, whereas translating maintained the awareness of difference by simultaneously interrelating what was historically divided, be it the split between one's own cultural past and present or between one's own culture and the alien ones to be encountered through a globally growing confrontation of cultures.

If one's own cultural past, as exemplified in Carlyle's *Past and Present* (1843), is totally alienated from the present,[5] translatability entails the effort to revitalize such an amputated past[6] by turning it into a mirror in which the present is refracted. As neither the past nor the present by itself is able to bring about such a mutual mirroring, a type of discourse has to be construed that allows for mutual interpenetration. Such a mutuality implies that the difference between past and present or between cultures can never be eliminated, for the past can never become a present again and one culture can never be totally encompassed by another. Consequently, whenever difference is eliminated, the encounter between cultures turns into a selective assimilation, guided by what is relevant for the culture concerned. In such instances, no interaction between cultures occurs, and the incorporation of alien features is at best pragmatically justified.

----

4. This may be one of the reasons that Carlyle is beginning to attract interest again. G. B. Tennyson started out a lecture to the Carlyle Society by saying, "I take some comfort in reporting that in the scholarly market Carlyle is now again on the upswing" (*Carlyle and the Modern World*, The Carlyle Society, Occasional Papers 4 [Edinburgh: Carlyle Society, 1971], 3).
5. See Ian Campbell, *Thomas Carlyle* (London: Hamish Hamilton, 1974), 109–110.
6. G. Robert Stange, "Refractions of *Past and Present*," in *Carlyle, Past and Present: A Collection of New Essays* (London: Vision, 19760, 97, gives a brief outline of how Carlyle conceived of the relationship between past and present. John D. Rosenberg, *Carlyle and the Burden of History* (Oxford: Oxford University Press, Clarendon, 1985), 121, points out the "circuitous way" that governs the linkup between past and present, which clearly reveals nascent hermeneutic features unconsciously employed by Carlyle.

Therefore the question arises as to the motivation underlying the translatability of cultures. If the experience of crises, issuing into a critique of one's own culture, is meant to balance out the deficiencies diagnosed, recourse to other cultures proves to be a means of therapy for a growing awareness of cultural pathology. The latter can be counteracted not just by taking over features and attitudes from different cultures but first and foremost by instilling a self-reflection into the stricken culture, thus providing scope for self-monitoring. Translatability is motivated by the need to cope with a crisis that can no longer be alleviated by the mere assimilation or appropriation of other cultures.

At such a historic juncture, a cross-cultural discourse begins to emerge. A discourse of this kind is not to be mistaken for a translation, as translatability is to be conceived as a set of conditions able to bring about a mutual mirroring of cultures. It is therefore a pertinent feature of such a discourse that it establishes a network of interpenetrating relationships. These in turn allow for a mutual impacting of cultures on one another.

Such a translatability is not motivated by assimilation, appropriation, or even understanding and communication, as each of these proves to be only a pragmatic exigency and hence points to an ulterior purpose. In each of these instances, a specific interlinking within the network is privileged, and this narrows down the very differentiation opened up by the network of the cross-cultural discourse. These instances testify to a prevailing need, which makes them subject to evaluation. The network itself is a web of mobile structures, functioning as an interface between different cultures. It is a clearing station in which cultural differences are juxtaposed and sorted out.

GENERIC FEATURES

Carlyle's *Sartor Resartus* (1836) is one of the first attempts at construing such a cross-cultural discourse. The concept-oriented philosophical culture of German idealism is transposed into the experience-oriented culture of British empiricism. The discourse devised for such an undertaking has to remain subservient to the transposition of cultures, and such a subservience is bound to have repercussions on the form of the discourse, not least because form exercises control and brings about determination. Consequently, such a discourse has to be permeated by a self-reflection, manifesting itself in the very subversion of its form.

The consequences of this undercutting are highlighted by the generic features of *Sartor Resartus*. Although dealing with a philosophical system, it is not cast as a treatise. Instead, we have an "English Editor" receiving from Germany several bags of notes and fragments from which he gets a rather disorderly glimpse of a highly speculative work, "Die Kleider, ihr Werden und Wirken,"[7] written by Diogenes Teufelsdröckh. This very introduction serves as a point of departure for exfoliating the density of a system in narrative terms that make *Sartor Resartus* almost appear to be a novel.[8] The narration, however, is constantly punctured by systematic expositions of this transcendental philosophy, which inhibit the narrative from unfolding. With the form of the treatise suspended and the narrative thwarted by arguments of philosophical disquisitions, *Sartor Resartus* pivots around an empty space that makes narrating and arguing constantly interchange. The narrative functions as a form of communication that strives to endow philosophical speculation with plausibility, whereas the abstractions that disrupt the narrative reveal transcendentalism as a mode of exceeding the familiar. Thus a British attitude permeates a systematic philosophy, just as German transcendentalism inscribes itself into a British disposition. Giving prominence to the empty space around which narrating and arguing revolve, Carlyle epitomizes in *Sartor Resartus* the telescoping of transcendentalism and empiricism. In doing so, he tries to make palatable to British readers the German import that in turn is bound to bring out something in the British readers of which they have hitherto not been aware.

The empty space as a generic feature of *Sartor Resartus* is further elaborated by an autobiographical account of Teufelsdröckh's spiritual growth,[9] to which one of the three books is devoted. Yet *Sartor Resartus* is not an autobiography either. The basic facts of Teufelsdröckh's development are grouped around his life-endangering crisis, which he eventually

---

7. Thomas Carlyle, *Sartor Resartus: The Life and Opinions of Herr Teufelsdröckh*, vol. 1 of the Centenary Edition of the Works (London: Chapman and Hall, 1897), 5. Unless otherwise specified, page references to *Sartor Resartus* are hereafter given parenthetically in the text.
8. Geoffrey H. Hartman considers the "genre of the book . . . at once commentary and fiction" (*Criticism in the Wilderness: The Study of Literature Today* [New Haven: Yale University Press, 1980], 48). Carlisle Moore quotes from Carlyle's correspondence (*Letters of Thomas Carlyle: 1826–1889*, ed. C. E. Norton [London: Macmillan, 1889], 365) that the book was to be "put together in the fashion of a kind of Didactic Novel; but indeed property *like* nothing yet extant" ("*Sartor Resartus* and the Problem of Carlyle's 'Conversion,'" *PMLA* 70 [1955]: 667).

solves by devising his Philosophy of Clothes. There is an intimate commerce between the facts of life and the ever-changing garments that epitomize Teufelsdröckh's philosophy. The more life eludes his grasp, the more concretely the Philosophy of Clothes takes shape. Thus the erstwhile self-inspecting autobiographer turns increasingly into a tailor, who designs new clothes or refashions garments inherited from the past in order to be able to capture himself. Clothing, however, is unable to eliminate the gap between a life lived and the attempt to fathom what that life is; instead, every garment turns into a propellant for an endless production of clothes, whose tailoring and retailoring are meant to narrow down the distance between 'being and having oneself.'

Thus *Sartor Resartus* is neither an autobiography nor an exposition of a philosophical system, although both form basic constituents of the work. The life narrated demands a philosophy in order to cope with its crisis, and the philosophy that addresses the crisis is more than just a remedy; it keeps changing that very life itself without, however, capturing it in its totality. The space between turns out to be a catalyst, evinced by the fact that Teufelsdröckh feeds his life into a philosophy that in turn feeds itself back into that life by changing it. This is the reason why *Sartor Resartus* unfolds as an unending proliferation of metaphors, which make both the life and the Philosophy of Clothes disperse into a welter of rather different designations. In such a dispersal, the catalytic effect of the space between becomes manifest, turning *Sartor Resartus* into a self-transforming piece of writing that on this microlevel already epitomizes the way in which a cross-cultural discourse is meant to function.

There are two consequences to be drawn from this interpenetration. First, as the density and accumulation of metaphors accrue into a critical mass, the metaphor indicates that it can never finally verbalize what it aims at, and consequently it accentuates the difference between itself and what it is designed to represent. It is this very difference, however, that triggers the exuberant proliferation of metaphors that not only unfolds this difference into a multifariousness of aspects but simultaneously indicates that representation must forever be separated from what it represents.

---

9. George Levine finds it hard to pinpoint the generic features of *Sartor Resartus*: "I prefer, therefore, in order to avoid the confusion that the word 'novel' . . . inevitably brings with it, to consider *Sartor* as a fiction belonging to the complex class of 'confession-anatomy-romance' " ("*Sartor Resartus* and the Balance of Fiction [1968]," in *Thomas Carlyle*, ed. Harold Bloom [New York: Chelsea House, 1986], 56f.).

Second, the profusion of metaphors deconstructs the received notion of representation, not least because representation entails giving presence to what is different in terms of what seems to be familiar. In this respect, the excessively proliferating metaphors delineate the space between as a "black box"[10] by making its very inexplicability explode into a self-transforming welter of aspects, by means of which a life is translated into a mainspring of philosophy and the emerging philosophy into a structure of life.

What is epitomized here in a nutshell holds equally true for the cross-cultural discourse as advanced in *Sartor Resartus*. A form of writing that constantly disperses itself reveals an inherent contradiction. The trial runs of the metaphors are marked by a duality. On the one hand, they strive to capture something, and, on the other, their density and dispersal cancel out the very representativeness they appear to have achieved. The countervailing movement signals that the cross-cultural discourse is not a third dimension under which the different cultures are to be subsumed. This would only be the case if the metaphors were accorded the quality of adequate representation, thereby establishing the cross-cultural discourse as a transcendental stance. The simultaneous undermining of what the discourse intends to achieve, however, imbues *Sartor Resartus* with a sense of comedy, whose ambivalence is not resolved by exposing German transcendentalism to ridicule but is meant to make the British readers see themselves in the mirror of such ridicule. The comedy is thus turned into a medium for the mutual transposition of cultures.This duality makes it necessary for the English Editor to intervene. His intervention, however, is not meant to provide a solution.[11] Instead, the Editor retailors the systematic exposition of German transcendentalism in such a manner that it can be conveyed to a British public. At the beginning Teufelsdröckh is praised

---

10. I use the term "black box" as defined by Gregory Bateson in *Steps to an Ecology of Mind* (New York: Ballantine, 1972): "A 'black box' is a conventional agreement between scientists to stop trying to explain things at a certain point. . . . So the 'black box' is a label for what a bunch of things are supposed to do. . . . But it's not an explanation of *how* the bunch works . . . . There's no explanation of an explanatory principle. It's like a black box" (39f.).

11. Concerning the various functions of the English Editor, see L. M. Findlay, "Paul de Man, Thomas Carlyle, and 'The Rhetoric of Temporality,' " *Dalhousie Review* 65 (1985): 172; Jerry A. Dibble, "Strategies of the Mental War: Carlyle and Hegel and the Rhetoric of Idealism," *Bulletin of the New York Public Library* 80 (1976): 100; and Rosenberg, *Carlyle and the Burden of History*, 10.

for adding a new name "to the first ranks of Philosophy, in our German Temple of Honour" (5), which causes the Editor to remark: "*Möchte es* (this remarkable Treatise) *auch im Brittischen Boden gedeihen!*" (6) The famous treatise, however, was published in "*Weissnichtwo*" by "*Stillschweigen und Co*" (5) and seems to be "a very Sea of Thought" (6).

In spite of the Editor's intention to transplant this "remarkable Treatise" into British soil, he nevertheless reports a few facts concerning this strange philosophy that make Teufelsdröckh appear a Don Quixote *redivivus*. Thus a British perspective dominates. After a short while, however, this seemingly ridiculous philosopher, whose loquaciousness was published by Stillschweigen and Co, turns out to be "*ein echter Spass- und Galgen-vogel*" (11) himself. This at least implies that there is no immediate need for the English Editor to poke fun at German transcendental philosophy, as Teufelsdröckh himself manifests a sense of superiority by ironizing himself. The ludicrous Don Quixote turns unexpectedly into a Tristram Shandy; this is also borne out by his work, which is of a "labyrinthic combination, each Part overlaps, and indents, and indeed runs quite through the other" (26–27). Just as Sterne made Tristram Shandy deconstruct the history of his own life in order to liberate life from the very confinements imposed on it by form, Carlyle makes Teufelsdröckh gamble away all existing forms of writing in order to bring out the fantastic multifariousness of his Philosophy of Clothes.

Thus Teufelsdröckh presents himself in a dual reading,[12] never coinciding totally with either a Don Quixote or a Tristram Shandy. Whenever one reading appears to become dominant, the other, lurking in the background, gradually asserts itself. This very assertion, however, which might do away with the equivocalness, is again tilted, and the salience of the displaced figure begins once more to loom large. Tilting between

---

12. Lore Metzger tends to confine Teufelsdröckh's "uneasy equilibrium between the two halves of his nature" to the antagonism of Faust and Mephistopheles, which makes him alternate between "divine inspiration of divinely begotten man and its eternal negation in the devil and the body's dross" ("*Sartor Resartus*: A Victorian Faust," *Comparative Literature* 13 [1961]: 317). Yet she also points out essential differences through which Carlyle diverged from Goethe (see esp. 325–336). Charles F. Harrold, *Carlyle and German Thought: 1819–1834*, Yale Studies in English 82 (New Haven: Yale University Press, 1934), 5–6, considers Teufelsdröckh a direct offspring of Jean Paul's humorous characters. See also Dennis Douglas, "Carlyle and the Jacobin Undercurrent in German Transcendentalism," *Bulletin of the New York Public Library* 80 (1976): 108.

incompatibles transforms Teufelsdröckh into an operator of the switches necessary when cultures have to be telescoped for the purpose of their mutual transmittance and reception. What initially appeared as an empty space manifesting itself in the constant interchange between narrating and arguing, and then as a space between a life lived and a philosophy capturing that life, now reappears as a constant tilting between mutually exclusive readings of the protagonist, thus setting cross-cultural operations in motion.

This tilting game endows the sense of comedy that permeates *Sartor Resartus* with a countervailing tendency. Teufelsdröckh is as much a target of comedy as he targets what has to be exposed. In this respect the black box between cultures assumes a different shape from those outlined so far in that it makes the ambivalence of comedy turn back on itself. Teufelsdröckh is not only a humorist but also sallies forth into irony. This irony is indicative of his having pierced through the naïveté, the ignorance, the superficiality, and the delusion dominating the world he wants to revolutionize by the philosophy he puts forward. As a humorist, however, he knows that the situation he finds himself in is marked by an ineluctable duality that makes his abstractions look absurd, although they are the remedy for the social ills of the very world that has made him a laughingstock. Irony and humor, however, equally measure out the distance between a concept-oriented culture and an empirically oriented one, highlighting Teufelsdröckh's helpless superiority and the world's inherent blindness, which his abstractions were meant to cure.

As far as the Editor is concerned, poking fun at German transcendentalism implicitly asserts a British attitude that allows transcendentalism to be channeled into empiricism. In the mirror of an experience-based attitude, the Philosophy of Clothes is reflected as convoluted craziness, and therefore the Editor appeals to "Experience" as "the grand spiritual Doctor" (145). To reshuffle the abstractions of transcendentalism in terms of experience, however, is not an easy task.[13] Although the Editor cannot

---

13. This is equally reflected in Carlyle criticism, which privileges either the idealist or the empiricist component of this cross-cultural relationship. Tom Lloyd, "Towards Natural Supernaturalism: Carlyle and Dual Vision," *Philological Quarterly* 65 (1986): 479–494, gives a balanced view of this situation. See also Lloyd's essay "Madame Roland and Schiller's *Aesthetics*: Carlyle's 'The French Revolution,' " *Prose Studies* 3 (1986): 39–53. Dibble indicates why the two components of Carlyle's thought are so intimately interlinked: "The conflict between 'English' realism and 'German' idealism . . . begins in earnest with Kant's first *Critique*, and it is there one sees most readily the rhetorical dilemma out of which *Sartor Resartus* came" ("Strategies of the Mental War," 90).

think of a "work nobler than transplanting foreign Thought into the barren domestic soil," he has to pull up "the Diligence and feeble thinking Faculty of an English Editor, endeavouring to evolve printed Creation out of a German printed and written Chaos, wherein, as he shoots to and fro in it, gathering, clutching, piercing the Why to the far-distant Wherefore, his whole Faculty and Self are like to be swallowed up" (63). The danger of being swallowed up in such an undertaking requires some kind of protection, and, in this respect, the sense of humor—deeply ingrained in the British attitude and brought to bear by the Editor—spells out the hope for survival.

This very hope, however, again makes the comedy leveled at that gibberish of abstractions ambivalent. The seemingly chaotic craziness is not meant to criticize the other culture but serves to protect one's own habitual attitudes, so that such a criticism says something not only about the foreignness of the other culture but also about the nature of one's own disposition. In this respect, the foreignness turns into a self-mirroring of those who encounter the alien culture.

Finally, the comic vein running throughout *Sartor Resartus* is in itself ambiguous.[14] Not only is Teufelsdröckh a humorist, but a great many of his statements are punctured by irony, and more often than not the things he says are tongue-in-cheek. The English Editor is fully aware of the German philosopher's mode of writing, summing it up in the pithy observation: "Nothing but innuendoes, figurative crotchets: the typical Shadow, fitfully wavering, prophetico-satiric; no clear logical Picture" (148). If this convoluted transcendentalism is permeated by streaks of satire that the author himself intersperses in his own writings, then a satiric or ironic treatment of Teufelsdröckh's endeavors as entertained by the English Editor is on the verge of becoming pointless.

Why poke fun at a humorist? Well, the Editor, who is sympathetically disposed toward German transcendentalism, anticipates an entrenched British aversion toward these seemingly intangible abstractions. Ridiculing these intellectual acrobatics, however, implies that one is in command of the proper solutions that Teufelsdröckh is groping for in vain. But because the humorist is not as naive as his seemingly ludicrous efforts

---

14. Harold Bloom sees Carlyle "in the tradition of Rabelais, Voltaire, and Swift, so far as his genre (or non-genre) can be determined, but he is less a satirist than the seer of a grotesque phantasmagoria" (introduction to *Thomas Carlyle*, ed. Harold Bloom [New York: Chelsea House 1986], 13). Tennyson maintains: "As always, Carlyle's method is, by exaggeration and caricature, to call attention to the truth" (*Carlyle and the Modern World*, 22).

appear to be, the sense of comedy, as practiced by the Editor, is of a twofold nature. On the one hand, it serves as a channel of communication through which German idealism can be transmitted into British empiricism. On the other, however, it makes the assumed superiority of satire and irony collapse in view of the fact that the humorist does not stand in need of being either unmasked or brought down to earth again. To frustrate an almost natural reaction of one culture when confronted with another proves to be a strategy on Carlyle's part to open the gate for the other culture to enter. This is the exact opposite of common cross-cultural relationships, whose operations are first and foremost guided by projecting one's own frame of reference onto the alien culture. By making the sense of comedy militate against itself, Carlyle suspends the natural urge for projections operative in cross-cultural relations.

This tendency is endorsed by what gradually happens to the Editor. He had considered it his commitment "to guide our British Friends into the new Gold-country, and show them the mines; nowise to dig-out and exhaust its wealth, which indeed remains for all time inexhaustible. Once there, let each dig for his own behoof, and enrich himself" (166). Yet this intention to provide guidance to the British reader makes the Editor cross the boundary to the "Gold-country" himself, in the course of which he becomes a proselyte, thereby lapsing into a metaphorical style of writing "with which mode of utterance Teufelsdröckh unhappily has somewhat infected us." Therefore it is not "hidden from the Editor that many a British Reader sits reading quite bewildered in head, and afflicted rather than instructed by the present Work. . . . Yes, long ago has many a British Reader been, as now, demanding with something like a snarl: Whereto does all this lead; or what use is in it?" (215). Although the Editor has apparently been sucked into Teufelsdröckh's manner of writing, thereby losing "much of his own English purity" (234), he nevertheless raises the question as to the purpose of the cross-cultural discourse that he meant to lay bare.

PHILOSOPHY OF CLOTHES

In this respect it is worth noting that Sartor Resartus is primarily a paradigm of translatability rather than an actual translation of one culture into another. Its paradigmatic quality has the advantage of exhibiting the workings of mutual transpositions of cultures in that they are not as yet guided, let alone determined, by a pragmatic purpose that would make the translatability subservient to a particular end, as exemplified in Carlyle's later work Past and Present.

The Philosophy of Clothes as put forward by Teufelsdröckh is to be conceived as an anatomy of representation. As representation presupposes a given of sorts, one can distinguish different modes of representation. *Imitation* is certainly the most time-honored, even though something is bound to happen to the pregiven when represented. Something similar occurs if representation is conceived in terms of *depiction*. What is pregiven will have to be fashioned. But in both these instances representation is to be considered rather as a modality, whose range of molding is limited by a set of qualities the pregiven appears to have prior to its being represented.

In this respect the Philosophy of Clothes can be confined neither to imitation nor to depiction.[15] Instead, it anatomizes the process of translatability itself, which, more often than not, is glossed over when imitation or depiction is the overriding concern of representation. Translatability is in itself something intangible; it does not have the nature of a pregiven object and hence can be tackled only by metaphors, as evinced in the Philosophy of Clothes. Clothing something is therefore neither a mode of imitation nor one of depiction. Although it seems that what is to be clothed must somehow preexist, this preexistence is never to be ascertained independently of its being clothed. This is why Carlyle makes it quite explicit that Teufelsdröckh is not a "new Adamite" (45); instead, he promulgates: "Without Clothes, without bit or saddle, what hadst thou been; what had thy fleet quadruped been? — Nature is good, but she is not the best: here truly was the victory of Art over Nature" (46).

If clothes cannot be considered forms of representation in the received sense of the term, as there is no one-way incline from something preexisting to its modes of conceivability, it would seem necessary to recast representation almost entirely. Right from the outset Carlyle keeps "regarding Clothes as a property, not an accident, as quite natural and spontaneous, like the leaves of trees, like the plumage of birds" (2). No doubt such a statement clears Teufelsdröckh from a possible charge of Adamitism. And yet it remains double-edged, because human beings do not enter the world with a "plumage" as animals do. Instead, as Teufelsdröckh confesses:

---

15. It is equally hard to trace the Philosophy of Clothes back to Swedenborg, as tentatively suggested by James C. Malin, "Carlyle's Philosophy of Clothes and Swedenborg's," in *Scandinavian Studies* 33 (1961): 155–68. Douglas is certainly right in stating that in this respect Carlyle's "basic orientation is Kantian" ("Carlyle and the Jacobin Undercurrent," 107).

"While I—good Heaven!—have thatched myself over with the dead fleeces of sheep, the bark of vegetables, the entrails of worms, the hides of oxen or seals, the felt of furred beasts; and walk abroad a moving Rag-screen, overheaped with shreds and tatters raked from the Charnel-house of Nature, where they would have rotted, to rot on me more slowly!" (44) Thus the apparent naturalness of wearing clothes is nevertheless a product of human tailoring and therefore definitely not something that comes naturally. What is natural in the kingdom of animals does not apply to human beings, although human beings do not exist apart from the clothes they wear. Obviously there is both identity and difference between clothes and human beings. Why stress difference, when it is made to collapse into an inseparable unity?

Representation as conceived by Teufelsdröckh's Philosophy of Clothes has a double trajectory: "For indeed, as Walter Shandy often insisted, there is much, nay almost all, in Names. The Name is the earliest Garment you wrap round the earth-visiting ME; to which it thenceforth cleaves, more tenaciously (for there are Names that have lasted nigh thirty centuries) than the very skin. And now from without, what mystic influences does it not send inwards, even to the centre; especially in those plastic first-times, when the whole soul is yet infantine, soft, and the invisible seedgrain will grow to be an all overshadowing tree!" (69) Garments, though they are a metaphor for something preexisting, simultaneously pattern what they are meant to represent. This is the plasticity of human nature, which, as such, not only remains intangible but appears to offer itself to being shaped and molded into kaleidoscopically changing forms. In this respect, each garment is a "plumage," although the very plasticity allows the plumage to be changed whenever necessity arises. Of course, such a patterning bears its own risks either by imprisoning the human being in one of the garments in which it has clothed itself or by deliberately reifying the clothes to which it has become endeared, as practiced by the "Dandiacal Body!" (229).

The Philosophy of Clothes is a kind of shorthand for the patterning and repatterning of human plasticity. It is initially conceived as a metaphor, because human plasticity is not accessible in itself. Yet the metaphor turns into a patterning and thus functions metonymically; otherwise, human beings would elude grasping. A metonymically functioning metaphor bears the inscription that whatever is, is constituted. Thus the Philosophy of Clothes ceases to be representation in the received sense, as a mere shifting of a pregiven into perceivability is no longer the issue. Instead, clothing itself translates the plastic human being into a definitive pattern in order to fathom what otherwise remains elusive. The metonymy therefore highlights the garment as a substitute that can be changed when worn out, not least in order to body forth aspects of human plasticity hitherto unthinkable.

The metonymic use of metaphors enables the Philosophy of Clothes to maintain the difference between the patterned and the patternings, thus allowing for the variability of patternings out of which human civilization arises. Simultaneously all forms of civilization are exposed to change as all the patternings that make up society can be repatterned. "Whatsoever sensibly exists, whatsoever represents Spirit to Spirit, is properly a Clothing, a suit of Raiment, put on for a season, and to be laid off. Thus in this one pregnant subject of CLOTHES, rightly understood, is included all that men have thought, dreamed, done, and been: the whole External Universe and what it holds is but Clothing; and the essence of all Science lies in the PHILOSOPHY OF CLOTHES" (58).

Thus the garment turns out to be a symbol of a special kind that presents itself as a representative of something intangible and simultaneously shapes that very intangibility, for which it is only a substitute.[16] In Teufelsdröckh's own words: "In a Symbol there is concealment and yet revelation: here therefore, by Silence and by Speech acting together, comes a double significance" (175). As far as the symbol conceals, it indicates through its visibility that "the thing Imagined, the thing in any way conceived as Visible, what is it but a Garment, a Clothing of the higher, celestial Invisible, 'unimaginable, formless, dark with excess of bright' " (52). And as far as the symbol speaks, it indicates that this formless unspeakability can be translated into multifarious aspects by imposing everchanging patternings on it. Out of this ineluctable duality arises the Philosophy of Clothes, which is an attempt at fathoming the unplumbable by translating it into a welter of

---

16. For the intimate relationship between symbol and silence, see Camille R. La Bossiere, "Of Silence, Doubt, and Imagination: Carlyle's Conversation with Montaigne," *English Studies in Canada* 10 (1984): 63–64, 72. This essay appears to be one of the rare occasions in Carlyle criticism that draws attention to the circularity of Carlyle's interpretive procedure: "The thought of *Sartor Resartus* and its complex of core images take the reader on a circular odyssey, the chart of which plots the progress of the Carlylean imagination" (67). There is still a difference between circularity and looping, however. For further evaluation of how Carlyle uses symbols in order to give voice to the unspeakable, see Findlay, "Paul de Man, Thomas Carlyle," 176–177, 179.

perceivable symbols whose very limitations expose them to change. Changes are all the more necessary because no particular type of garment can ever be equated with the inaccessibility it tries to capture. And therefore every garment is subject to critical inspection in order to find out the ulterior motivation operative in the patterning of the "invisible and unspeakable."

The reason for this duality of the symbol as substitute and patterning is that the "secret of Man's Being is still like the Sphinx's secret" (42). Such a concealment, however, is not something to be penetrated or even tackled, because the unfathomableness of the human being results from a basic ignorance of humankind:

> Was Man with his Experience present at the Creation, then, to see how it all went on? Have any deepest scientific individuals yet dived down to the foundations of the Universe, and gauged everything there? Did the Maker take them into His counsel; that they read His ground plan of the incomprehensible All; and can say, This stands marked therein, and no more than this? Alas, not in anywise! These scientific individuals have been nowhere but where we also are; have seen some handbreadths deeper than we see into the Deep that is infinite, without bottom as without shore. (204)

Such an impenetrableness translates itself into a Philosophy of Clothes, because human beings have to live, to interact, to establish organizations, societies, and religions, which obtain their stability by a differentiated system of clothes. Therefore clothing itself "has more than a common meaning, but has two meanings" (52). On the one hand, it can conceal the groundlessness from view, which results in a reification of the garment; on the other, it can heighten the awareness that, as a substitute, it is a patterning of the unfathomable, guided or even caused by pragmatic exigencies. Thus the groundlessness inscribes itself as duality into the garment.

This may have been one of the reasons that the Editor, when first encountering Teufelsdröckh, took him to be a kind of philosopher, who, if he were to publish anything at all, would come out with "a refutation of Hegel" (10). The Editor anticipated correctly that a Philosophy of Identity would be anathema to someone advocating a Philosophy of Difference.[17] Instead of identifying the "Spirit" with its manifestations, the

---

17. For a different view of the assumed parallels between Carlyle and Hegel, especially between *Sartor Resartus* and *The Phenomenology of Mind*, see Dibble, "Strategies of the Mental War," 97–102.

Philosophy of Clothes emphasizes difference between an impenetrable groundlessness and the ensuing necessity to constitute human life by constantly clothing it and then retailoring the clothes.

Trying to chart what remains hidden from view turns the Philosophy of Clothes into a systematic attempt at coping with openness. Such an attempt implies that the metonymic patterning can never be a projection covering up the groundlessness. Rather, it develops as a recursive loop feeding forward the garment in order to clothe openness, an openness that in turn becomes a negative feedback loop by exposing the garments to change when they no longer fit. Thus the recursive loop adjusts future clothing according to the past performance of the garments. This loop keeps the Philosophy of Clothes from reifying the garments and simultaneously activates the groundlessness as a form of retailoring.

Such a mutual translatability might be conceived as the hallmark of culture, not least because the latter, since the advent of the modern age, can no longer be grounded in an etiological myth. If an impenetrable groundlessness replaces the etiological myth as the mainspring of culture, the necessary stability can only be provided by a network of translatabilities, as exemplified by the Philosophy of Clothes. The life of culture realizes itself in such recursive loops, and it begins to dry up whenever the loop is discontinued by elevating one of the achievements of its interchange into an all-encompassing form of representation. Representation runs counter to translatability, whose ongoing transformations are brought to a standstill by equating culture with one of its conspicuous features. The recursive loop, however, is able to process groundlessness, and as there is no stance beyond this loop for ascertaining what happens in its operations, the Philosophy of Clothes presents itself as a paradigm for spelling out the blueprint of culture. This paradigm has a dual coding: it makes tangible what analytically remains ungraspable, and as a mode of translatability it provides access to what is beyond the terms of empiricism.

VALIDATION BY PERSONAL EXPERIENCE

To allegorize German transcendentalism—at least as Carlyle understood it—allows the transposition of something alien into a mode of perception familiar to the receiving culture. This is stressed right at the beginning by the Editor, who keeps pondering, "How could the Philosophy of Clothes, and the Author of such Philosophy, be brought home, in any measure, to the business and bosoms of our own English Nation?" (6).

He tackles it basically by translating the convolutions of transcendentalism in terms of the philosopher's own life, in order to demonstrate that he did not just concoct these seeming absurdities out of nothing; instead, they arose out of personal experience. This allows transcendental speculations to be validated by what happened to their author: "But indeed Conviction, were it never so excellent, is worthless till it convert itself into Conduct. Nay properly Conviction is not possible till then; inasmuch as all Speculation is by nature endless, formless, a vortex amid vortices: only by a felt indubitable certainty of Experience does it find any centre to revolve round, and so fashion itself into a system" (156). Such a linkup, however, provides a different referent for transcendentalism; it is no longer considered a holistic system but conceived as an impact able to turn one's whole life around. The possibility of experiencing what appears to be speculative and of perceiving the invisible are frames of reference different from what may be considered the basic premises of German transcendentalism. The emphasis on experience makes it obvious that German transcendentalism, when transposed into British empiricism, has to be executed in terms the British reader is familiar with. Yet simultaneously Carlyle reflects on this familiarity when castigating what he calls "a dead Iron Balance for weighing Pains and Pleasures on" (176) as deeply ingrained in the British disposition. Much as an empirically oriented attitude prevails in order to make this constant trading in abstractions conceivable, if not palatable, to an English audience, Carlyle nevertheless battles against such an attitude, because it tends to congeal into a custom, and as "we do everything by Custom, even Believe by it," he continues quoting from the work of his hero: "Nay, what is Philosophy throughout but a continual battle against Custom; an ever-renewed effort to *transcend* the sphere of blind Custom, and so become Transcendental?" (206). Such a transcendentalism is actually meant to monitor what human beings are doing, and, though experience-oriented, they should nevertheless be able to distance themselves from what they are involved in, in order to be able to process experience itself.

Teufelsdröckh's life illustrates this overriding aim, because what happens to an individual carries much more conviction than the mere exposition of a philosophical system. Teufelsdröckh himself, although the engineer of the Philosophy of Clothes, nevertheless has reservations about abstractions that are in no way tied to the mastery of life. If being transcendental implies monitoring oneself, then German transcendentalism is turned into an instrument for processing experience as exemplified by

Teufelsdröckh's life. Such a life becomes an epitome of how different cultures may be translated into one another.

Highlighting such a process in terms of an individual life is an offshoot of romanticism, which elevated the self into a be-all and end-all. What triggers the necessity of translating cultures into one another is again the moment of crisis that Teufelsdröckh experiences by moving from the stage of the *"Everlasting No"* through the *"Centre of Indifference"* to the *"Everlasting Yea"* (italics mine). At the outset "the universe" was for him "as a mighty Sphinx-riddle," of which he knew "so little . . . , yet must rede or be devoured." And he continues: "In red streaks of unspeakable grandeur, yet also in the blackness of darkness, was Life, to my too-unfurnished Thought, unfolding itself. A strange contradiction lay in me; and I as yet knew not the solution of it" (102). This situation plunges Teufelsdröckh into a crisis, and, long before Plessner and Lacan described the decentered position of the human being,[18] he made the pithy remark "WE are — we know not what" (43). Such a split between being and not knowing what it is to be is at the bottom of Teufelsdröckh's crisis, which develops into an almost unmanageable duality: "It is because there is an Infinite in him, which with all his cunning he cannot quite bury under the Finite" (151–152).

This growing awareness that he is also the other of himself triggers the necessity to resolve the duality by translating the decentered positions into one another. Out of this effort arises the Philosophy of Clothes, whose main thrust is not philosophical speculation but an attempt to deal with "their *Wirken*, or Influences" (40). This focus on the impact that the Philosophy of Clothes is meant to exercise arises from Teufelsdröckh's experience that his own life appears to him impenetrable, as manifested in his crisis, and consequently has neither to be explained nor to be understood but to be mastered. Such a mastering has a dual reference. On the one hand, the garment patterns what it clothes, and, on the other, the garment exercises an impact on the social conditions in which it is displayed. In a "Society . . . to be as good as extinct," in which "the CHURCH [has] fallen speechless, from obesity and apoplexy; the STATE shrunken into a Police-Office, straitened to get its pay!" (184–185), the Philosophy of

---

18. See Helmuth Plessner, "Die anthropologische Dimension der Geschichtlichkeit," in *Sozialer Wandel: Zivilisation und Fortschritt in der soziologischen Theorie*, ed. Hans Peter Dreitzel (Neuwied: Luchterhand, 1972), 160; and Jacques Lacan, *Écrits* (Paris: Éditions du Seul, 1966), 93–94, 97.

Clothes is, according to the Editor, meant to excite "us to self-activity, which is the best effect of any book" (21). Inciting self-activity means changing worn-out clothes, and the subsequent divesting of society is simultaneously a redressing of its ills, because garments pattern what is otherwise impenetrable and therefore can be exchanged for a more adequate patterning.

Teufelsdröckh's life serves as the living emblem for such a perpetual rejuvenation. The *Centre of Indifference* is the black box of his own life, a gulf that yawns between his being alive and not knowing what it means to live. This unplumbable *Centre* that divides him from himself defies cognition and thus translates itself into activity, feeding the *No* into a nascent *Yea*, whose feedback makes the *No* vanish; this evaporation in turn feeds the strength of conviction into the *Yea*. Teufelsdröckh's life provides a vivid illustration of the fact that even an individual life is marked by a black box that may be cast as an empty space, a space between, or a *Centre of Indifference*, whose impenetrableness gives rise to recursive loops of human self-fashioning. Thus human life mirrors the very structure out of which culture arises. Yet Carlyle left no doubt that the elevated self inherited from romanticism had to be transformed into a hero who testifies that only an outstanding individual is able to endure the crisis by translating it into a mastery of life.

The experience of crisis gives rise to the Philosophy of Clothes in order to process human life, whose ground is sealed off from cognitive penetration. Just as life is unfathomable, so is culture, which in the final analysis manifests itself as a mastery of life. In proportion to a growing awareness that the assumed fundamentals of life and culture are exposed to erosion, repair becomes necessary, and this can no longer mean exchanging one set of fundamentals for another. Instead, life and culture have to be reshuffled: in Teufelsdröckh's case, by coming up with the Philosophy of Clothes; in Carlyle's case, by designing the cross-cultural discourse of *Sartor Resartus*.

As long as there is an overriding conviction that a culture rests on a firm foundation, the necessity for a cross-cultural discourse does not arise. For such a self-understanding of culture, a cross-cultural discourse can only mean a foreign intrusion. The very fact, however, that a mutual assimilation, incorporation, or appropriation of cultures is always going on bears witness to exigencies that have to be met. This mutual commerce, however, is at best a patching-up of what has been eroded or lost, and it does not substantively contribute to a revitalization of what has become defunct.

A cross-cultural discourse distinguishes itself from assimilation, incorporation, and appropriation, as it organizes an interchange between cultures in which the cultures concerned will not stay the same. A foreign culture is not just transposed into a familiar one; instead, as in the Philosophy of Clothes, a mutual patterning and repatterning is effected by the discourse. First of all, the foreign culture is modeled on conditions set by the receiving one and thus becomes defamiliarized. This defamiliarization is due to the terms imposed on otherness for its reception, as German transcendentalism is meant to resuscitate the dying culture of laissez-faire. That is the service to be rendered in face of the crisis that emerged in an agrarian society plunged into industrial production. In such a takeover of German transcendentalism, its very abstractions are recast. They no longer figure and delineate the manifestations of the Spirit on its way to becoming conscious of itself but are transformed into tools for processing a crisis-ridden culture no longer able to cope with the situation on its own terms. Transcendentalism therefore is neither assimilated nor appropriated but "clothed" in such a manner that its repatterning can serve the self-regeneration of an empirically oriented culture.

To accommodate transcendentalism for such a purpose, some kind of fashioning is necessary in order to make its transmittance feasible. Therefore the Editor pokes fun at the convoluted abstractions of this "written Chaos." The sense of comedy that pervades *Sartor Resartus* strangely loses its impact whenever it hits its target, however, thus invalidating habitual reactions to the absurd musings of German philosophy. The frustrated comedy turns into a trajectory along which the otherwise unpalatable abstractions are able to travel.

The operations of such a cross-cultural discourse are realized in loops; by eclipsing the convention-bound features of the cultures concerned, they feed the crisis of a defunct society into transcendentalism, and by feedback they loop self-activity into empiricism. These loops work chiastically, thus converting the black box between cultures into a dynamism, exposing each one to its otherness, the mastery of which results in change. In this respect, the cross-cultural discourse is a means of mutually supportive self-regeneration of cultures and provides an opportunity to extend their life span. As a propellant for change, the discourse bears witness to the fact that no culture is founded on itself, which is evinced not least by the array of mythologies invoked when the assumed foundation of a culture has to be substantiated.

The interlinking of cultures brought about by a cross-cultural discourse enacts one culture in terms of the other. German transcendentalism is staged in terms of British empiricism and vice versa. Such a staging prevents one culture from dominating the other, and such a mutual enacting simultaneously implies a suspension of the frames of reference pertaining to the cultures telescoped. If empirical criteria guide the takeover of German transcendentalism, an alien set of references is applied that both dwarfs and enlarges features of transcendentalism. Something similar happens to empiricism when transcendentalism provides the criteria. This mutuality has repercussions for the cross-cultural discourse.

With traditional references suspended, new ones have to be established, which is all the more difficult as the mutual enacting of cultures exposes them to change. The change appears to be necessary, as the old orientation of the respective culture has crumbled and can no longer serve as a guideline for coping with the crisis. The Philosophy of Clothes gives a very vivid impression of such a situation. Teufelsdröckh writes: "The sight reaches forth into the void Deep, and you are alone with the Universe, and silently commune with it, as one mysterious Presence with another. Who am I; what is this ME? A Voice, a Motion, an Appearance; — some embodied, visualised Idea in the Eternal Mind? *Cogito, ergo sum.* Alas, poor Cogitator, this takes us but a little way" (41).

When the inherited frameworks are invalidated, the cross-cultural discourse has to establish its own guidelines, and this endeavor is paradigmatic for cross-cultural discourse in general. It cannot exchange one frame of reference for another; instead, it has to establish multiple references in order to provide sufficient orientation for both the remedy of crisis and the control of change. Therefore routes of reference have to be explored and linked up in chains of kaleidoscopically changing modes of reference.[19]

Teufelsdröckh's Philosophy of Clothes is initially meant to designate German transcendentalism. This very designation, however, is used to exemplify how human plasticity is to be shaped. The shifting of references continues when this particular exemplification serves as an expression of how a crisis is to be tackled. Designation, exemplification, and expression are no longer tied to a pregiven frame of reference within which they exercise their function. Instead, they are made to substitute for one another, and the ensuing interchange of their referential modes produces the very guidelines along which the cross-cultural discourse

---

19. Concerning the notion and function of routes or chains of reference, see Nelson Goodman, *Of Mind and Other Matters* (Cambridge: Harvard University Press, 1984), 54–71.

unfolds its operations. Consequently, one culture designates something in another in order to exemplify what cannot be seen by the culture concerned, and thus it may turn into an expression of what the culture is like and why—in view of what it is—it is liable to lapse. Designation of a crisis could then also turn into an exemplification of the remedy, which in turn may give expression to the other culture invoked. And in doing so, it designates something in that culture to which the culture itself appears to be blind.

A cross-cultural discourse has thus to bring about its own referentiality, which is indispensable, as such a discourse can only operate within but not beyond reference. The only control to be exercised over the establishment of its own referentiality is the mutual mirroring of the cultures concerned, and this makes the cross-cultural discourse into a stage on which different cultures are enacted under mutually alien conditions. A discourse that liberates its referential control from any pregiven frame of reference in order to generate its own control by constantly shifting modes of reference assumes aesthetic features. What keeps it, however, from turning into an artwork is its amphibolic nature, as manifested by its inherent duality. It stages a mutual mirroring of cultures and disappears when it has wrought the transformation of the cultures concerned. This highlights its quality as a catalyst, emphasized at the end of *Sartor Resartus*: "Professor Teufelsdröckh, be it known, is no longer visibly present at Weissnichtwo, but again to all appearance lost in space!" The only trace left is his last saying: "*Es geht an* (It is beginning)" (236).[20]

Enfoldings in Paterian Discourse: Modes of Translatability

Nowadays Walter Pater's writings are no longer taken for "the discovery of a gospel, of a new way of living,"[21] as Logan Pearsall Smith took them to be. Voices like that of Yeats, who maintained for himself and his friends that "we looked consciously to Pater for our philosophy,"[22] have fallen

---

20. Moore stresses Carlyle's commitment to action: "Action not only removes religious doubt, it creates faith and happiness and, in the form of work, creates order and belief in a dynamic society" ("Carlyle's 'Conversion,' " 674).
21. Logan Pearsall Smith, *Reperusals and Recollections* (London: Constable, 1936), 67.
22. Quoted in Edmund Wilson, *Axel's Castle: A Study in the Imaginative Literature of 1870–1930* (London: Collins, 1961), 34.

silent. *Marius the Epicurean*, which George Moore avowed to be "the book to which I owe the last temple in my soul,"[23] no longer provides the spiritual awakening he believed he had experienced. And it is even more than doubtful whether the statement made by the Anglican clergyman J. A. Hutton in 1906 could still claim any validity: "There is a stage, and in our day amongst educated people it has come to be almost a necessary stage, at which the writings of Pater are able to define our troubles to ourselves, and, in a way, to deal with them as no writer whom I know can with equal discernment."[24]

For a few decades after his death Pater enjoyed a somewhat mixed reception in relation to the guidance he provided for living in a world in which "we are all under sentence of death but with a sort of indefinite reprieve,"[25] as well as for monitoring the self that had "to burn always with this hard, gemlike flame" (236). Increasing distance made his achievements shrink, as pinpointed by Chesterton, who still maintained with some sympathy that "Pater may well stand for a substantial summary of the aesthetes."[26] It was exactly such a "summary" that T. S. Eliot both contested and downgraded:

> The right practice of "art for art's sake" was the devotion of Flaubert or Henry James; Pater is not with these men, but rather with Carlyle and Ruskin and Arnold, if some distance below them. *Marius* is significant chiefly as a reminder that the religion of Carlyle or that of Ruskin or that of Arnold or that of Tennyson or that of Browning, is not enough. It represents, and Pater represents more positively than Coleridge of whom he wrote the words, "that inexhaustible discontent, languor, and homesickness . . . the chords of which ring through all our modern literature."[27]

---

23. George Moore, *Confessions of a Young Man* (London: Heinemann, 1952), 139.

24. J. A. Hutton, *Pilgrims in the Religion of Faith* (Edinburgh: Oliphant, Anderson, and Ferrier, 1906), 66f.

25. Walter Pater, *The Renaissance: Studies in Art and Poetry* (London: Macmillan, 1919), 238.

26. G. K. Chesterton, *The Victorian Age in Literature* (London: Oxford University Press, 1966), 28.

27. T. S. Eliot, *Selected Essays* (London: Faber and Faber, 1951), 443.

Pater's writings are no longer to be viewed as a gospel, and what used to be a guiding philosophy has faded into the weariness of unattainable longings. Such a kaleidoscopically shifting reception points to the fact that Pater was primarily viewed as a representative either of the aestheticism he advocated or of the secular religion he failed to achieve.

This approach to Pater has inevitably relegated him to the past, making him at best into an epitome of concerns no longer relevant. Meanwhile, however, these very assessments have themselves become historical, not least as they have so exclusively focused on what Pater stood for. Privileging the idea of representation is symptomatic of the fact that the reception of a past is dominated by a desire to classify, but such dominance screens off all the details that defy integration into the organizing patterns. Consequently, these details are bound to emerge again when the horizon of expectation changes. We may no longer be interested in what Pater represented but rather in what he might have anticipated. Did he throw light on something we are preoccupied with, and, if so, to what extent did he address issues that are now current?

Toward the end of his career, Pater reflected both on the modes and on the generic features of the various types of discourse he had either practiced or opposed. In *Plato and Platonism* we read:

> The poem, the treatise, the essay: you see already that these three methods of writing are no mere literary accidents, dependent on the personal choice of this or that particular writer, but necessities of literary form, determined directly by matter, as corresponding to three essentially different ways in which the human mind relates itself to truth. If oracular verse, stimulant but enigmatic, is the proper vehicle of enthusiastic intuitions; if the treatise, with its ambitious array of premiss and conclusion, is the natural out-put of scholastic all-sufficiency; so, the form of the essay [is] the literary form necessary to a mind for which truth itself is but a possibility, realisable not as general conclusion, but rather as the elusive effect of a particular personal experience; to a mind which, noting faithfully those random lights that meet it by the way, must needs content itself with suspension of judgment, at the end of the intellectual journey, to the very last asking: *Que scais-je?*[28]

28. Walter Pater, *Plato and Platonism: A Series of Lectures* (London: Macmillan, 1920), 175f.

Such a reflection highlights an awareness of how the very modality of discourse predetermines the way in which subject matter is captured. If the human mind's relation to truth is dependent on the form of discourse chosen, then Pater opened up an issue that has become prominent in our own fin de siècle, namely, what actually happens in interpretation. Pater provided, almost in a nutshell, an anatomy of interpretation, and, even more important, he fed his insights back into his own writings, thus splitting them up into a diversity of differently operating discourses. Having made interpretation itself into an object of scrutiny and having retooled the mechanics of discourse gives Pater an unprecedented presence one hundred years after his death.

Why has interpretation become such an overriding concern, and to what extent do the types of Paterian discourse epitomize basic structures of interpretation to which we have only now become alert? Each interpretation, we have to remind ourselves, translates something into a different register. Or, as Pater phrased it: "Well! all language involves translation from inward to outward."[29] If that is so, then we should shift our focus away from underlying presuppositions to the space that is opened up when something is translated into something else. As each act of interpretation creates such a space, its intent will realize itself in the way in which this space is negotiated. If interpretation is primarily a form of translation, clearly it is dependent on what is translated, and Pater was well aware of this when he stated that "methods of writing are . . . determined directly by matter."[30]

How Pater practiced interpretation as modes of translatability is revealed by his different "methods of writing," which in turn are marked off from one another according to the way in which that in-between space is coped with. What makes him exemplary for current concerns is his rejection of axioms and definitions as starting points of interpretation; instead, he prefers to measure the distance caused by any transposition of something into something else and to incorporate that distance into his own discourse.

---

29. Walter Pater, *Appreciations, with an Essay on Style* (London: Macmillan, 1920), 34. In his book *Plato and Platonism*, Pater already voiced his criticism against a type of interpretation that laid claim to a monopoly by stating: "The treatise as the instrument of dogmatic philosophy begins with an axiom or a definition" and is bound to end in "a system of propositions" (188).
30. Pater, *Plato and Platonism*, 175.

This is most strikingly to be observed in one of his last works, *Plato and Platonism*, which Pater considered the best of all his writings.[31] The fairly systematic exposition of Plato's philosophy and its antecedents is cast in a form that strangely deviates from any philosophical "methods of writing," such as the treatise, on which Pater expressly reflected in his presentation of Plato's philosophy. He considered the philosophical armory of writing inadequate for his undertaking, not least as in "the history of philosophy there are no absolute beginnings," and whatever may be taken for such a beginning either slides back into "forethoughts" or turns out to be nothing but an abstract concept that is identified with a supposed origin.[32] If origins are unplumbable, all our umbrella concepts such as "organism and environment, or protoplasm perhaps, or evolution, or the *Zeitgeist* and its doings, may, in their turn, come to seem quite as lifeless and unendurable" (154). With no overriding frame of reference available, no axioms and definitions to begin with, Pater's interpretation of Plato is confronted with the distance between now and then, between fragmentary, mythological philosophizing and systematic conceptualization, and also between Plato's texts and the other register into which Pater intended to transpose them. For Pater, moreover, the space opened up by interpretation between the subject matter and the register into which it is translated could no longer be glossed over by any abstract notions or presuppositions, whose claim to reality Pater never espoused. Consequently, the space between proved to be ineradicable, not least as all translations produce a residual untranslatability that can only be narrowed down in the act of interpretation.

Being aware that the space opened up by interpretation itself could never be eliminated, Pater incorporated that space into his own discourse. "Plato is to be explained, as we say, or interpreted, partly through his predecessors, and his contemporaries; but in part also by his followers, by the light his later mental kinsmen throw back on the conscious or unconscious drift of his teaching" (193). Thus Plato is viewed from a mobile array of standpoints, none of which is equated with his philosophy, as each of them is different from what they are meant to focus on. Such mobility of shifting angles points to the fact that there is no bird's-eye view for interpreting Plato, who is conceived neither as a result of a Hegelian

---

31. See A. C. Benson, *Walter Pater*, English Men of Letters 59 (London: Macmillan, 1906), 162.
32. Pater, *Plato and Platonism*, 5.

evolution nor as a focal point for unforeseeable historical disseminations. Instead, Pater inscribes into his own discourse the multiple differences that distinguish Plato both from those to whom he reacted and from the processing of Platonic ideas in history. Overarching presuppositions are replaced by the indication of differences, which are enfolded into interpretation itself. The various differences highlighted are individual manifestations of this enfolding, in consequence of which Pater's interpretation of Plato develops as a discourse of many layers. A layered discourse is not structured by a guiding principle, it rather "interfuses"—to use a favourite word of Pater's—its seemingly independent strands. Such an interfusion in turn is in no way determinate; it leaves the suggested interpenetration of the various layers open-ended.

Right at the beginning of *Plato and Platonism*, Pater epitomizes such a procedure, which forms the guideline for his exposition of Plato's philosophy.

> It is hardly an exaggeration to say that in Plato, in spite of his wonderful savour of literary freshness, there is nothing absolutely new: or rather, as in many other very original products of human genius, the seemingly new is also old, a palimpsest, a tapestry of which the actual threads have served before. . . . Nothing but the life-giving principle of cohesion is new; the new perspective, the resultant complexion, the expressiveness which familiar thoughts attain by novel juxtaposition. In other words, the *form* is new. But then, in the creation of philosophical literature . . . *form*, in the full significance of that word, is everything, and the mere matter is nothing. (8)

The palimpsest highlights the layered structure in terms of difference and interpenetration. It also creates a fold in both senses of the dictionary entry: "laying together, so as to overlap" and "the space or hollow at the junction of two folded parts." Thus the fold bears a dual inscription: it simultaneously marks an overlapping and an empty space. Pater made this inherent duality operative in his interpretation of Plato through a continuous interfolding of the layers. Such an interfolding is not confined to a juxtaposition of historical strands as initially indicated. Instead, Pater develops ever-new variations of the way in which his multilayered discourse telescopes obviously disparate references.

Pre-Socratic philosophy is enfolded into the doctrine of Plato insofar as Plato reacted to the doctrines of motion, rest, and number. What his predecessors had thought is present as a layer in Plato's own thinking and thus conditions the way in which he outstripped them. Challenge and response make up Pater's formula for capturing such a relationship, which heeds not only the difference between Plato and the Pre-Socratics but also the space opened up by transposing Plato into Pater's own terms of understanding. If Plato is dependent on what he responds to, then the various "influences" to which he was subjected "made him, incurably (shall we say?) a dualist" (46). Thus duality becomes the hallmark of Plato for Pater, who—in trying to grasp what such a duality might entail—explores its kaleidoscopically shifting manifestations. "The eternal Being, of Parmenides, one and indivisible, has been diffused, divided, resolved, refracted, differentiated, into the eternal Ideas. . . . It was like a recrudescence of polytheism in that abstract world; a return of the many gods of Homer, veiled now as abstract notions, Love, Fear, Confidence, and the like [that] would rank the Platonic theory as but a form of what he calls 'animism' " (168f.). What used to be the abstract notion of Being is translated into an array of different ideas that in turn fade into a reemerging animism, thus translating the ontological difference into terms of perception and experience.

Something similar happens to "the Socratic 'universals,' the notions of Justice and the like[, which] become, first, things in themselves—the real things; and secondly, persons, to be known as persons must be" (166). This gradual sliding of lofty universals into corporeal shapes does not do away with the ontological difference but transposes it through an imbrication of the invisible and the visible into tangibility. In each of these instances, duality is maintained, though the empty space between abstractions and realities as well as that between concepts and personifications are fashioned in different manners. It is a graduated transposition in the first case and a transmogrification in the second.

This very duality, which marks Plato's philosophizing as foreshadowed in Socrates, finds its counterpart in the duplicity of the Sophists. If Socrates "with all his singleness of purpose, had been . . . by natural constitution a twofold power, an embodied paradox" (87), the Sophists "are partly the cause" and "still more the effect of the social environment" (107) in the pursuit of their highly ambivalent purposes. To be the effect of one's own cause makes the duality chiastic, and to such a manifestation Plato, the dualist, was opposed. For Pater, however, this duplicity serves as a foil for narrowing down the shades of duality that he believed constituted Plato's thinking. Duality versus duplicity highlights the countervailing tendency operative in Plato's double-sidedness, which is not to be confined to a split, a dividedness, a graduated interlinking, a shading of opposites into one another, or a telescoping of what is mutually exclusive.

Instead, each of these manifestations testifies to the fact that Platonic duality defies conceptualization. No overriding notion for the multiple enfoldings of "antecedent and contemporary movements of Greek speculation" (11) is traceable in Platonic discourse, which is dotted with 'hollow' spaces that mark the junction of folded parts. The fold is an indication for Pater that Plato himself did not gloss over the space that separated him from his predecessors and contemporaries when—in relating to them—he was formulating his doctrine. Plato—as Pater contends—inscribed this space into his own discourse, and only by highlighting that procedure can "the proper aim of the historic, that is to say, of the really critical study of" Plato be achieved (11).

One might be tempted to say that Pater took the cue for his own discourse from what he believed to be the structure of the Platonic doctrine. By holding the mirror of history up to Platonic philosophy, his interpretation seems to duplicate the presumed preoccupations of Plato himself. In this way Plato became both an antecedent and a contemporary of what came after him, just as he himself enveloped the Pre-Socratics, Socrates, and the Sophists. The historical references permeating Pater's discourse again bear a dual inscription by simultaneously highlighting and bridging the differences between Plato and subsequent historical events. Enfolding Plato in what was historically beyond his pale and equally enfolding subsequent history into the Platonic doctrine convert the space between into a continuous oscillation of the seemingly incompatible.

This oscillation produces changing features. Sometimes it assumes a pattern of figure and ground in order to offset aspects of Plato from those of history and vice versa. Sometimes it assumes a relation between theme and horizon by refracting Plato in the mirror of history, in which case Plato becomes the theme. Or it points up the extent to which Platonic ideas have been distorted, in which case history becomes the theme. This switching between theme and horizon allows the emergence of the reverse side,[33] be it through a facet of Plato's doctrine or through a related historical incident. And this reverse side can be either a disclosure of something that has remained hidden or a transformation of the familiar when it is overshadowed by what had previously been eclipsed. A good example of how phenomena became intensified is Pater's juxtaposition of the Platonic and the Danteesque sensibilities to light and color:

---

33. "Theme" and "horizon" as a pair of terms regulating the change of focus were coined and elaborated by Alfred Schütz, *Das Problem der Relevanz*, trans. A. von Baeyer (Frankfurt/Main: Suhrkamp, 1971), 30f., 104ff., 145ff.

A matter of very lively and presentable form and colour, as if making the invisible show through, this too pleased the extremely visual fancy of Plato; as we may see, in many places of the *Phaedo*, the *Phaedrus*, the *Timaeus*, and most conspicuously in the tenth book of *The Republic*, where he relates the vision of Er—what he saw of the other world during a kind of temporary death. Hell, Purgatory, Paradise, are briefly depicted in it; Paradise especially with a quite Dantesque sensibility to coloured light—physical light or spiritual, you can hardly tell which, so perfectly is the inward sense blent with its visible counter-part, reminding one forcibly of the *Divine Comedy*, of which those closing pages of *The Republic* suggest an early outline.[34]

This mutual spotlighting transfigures the *Republic*, just as it suffuses the *Divine Comedy* with an Apollonian luminosity. If theme and horizon form a fairly stable pattern, in spite of the tilting that occurs between them, telescoping and overlapping—whether of pagan and Christian strands or of Platonic and subsequent philosophizing—constitute a less controlled oscillation of the space between Plato and history. The diminishing control of what is to be epitomized by the telescoping and overlapping of incidents that are worlds apart, however, brings forth traces of the inexpressible and at the same time gives voice to such inexpressibility. Traces of this kind have a definite aesthetic quality, not least as they engage the recipient. Plato himself appears to have endorsed such a view, as for him (according to Pater), the ideal artist increases "his power by reserve" that is "to express more than he seems actually to say" (281). And the implication of such a "reserve" Pater finds epitomized in Pindar's art, which reveals "how much he leaves for a well-drilled intelligence to supply in the way of connecting thought" (283).

On virtually the last page of his lecture series, the implications underlying Pater's own interpretation of *Plato and Platonism* come fully into the open. The multiple folds that mark his discourse are dually coded. On the one hand, they testify to the fact that each interpretation opens up a space between the subject matter and the register into which the subject matter is translated. On the other, Pater folds this space back into his own discourse, which thus becomes one of multiple folds, highlighting the empty spaces between the folded parts out of which Plato's doctrine arose and also between Pater's own enfoldings of Plato into subsequent history. Each of these folds expresses more than it says, as the junction of folded parts

---

34. Pater, *Plato and Platonism*, 69.

invites "connecting thoughts" for the hollow space to be filled. Interpretation therefore is no longer a cognitive explanation but a guided conceivability. This accounts for the fact that Pater was opposed to axioms and definitions, from which the treatise as a form of philosophical interpretation is bound to start out. Instead of superimposing presuppositions on the matter to be interpreted—thereby colonizing the space opened up by any interpretation as an act of translation—Pater negotiated that space by inscribing it in terms of multiple foldings into his own discourse.

Such a procedure allows the recipient to participate in working out what is translated in any interpretation. The fold, we might say, is a counterconcept to all the overarching frames of reference otherwise so frequently operative in interpretation. It further indicates that any third dimension in interpretation can only predetermine what in actual fact has to be explored in the first instance. And, finally, it brings out into the open the residual untranslatability produced by the very act of interpretation. This residual untranslatability, however, energizes the drive to overcome what resists transposition into a different register, as revealed by the variegated shapes assumed by the folds in Paterian discourse. The extent to which Pater was aware of this interrelationship can be gauged from his definition of his position as an interpreter when he states that his "own stand as to this matter [is] somewhere between the realist and the conceptualist" (151). The hallmark of Pater's discourse is the fact that the ineradicable space caused by any interpretation is folded back into the discourse itself.

In *Plato and Platonism* Pater also reflects on a form of writing that was most congenial to him: the essay. He considers it "the literary form necessary to a mind for which truth itself is but a possibility" (175), because the essay "does in truth little more than clear the ground, as we say, or the atmosphere, or the mental tablet, that one may have a fair chance of knowing, or seeing, perhaps" (188). What that may entail is best discerned in the book through which Pater established his fame: *The Renaissance*. As a collection of essays, it gains its coherence through the structure that each of the individual essays varies in its own way. If *Plato and Platonism* unfolds the doctrine of Plato in terms of multiple enfoldings, *The Renaissance* highlights the interval, which as a pause marks a transition. The interval is identical neither with what has gone before nor with what is to follow. Although it separates a past from a future, it does not make the past vanish or the future become present. Articulating the interval means giving voice to what is basically silent and giving form to what is basically featureless. Such an articulation is Pater's achievement in his loosely connected series of essays depicting a historical shift.

Right at the beginning, Pater rejects all abstract definitions as starting points for such an undertaking, because there can be no "universal formula";[35] instead, he maintains that such an exploration requires for the most part "different starting-points" and has to proceed "by unconnected roads" (xiii), for which, we may note, the essay proves to be the appropriate form. The essay—as Hugo Friedrich once described it, explicitly referring to Pater—"is the medium for a mode of writing that seeks to be not a result but a process. . . . It describes, narrates, articulates, and thus testifies to its capability of pointing towards truth more adequately and less imposingly than any discursive analysis is able to achieve."[36]

What runs like a thread through all these essays on the Renaissance is a sense of "antinomianism"[37] which does not call out for any decisions but exercises a peculiar attraction. "Theories," Pater maintains in his first essay, "which bring into connexion with each other modes of thought and feeling, periods of taste, forms of art and poetry, which the narrowness of men's minds constantly tends to oppose to each other, have a great stimulus for the intellect, and are almost always worth understanding" (3). To capture such a situation in writing requires an open-ended form, allowing the potential recipient to provide the closure necessary for understanding. The essay fulfills these conditions, not least because by suspending judgment, it requires the recipient to cooperate in arriving at an insight into what happens when opposites meet.

The "uncertain twilight" (6) of the so-called renaissance of the twelfth century arouses a "curious interest of the *Doppelgänger*" (9), as evinced in the story of Amis and Amile, and manifests itself again in the "mixture of simplicity and refinement" (18) in the story of Aucassin and Nicolette, in which "the note of defiance, of the opposition of one system to another, is sometimes harsh" (27). In the fifteenth century we encounter Pico della Mirandola, who juggles with "the double meanings of words" when trying to explain the relation between Plato and Moses (45). What "Dante scorns as unworthy alike of heaven and hell, Botticelli accepts, that middle world in which men take no side in great conflicts, and decide no great causes, and make great refusals" (55), and Pater continues in the same vein: Botticelli "paints the story of the goddess of pleasure in other episodes besides that of her birth from the sea, but never without some

---

35. Pater, *The Renaissance*, vii.
36. Hugo Friedrich, *Montaigne* (Berne: Franke, 1949), 430; see also 443.
37. Pater, *The Renaissance*, 24.

shadow of death in the grey flesh and wan flowers. He paints Madonnas, but they shrink from the pressure of the divine child, and plead in unmistakable undertones for a warmer, lower humanity" (60).

One could continue to fan out the multiplicity of opposing tendencies, clashes, mutual displacements, interfusions of extremes on which almost all the essays in this volume pivot without necessarily fine-tuning whatever else that age of transition might still reveal. What the remarks on Botticelli indicate, however, is a noticeable shift in perspective away from the multifarious manifestations of that all-pervading "antinomianism" toward the "middle world," as Pater termed it, that is between the opposites. Such an in-betweenness may sometimes mark a point of intersection, sometimes an interval in time, and gains its substance only through a meeting of opposites.

It is now possible to pinpoint the constitutive features of the essay as a discursive practice by means of which Pater tries to capture this age of transition. The component parts of the essay are made up of countervailing trends, which cause a blank whenever they collide. This blank is as important to the essay as the opposing tendencies by which it is caused. "Opposing," however, does not mean that binarism is the basic constituent, because the essay is a form of discourse in which "many persons, so to speak, will necessarily take part; so many persons as there are possible contrasts or shades in the apprehension of some complex subject."[38] Consequently, the blanks will increase proportionately to the conflicting tendencies that the essay is meant to accommodate.

Interpreting an age of transition—as undertaken in *The Renaissance*— implies translating something intangible into terms of apprehension. For such a transposition the Paterian essay is a suitable form, as it incorporates into itself not only the intangible element of transition but also the space opened up by interpreting an age of transition in terms of its constitutive blank. Such a blank has many shades: it corresponds to the subject matter to be depicted; it retains the ineradicable space between the subject matter and the register into which it is to be translated; and as the point where what appears to be mutually exclusive intersects, it invites and allows for unforeseeable combinations.

This can best be illustrated by a passage from Pater's essay "The Poetry of Michelangelo," in which he tries to capture Michelangelo's achievement in the sacristy of San Lorenzo.

---

38. Pater, *Plato and Platonism*, 183f.

The tombs in the sacristy of *San Lorenzo* are memorials . . . of Giu-
liano, and Lorenzo the younger, noticeable chiefly for their somewhat
early death. It is mere human nature therefore which has prompted the
sentiment here. The titles assigned traditionally to the four symbolic
figures, *Night* and *Day*, *The Twilight* and *The Dawn*, are far too definite
for them; for these figures come much nearer to the mind and spirit of
their author, and are a more direct expression of his thoughts, than any
merely symbolical conceptions could possibly have been. They con-
centrate and express, less by way of definite conceptions than by the
touches, the promptings of a piece of music, all those vague fancies,
misgivings, presentiments, which shift and mix and are defined and
fade again, whenever the thoughts try to fix themselves with sincerity
on the conditions and surroundings of the disembodied spirit. I suppose
no one would come to the sacristy of San Lorenzo for consolation; for
seriousness, for solemnity, for dignity of impression, perhaps, but not
for consolation. It is a place neither of consoling nor of terrible
thoughts, but of vague and wistful speculation.[39]

All the basic constituents of the Paterian essay are discernible here: the
polarities; the space between which they adumbrate; the intensified interfusions they seem to trigger. The "touches" and the "promptings," the "misgivings" and the "presentiments" shift, mix, fade, and finally evaporate into
"wistful speculations," so that, in spite of the multifarious interpenetrations
of opposites, no resolution emerges. The space between is thus itself highlighted, and instead of vanishing into a definite combination of the opposites, it makes all the overlappings and telescopings run out of control,
plunging even "terrible thoughts" into vagueness.

A similar procedure is to be observed in Pater's essay "Leonardo da
Vinci." Apart from the purple patch on Mona Lisa,[40] Pater minutely delineates what happens when "womanly beauty" is transposed into painting:

Daughters of Herodias, with their fantastic head-dresses knotted and folded so strangely to leave the dainty oval of the face disengaged, they are
not of the Christian family, or of Raphael's. They are the clairvoyants,

---

39. Pater, *The Renaissance*, 94f.
40. I tried to analyze Pater's vision of Mona Lisa in my book *Walter Pater: The
Aesthetic Moment*, trans. David H. Wilson (Cambridge: Cambridge University Press, 1987), 43–46.

through whom, as through delicate instruments, one becomes aware of the subtler forces of nature, and the modes of their action, all that is magnetic in it, all those finer conditions wherein material things rise to that subtlety of operation which constitutes them spiritual, where only the final nerve and the keener touch can follow. It is as if in certain significant examples we actually saw those forces at their work on human flesh. Nervous, electric, faint always with some inexplicable faintness, these people seem to be subject to exceptional conditions, to feel powers at work in the common air unfelt by others, to become, as it were, the receptacle of them, and pass them on to us in a chain of secret influences.[41]

What "womanly beauty" represents is not the thrust of the description here but what the beholder of the painting is given to experience. Such an experience, however, can hardly be processed, as the many countervailing impressions appear to clash and begin to transform one another, so that all emerging points of reference keep vanishing. We are confronted by a whirlpool of kinetic energy; perception is equally dispersed and enriched without finding the suggested guidance. This makes Pater's description into a subtle form of translation as he seeks to convey in cognitive terms how Leonardo transposed "womanly beauty" into an artistic medium and how that transposition in turn is translated into terms of experience for the beholder.

This effort is permeated by an awareness that the space between the subject matter and its rendering cannot be wiped out but has to be inscribed into the very language that effects the translation. Thus Pater's description is punctured by disconnections or even blanks that not only spur the beholder into action but also manifest the space that is opened up in any act of interpretation.

Such a space draws both its information and its energy from the polarities that initially have marked it out. The information, however, seems to be selected and even processed according not to what the polarities represent but to an inexplicable drive that wells up in the space itself. This accounts for the element of uncontrollability to be observed in the kaleidoscopically shifting interpenetrations, a process that Pater tries to grasp without ever bringing it to a standstill. And Pater is right to refrain from doing so, as otherwise the space would be colonized by the presuppositions brought to bear. Maintaining the space created by polarities makes the essay itself into a process in which judgment is suspended, in which guidelines

---

41. Pater, *The Renaissance*, 115f.

provide no definite orientation, and in which the ongoing interplay of what is different allows continuous new explorations. "It is the mistake," Pater therefore contends, "of much popular criticism to regard poetry, music, and painting . . . as but translations into different languages . . . as art addresses not pure sense, still less the pure intellect, but the 'imaginative reason' " and has "its own peculiar and untranslatable sensuous charm" (130). The essay uncovers something of that untranslatability, not least as it remains a cognitive attempt to transpose the "sensuous charm" of art into forms of apprehension. Therefore the space between the artwork and its understanding created by any interpretation contains a residual untranslatability that, however, powers the drive to overcome it, without ever being able to do so. Such a space—which can be qualified in terms neither of subject matter to be interpreted nor of the register into which the subject matter is to be translated—turns out to be autopoietic in nature. The space is autopoietic because it produces its own shifting forms of organization, as evinced by the quotation from the Michelangelo essay. Owing to this self-organization, the space may explode into unforeseeable iterations of the features that have adumbrated it and whose respective counterposition it has absorbed.

The extent to which Pater has made the autopoietic space constitutive for his own mode of writing can be inferred from the way he focuses on such self-organizing spaces in the artworks under consideration. For him these works are models that he tries to emulate. Giorgione produced "exquisite pauses in time, in which, arrested thus, we seem to be spectators of all the fullness of existence" (150).[42] In another painting of the

---

42. In the introductory section of his essay "The School of Giorgione," Pater emphasizes that the "pictorial quality" of painting resides neither in the "mere technical acquirement in delineation or touch, working through and addressing itself to the intelligence" nor in "what may be called literary interest, addressed also to the pure intelligence" but in "that . . . which lies between" (131f.). This is a further qualification of what the "exquisite pauses in time" entail. They are not just gaps but are autopoietic by nature, bringing about on their own rather impenetrable terms an interfusion of what is separate. Likewise the "pictorial quality" of painting cannot be captured in either formalistic or cognitive terms but emerges as something that sits in between and can thus only manifest itself in a continual dispersal of perceptual and conceptual description, as Pater has so successfully practiced in his essays. What makes the "pictorial quality" elude cognitive grasp is its aesthetic nature, which can at best be defined as in-betweenness. This aesthetic nature is likewise preponderant in the "exquisite pauses in time" as evidenced by the self-organization that the autopoietic intervals generate.

school of Giorgione these "exquisite pauses in time" turn into an "airy space, as the eye passes from level to level, through the long-drawn valley in which Jacob embraces Rachel among the flocks!" (153). Such spaces or intervals generate a fullness of vision, and they are autopoietic insofar as they yield something that may well go beyond "the intention of the composer" (133). Simultaneously, the self-organizing operations of the autopoietic space guide the gaze of the beholder and thereby make him or her participate in working out whatever may be suggested by that uncontrollable process. The autopoietic space is not empty because it feeds on the positions that have carved it out, although none of these can exercise control over the way the selected features are reorganized through shifting combinations.

It is interesting to note the extent to which Pater's keen awareness of the space opened up by any act of interpretation also pervades his fictional writings, of which *Gaston de Latour* is a revealing example. The main focus of this novel, which was never completed, is identical to Pater's basic concern, as C. L. Shadwell remarks in his preface to the fragment edited under his supervision. It deals with "another age of transition, when the old fabric of belief was breaking up, and when the problem of man's destiny and his relations to the unseen was undergoing a new solution." This solution, however, was precarious for someone like Gaston, who was "capable of keen enjoyment in the pleasures of the senses and of the intellect, but destined to find its complete satisfaction in that which transcends both."[43] Being focused on the "unseen" and simultaneously transcending "the pleasures of the senses and of the intellect" makes Gaston hang between what he has abandoned and what he is striving for. The novel is therefore dotted with opposites and dualities, ranging from Gaston's home, which is a Château of Deux-manoirs, through "the twin spires of Chartres,"[44] under whose shadow Gaston becomes a clerk in orders, where "human experience . . . in its strange mixture of beauty and evil" (38) dawns on him, through the "two rival claimants upon him, of two ideals" (71) that he feels in his encounter with Ronsard, to the final amazement he experiences vis-à-vis Bruno's "famous axiom of 'indifference,' of 'the coincidence of contraries' " (143). Whatever move in life he makes,

---

43. Charles L. Shadwell, preface to Walter Pater, *Gaston.de Latour*, ed. Charles L. Shadwell (London: Macmillan, 1920), vi.
44. Walter Pater, *Gaston de Latour*, ed. Charles L. Shadwell (London: Macmillan, 1920), 19.

Gaston finds himself unavoidably plunged into a space between dualities. This makes him into a vehicle for measuring out that space, which Pater in his critical writings enfolded into his discourse. One might be inclined to assume that Pater switched to fiction in order to explore the possible ways for this space to be overcome. The quandary in which Gaston finds himself may be a pointer to such an intention: "Two worlds, two antagonistic ideals, were in evidence before him. Could a third condition supervene, to mend their discord, or only vex him perhaps, from time to time, with efforts towards an impossible adjustment?" (38f.). Obviously, there is no third dimension that might eliminate this in-between state, which for Gaston is impossible to endure. But how can the unendurable be endured?

There are moments in Gaston's life when he seems to be able to transcend the dualities between which he feels himself so irrevocably wedged. When he climbs the tower of Jean de Beauce, a vast panorama opens up to him:

> At each ascending storey, as the flight of the birds, the scent of the fields, swept past him, till he stood at last amid the unimpeded light and air of the watch-chamber above the great bells, some coil of perplexity, of unassimilable thought or fact, fell away from him. He saw the distant paths, and seemed to hear the breeze piping suddenly upon them under the cloudless sky, on its unseen, capricious way through those vast reaches of atmosphere. At this height, the low ring of blue hills was visible, with suggestions of that south-west country of peach-blossom and wine which had sometimes decoyed his thoughts towards the sea, and beyond it to "that new world of the Indies," which was held to explain a certain softness in the air from that quarter, even in the most vehement weather. Amid those vagrant shadows and shafts of light must be Deux-manoirs, the deserted rooms, the gardens, the graves. In mid-distance, even then a funeral procession was on its way humbly to one of the village churchyards. He seemed almost to hear the words across the stillness. (41f.)

It is as if Gaston were lifted out of the narrow confines of his life in Chartres. The higher he climbs, the freer he feels, until finally the "coil of perplexity" falls away, and the irreconcilability of his environment with his longing disappears as he gazes on the ever-expanding landscape. Here is something that seems to embrace all opposites. Not even the blue hills on the horizon can close off his view but indeed, paradoxically, seem to open it wider still. The world stretching in front of him points to another world, distant and unseen, but imaginable.

Pater employs a technique of juxtaposition in depicting Gaston's heightened experience of this landscape. The horizon is Gaston's equator, simultaneously enclosing the physical country on the near side and pointing to the visionary beyond. Thus what is limited expands into the unbounded, with the Indies, Deux-manoirs, and the funeral procession merging into a single experience. Permeating this is the promise that divisions and opposites can all be embraced and reconciled. Small wonder that Gaston almost immediately asks himself: "Would it always survive, amid the indifference of others, amid the verdicts of the world, amid a thousand doubts?" (42).

The landscape figures as an epiphany of duality overcome, which assumes a numinous character heralding the advent of something extraordinary. This entails the transfigured landscape turning into a sign for something other than itself. The resolution of dualities that eliminates the space between what is different tends to produce that 'supervening third condition' for which Gaston keeps yearning. The interpenetration, however, of what is far and near, seen and unseeable, perceived and imaginable is highly volatile and falls apart again when it does not change into a pointer to something beyond itself. Pater makes this longed-for "coincidence of contraries" into a fleeting moment that is repeated in Gaston's vision of another landscape: the Loire valley (78f.). The eliminated separations, divisions, distances, and juxtapositions of these moments are paid for by their discontinuity, in which the suspended in-between state reasserts itself. Consequently, Gaston's vision strikes him as a "stage-play" (79), indicating that whatever overarches dualities has no reality of its own but can at best only be enacted. If the space between dualities and juxtapositions reveals itself as a drive for enactment, then its autopoietic impulse becomes apparent. In thematizing the interpenetration of dualities in two visionary scenes Pater illuminates the ever-expanding self-organization of the autopoietic space that only the imagination is able to spell out. Pater seems to be striving for nothing less than an idea of how to conceive this space and the manifold operations it triggers. Such an undertaking, however, could only be executed in terms of fiction, because critical discourse opens up the very space that it can never eliminate, let alone show in all its workings.

What remains remarkable for us today is not only the fact that more than one hundred years ago Pater reflected on different modalities of discourse in relation to what they were able to grasp but also that he developed types of discourse that anticipate a late-twentieth-century concern with the anatomy of interpretation. Pater spotlighted the autopoietic space

as the generative matrix of the artwork and made it into a constitutive feature of the essay in order to translate the emergent potentialities of a work
of art into terms of conceivability. In *The Renaissance*, the essay pivots
around an evocative blank; in *Plato and Platonism*, this space is cast as
one of multiple enfoldings. Each of these types of discourse bears the
inscription of the space between. In this respect, Pater is very much in
line with present-day concerns regarding interpretation. Both the resur-
gent and the newly developed types of interpretation are preoccupied
with the handling of the space that opens up when something is transposed into something else. The hermeneutic circle, the cybernetic loop,
and the traveling differential have emerged as prominent structures in
tackling that space.

Pater's own procedure is closely akin to those procedures. Circle, loop,
and differential, irrespective of whether they operate separately or in combination, do not determine the autopoietic space but function as strategies for the otherwise ungovernable self-organization, just as the evocative
blank in the Paterian essay and the multiple enfoldings in his lecture on
Plato fulfill the same ends. Pater not only conceived the autopoietic space
as fundamental to any interpretation but enriched the armory available
for coping with such space by the elaborate evocativeness of the blank
and the multiple enfoldings of cognitive discourse.

INDEX*

Abel, Günter, 1
Aestheticism, 183
Akiva, Rabbi, 27
All, the (Rosenzweig), 118, 121, 137, 138, 141
Analytic philosophy, 12
Ancients, 160
Aquinas, Thomas, 45
Aristotelian poetics, 33, 34
Aristotle, 142
Arnold, Matthew, 38, 182
Atlan, Henri, 103, 152
Aught, the (Rosenzweig), 120–22, 123, 124, 126, 129, 130,
    134
Augustine, 18
Authority, 9, 13–15, 17–21, 23, 25, 27–28, 30–32, 45,
    47–48, 53–54, 58, 115, 118, 145; and the sealed canon,
    18–20, 21; problem of, 27; replacement of by herme-
    neutic circle, 53; secular, 35, 37; vs. brisur, 48

Bahn (Rosenzweig), 137–38
Bakhtin, Mikhail, 46
Barstone, Willis, 5
Bate, Walter Jackson, 29, 32, 33
Bateson, Gregory, 103, 127, 156, 166
Beethoven, Ludwig van, 98
Benson, A.C., 185
Benveniste, Émile, 71
Blank/Blanks, 31, 54, 58, 93–94, 121, 156, 158, 192, 194,
    199. See also Gap
Bloom, Harold, 5, 169
Bible, 16, 18, 22, 23, 25, 27, 43, 44; doctrine of fourfold
    senses, 43–44

---

* Compiled by Richard van Oort